AGORAPHOBIA

One of the commonest of the phobias, agoraphobia is also one of the most difficult to treat, and is often ill-understood. This valuable up-to-date review of the effectiveness of various approaches to agoraphobia brings together contributors from all the major mental health professions.

The topics dealt with range widely, from discussions of the nature of the syndrome, through assessments of the effectiveness of exposure (behavioural) treatment and drug treatment, to an analysis of the part played by sex-role stereotyping and social factors in treatment failure and in treatment outcome generally. The contributors' accounts of the nature and treatment of this crippling problem will be of particular interest to those specializing in the research and treatment of agoraphobia.

THE EDITOR

Dr Kevin Gournay is Behavioural Psychotherapist for Barnet Health Authority. He also co-directs a major research programme at the Institute of Psychiatry, London.

AGORAPHOBIA

Current Perspectives on Theory and Treatment

EDITED BY KEVIN GOURNAY

ROUTLEDGE

London and New York

First published 1989
by Routledge
11 New Fetter Lane, London EC4P 4EE
29 West 35th Street, New York, NY 10001

Typeset by LaserScript Limited, Mitcham, Surrey
Printed and bound in Great Britain by
Mackays of Chatham PLC, Chatham, Kent

British Library Cataloguing in Publication Data

Gournay, Kevin, 1946–
Agoraphobia: current perspectives on theory and treatment
1. Man. Agoraphobia. Therapy
I. Title
616.85'225

Library of Congress Cataloging in Publication Data

Agoraphobia: current perspectives on theory and treatment /
edited by Kevin Gournay.
p. cm.
Includes index.
1. Agoraphobia—Treatment. 2. Behavior therapy.
I. Gournay, Kevin, 1946–
[DNLM: 1. Phobic Disorders—therapy. WM 178 A2759]
RC552.A44A38 1989
616.85'225—dc 19
DNLM/DLC
for Library of Congress
88-36568
CIP

ISBN 0-415-01886-2

For Alexander

CONTENTS

TABLES AND FIGURES

TABLES

FIGURES

NOTES ON CONTRIBUTORS

Cherrie Coghlan
Senior Registrar and Honorary Lecturer, University College and Middlesex Hospital, London.

H. Gordon Deakin
Director, Nurse Therapy Training Programme, Plymouth Health Authority, Devon.

Kevin Gournay
Behavioural Psychotherapist, Barnet Health Authority/Institute of Psychiatry, University of London.

Barbara Hudson
Lecturer, Department of Social and Administrative Studies and Fellow of Green College, University of Oxford.

David Winter
Top Grade Clinical Pychologist, Barnet Health Authority, Barnet, Herts.

EDITOR'S ACKNOWLEDGEMENTS

Apart from the authors of the various chapters, there are many people to whom I owe thanks and who in many diverse ways have helped me with this book

Dr Kevin Howells guided me as a friend and supervisor. Prof. Isaac Marks, Dr Julian Bird, Dr Din Master, and Mr Peter Lindley were my original sources of inspiration. My membership of the British Association for Behavioural Psychotherapy has provided continuous peer support and education.

The following friends and colleagues are gratefully thanked for the work they put in as therapists, assessors, secretaries, and advisors: Ms Kate Adams, Mr Ken Allen, Mrs Val Curtis, Dr Sue Davenport, Ms Jill Davis, Mr Bill Drysdale, Mr Richard Elliot, Ms Janis Flint, Dr Fakhir Hussain, Ms Lucy Johnstone, Prof. Andrew Mathews, Mrs Pam McCarthy, Dr Lawrence Ratna, Ms Michelle Roitt, Ms Lynda Simpson, Mrs Jo Todd, and Dr David Winter. The research on which my chapters are based was aided by a two-year grant from the North West Thames Regional Health Authority.

PREFACE

This book is an attempt to present a number of different perspectives on an interesting but ill-understood syndrome. Agoraphobia is, to most people, a fear of open spaces, a woman's complaint, a minor neurotic problem, a manifestation of modern stress, and so on. These descriptions are largely erroneous and are believed by not only the general public, but also by many health professionals. This book will, it is hoped, correct these misconceptions and inform about both the nature and treatment of this crippling problem. It was inspired by a number of sources. First, it stems from the research I carried out between 1980 and 1986. While this work confirmed my belief in the powerful principle of exposure, it also demonstrated that current behavioural methods, while dramatic in effectiveness, have a number of limitations. It is true that many patients in this study, who were treated by exposure, were up to 95 per cent improved and that this contrasts with the picture in the 1960s when agoraphobia was such an intractable problem that leucotomy was routinely carried out. However, set against this are two sobering facts. First, 44 per cent of our original sample could be categorized as treatment failures either by refusing treatment, by dropping out, by failing to achieve predetermined criteria on a number of measures, or by relapsing once the treatment period was over. Second, of the 132 patients taken into the trial, not one achieved anything amounting to a total abolition of symptoms. Thus I now share the view of others, most notably Rachman, who have cautioned against complacency.

The second source of encouragement to produce such a book has been my experience since 1985 of carrying out work preparatory to a large outcome study involving psychiatry in primary health care. This has necessitated the observation of GPs and community psychiatric nurses and also caused me to look at the practice of psychiatrists, psychologists, and social workers. Unfortunately, the overwhelming impression is that these skilled and highly trained professionals generally ignore the voluminous evidence and treat agoraphobia as if the syndrome is merely reflective of another 'deeper' psychopathology (either intra- or interpersonal) and, to compound the error, then deliver treatment which carefully omits any exposure. I have therefore tried to do more than pay lip-service to multidisciplinary approaches by assembling representatives of all of the major mental health professions to contribute chapters.

Barbara Hudson looks at the syndrome from the perspective on the social worker. Her incisive literature review helps to debunk many of the myths that have become clinical lore. Hudson looks at social factors and puts them into the context of social work practice. Her chapter is notable for her clear account of behavioural social work with people with agoraphobia.

Gordon Deakin gives an excellent account of how exposure treatment should be delivered. This includes a meticulous step-by-step account of treatment sessions which should prove invaluable to both therapists in training and indeed to trained and experienced professionals who should continually be evaluating their own performance. Deakin's chapter is testimony to the excellence of nurse behaviour therapy in the UK and provides a model which could easily be extended worldwide.

David Winter describes how personal construct psychology can provide a refreshingly novel perspective of agoraphobia. His chapter focuses on the very individual perceptions of agoraphobia by the patient and how these may change in therapy. Implicit in his views are cogent arguments for the experimental testing of many of the 'softer' cognitive hypotheses. While his chapter is far from uncritical of behavioural approaches, he demonstrates that behaviour therapy produces significant cognitive change. Furthermore, in arguing the case for using Kelly's theory, he states the main aim of personal construct approaches as the encouragement of experimentation by the individual client who should venture forth as a personal scientist. This ideal should not prove distant from that of the behaviour therapist.

Cherrie Coghlan reviews the role of drugs in the management of agoraphobia. She gives an overview of the research carried out over the last quarter of a century and suggests a small but significant role for medication in treatment. Her description of mechanisms and research findings will provide an interesting account for non-medical therapists who often have knowledge gaps in this area.

My own chapters on exposure treatment, cognitive change, treatment failure, and sex roles are based on six years of research, which I should say was inspired by my training at Isaac Marks's unit at the Maudsley Hospital.

My hope is that the readers of the following chapters will take the relevant research and apply it to their clinical work.

Kevin Gournay
March 1988

Chapter One

INTRODUCTION: THE NATURE OF AGORAPHOBIA AND CONTEMPORARY ISSUES

KEVIN GOURNAY

Because there are now so many excellent texts (e.g. Mathews *et al.* 1981, Chambless and Goldstein 1982, Thorpe and Burns 1983, Marks 1987a) which describe the nature of agoraphobia, it is not intended to compete with them in this chapter. Rather, the main issues will be summarized and some more attention will be given to some topics which are either of contemporary interest or are relevant to the rest of the book.

CLINICAL FEATURES OF THE SYNDROME – A SUMMARY

The syndrome is not a trivial neurosis, but a truly distressing and handicapping state which places enormous demands on treatment services. Having said that, it is likely that only a minority of sufferers receive adequate treatment (Agras *et al.* 1969, Marks 1987a) and that the majority continue to live in permanent misery, or worse still, suffer iatrogenic effects via long-term benzodiazepine use.

The problem usually starts in early adult life, with two probable peaks of onset at about twenty and thirty years of age (Thorpe and Burns 1983, Marks 1987a). The onset may vary from a panic attack which is followed within hours by incapacitating anxiety and avoidance, to a very insidious course with avoidance behaviour growing over many years. The patient is, in the full-blown syndrome, incapacitated by anxiety linked to situations away from a secure base.

This then leads to a whole range of life restrictions which affect both the patient and family. Thorpe and Burns (1983) reported the results of a survey of 818 women and 112 men suffering from agoraphobia and demonstrated a wide range of problems which were a direct consequence of the condition. There were some clear sex differences, but overall there was a very high incidence of inability to work, lack of social contacts, secondary psychological problems such as poor self-esteem, marital disharmony, and several other difficulties. It is clear that these problems are consequential rather than causal, as successful treatment is usually followed by an abolition of these phenomena.

The clinical picture is probably best described by looking at the symptoms according to response system.

Physical symptoms

The physical symptoms experienced are those of anxiety. They commonly include palpitations, sweating, dry mouth, gastrointestinal overactivity, and shaking. In addition, the hyperventilation which is part of the more general arousal can produce a miscellany of symptoms which in themselves are frightening. Pins and needles or tingling, yawning, sighing, feeling lightheaded and faint, feeling unable to breathe, are all classic symptoms of hyperventilation. There are, in addition, many other symptoms of lower $pCO2$ and as Rapee (1987) describes, these hyperventilation-induced sensations produce a vicious circle of panic and more hyperventilation. Some patients may focus on one particular symptom, such as 'jelly legs' or visual disturbance, and be unaware of sweating or tachycardia. During bouts of anxiety, the patient often feels that the symptoms of anxiety herald a heart attack, a fainting episode, a stroke, or other catastrophic physical event. They may, however, worry that they will suddenly lose control, go mad, become homicidal and so on. Some patients may go to great lengths to prevent this happening and the author actually witnessed one case where a man had tied himself up and, with the reluctant co-operation of his wife, bound himself to a chair, lest he lose control and inflict harm on others. The degree of muscle tension caused in such patients can obviously lead to physical pain. Commonly this pain is headache, which may have been diagnosed as migraine and been extensively investigated. Sometimes tension pains occur in the chest and some patients may have been seen by countless cardiologists. Likewise, tingling and visual disturbances may be suspected as a sign of multiple sclerosis and neurological opinion sought. In cases where there has been extensive medical investigation, there does seem to be a secondary problem of illness behaviour. Whether this is due to a predisposition in the patient, or is induced by the procedures themselves, or is a mixture of these factors, is unclear. The visual perception changes of over-arousal probably lead to a sensation that oneself or the outside world has changed. These sensations are called depersonalization and derealization, respectively.

The physical symptoms described by agoraphobics are countless and obviously an important part of helping the patient is a careful explanation of how these phenomena occur.

Behavioural aspects

The behavioural aspect of avoidance is of situations where escape is no readily possible, or where help is not readily available in the case of panic. Thus, as Chambless (1978) argues, the central element is 'fear of fear' and avoidance is the coping strategy used by sufferers. The help described in the DSM III definition (see p.9 in 'Classification issues') may be a companion or spouse in whom the patient trusts; it may be a bottle of vodka in a handbag which potentially provides almost instant anxiolysis; it may be a Valium tablet, always in the pocket but never taken; it may be a walking stick to use when feeling unsteady; it may be the proximity of a doctor or hospital; it may be access to a telephone, and so on. These modifying factors, if present, may make trips to the supermarket or holidays abroad possible. There- fore, people with very severe agoraphobic anxiety may, by the use of these props, appear to lead normal lives. Commonly, however, the avoidance behaviour leads to disablement in many areas, and most notably to severe social and occupational handicap (Thorpe and Burns 1983).

Cognitive aspects

The central fear suffered by agoraphobics is generally that of losing control in some way. The commonest fears are of fainting, running amok, going mad and being 'taken away', vomiting, becoming incontinent of urine or faeces, and so on. Sometimes there is a fear of dying during a panic attack and the commonest fears are that death may occur from a heart attack or stroke. On close questioning, some patients cannot volunteer any feared consequence during episodes of anxiety, while others may fear a range of outcomes, these varying over both time and situation.

Agoraphobics commonly have a range of other cognitive symptoms. Many describe themselves as natural 'worriers' and say that they anticipate, with anxiety, all kinds of life events. As Thorpe and Burns (1983) and Marks (1987a) point out, agoraphobics are often hypochondriacal, generally anxious, and may be prone to obsessive rituals and ruminations.

Panic attacks are a variable feature of the syndrome and may be present only in specific situations, or may arise spontaneously. This distinction forms the basis of current taxonomy and is discussed on p.9. As Marks (1987b) points out, panic may be absent in the clinical picture because of the ability of the person to avoid all situations which act as triggers for the attack. However, most agoraphobics suffer panic attacks at some time, although again, as Marks (1987b) observes, whether anxiety is labelled as panic is really a matter for the sufferer.

While depressive illness and the agoraphobic syndrome are separate entities, depressive symptoms in agoraphobia are extremely common. In Buglass *et al.*'s (1977) study more than 30 per cent of their sample were clearly depressed and in Gournay's (1985) study, just over half of all subjects (of a total of 132) had clear depressive symptomatology. In most cases depressive symptoms are a direct consequence of the agoraphobia. This is not surprising given the severe handicaps that accrue from the syndrome. That depressive symptoms are secondary, is clear from the results of exposure programmes. In the great majority of cases, direct treatment of the agoraphobia leads to a reduction or abolition of depressive symptoms. Apart from this, there is clear evidence from factor-analytic and epidemiological studies (reviewed by Marks 1987a) that the problems are separate. There are, however, cases of primary depression where agoraphobic symptoms are present and this is so in other problems such as obsessive compulsive disorder and schizophrenia. In these cases it is usually clear from the history that avoidance of situations away from a secure base is a consequence of other (separate) difficulties and differential diagnosis is usually no problem.

Prevalence

Marks (1987a) has carried out a very detailed analysis of the incidence of agoraphobia, and provides evidence that the syndrome, in some shape or form, is extremely common, with up to 20 per cent of the population suffering some agoraphobic avoidance. In the same analysis, Marks concludes that the incidence of full-blown agoraphobia in western cultures is between 1.2 and 3.8 per cent and a similar prevalence may occur in Asian and African cultures. The overwhelming evidence, therefore, opposes the view that agoraphobia is a reflection of the stress of urban life.

Gender

This area will be discussed specifically in Chapters 3 and 9, but it is worth pointing out that agoraphobia may be more frequent in males than treatment statistics indicate. There are several reasons for this. First, as Rachman (1978) indicates, males are far more likely to deny or hide their fearfulness. Second, many male agoraphobics may drink to cover up their fears. This hypothesis is strengthened by studies such as Mullaney and Trippett (1979) who demonstrated large numbers of agoraphobics in a sample of patients being treated for alcoholism. Thus, to quote Chambless (1982), 'Many male agoraphobics may be found in bars and the rooms of Alcoholics Anonymous rather than Phobia societies or Psychiatric Clinics.' Third, male agoraphobics may, of occupational necessity, be forced to expose themselves to phobic situations and thus, so to speak, treat themselves.

Classification issues

The two main classifications of agoraphobia are found in the *Diagnostic and Statistical Manual* III (DSM III) (American Psychiatric Association 1980) and the International Classification of Diseases 10 (ICD-10) of the World Health Organization. ICD-10 simply defines, under phobic avoidance, three main phobic syndromes, i.e. social phobia, specific phobia, and agoraphobia. However, in the new version of the more widely used DSM III, i.e. DSM IIIR, agoraphobia is classified as occurring without panic disorder, and panic disorder is defined with or without agoraphobia.

Agoraphobia is defined in DSM IIIR as:

fear of being in places or situations from which escape might be difficult (or embarrassing) or in which help might not be available, in the event of a panic attack. As a result of this fear, there are either travel restrictions or need for a companion when away from home, or there is endurance of agoraphobic situations despite intense anxiety. Common agoraphobic situations include being outside of the home alone, being in a crowd or standing in a line, being on a bridge, travelling in a bus or car.

The assessor is also asked to specify whether the agoraphobic avoidance is mild, moderate, or severe.

As Marks (1987b) points out, DSM IIIR has elevated panic into an organizing principle. This, to some extent, is the product of the work of Americans such as Klein (e.g. Klein 1964, 1981) and others (e.g. Di Nardo *et al.* 1983) who have made out a not entirely convincing case for viewing panic disorder as an entity. Marks, in his extensive critique (1987b), has pointed out that there is ultimately only the patient's labelling which delineates panic and anxiety. Further, he has added that the absence of panic may simply be a measure of avoidance. Marks is also unhappy that the agoraphobic cluster of fears is under-emphasized, and that the DSM IIIR definition of agoraphobia could also embrace specific phobias or obsessive compulsive disorder.

The validity of the syndrome

There is overwhelming evidence that agoraphobia is a distinct problem, separate from other anxiety states, phobias, and depression. A number of factor-analytic studies have consistently demonstrated an independent cluster of symptoms (e.g. Marks and Herst 1970, Schapira *et al.* 1970, Arrindell 1980). However, there is one author who has challenged the view that agoraphobia is a distinct entity. Hallam (1978, 1983, 1985) has questioned two main assumptions. First, he has challenged the view that agoraphobia is a phobia, where the term phobia is used in the sense of fear attached to a discrete set of cues. Second, he has disagreed that the agoraphobic syndrome can be clearly differentiated from states of general anxiety. Hallam argues that, although there are clusters of fear which have been called the agoraphobic syndrome, a simple fear-avoidance relationship is not a central feature of subjects suffering from agoraphobia. He cites evidence of not only the differences between agoraphobics and specific phobics, but the similarities between agoraphobia and affective disorders. In his 1978 paper, Hallam argued that the phobic avoidance found in agoraphobia merely represented a variation of coping behaviour in subjects with neurotic anxieties. In the conclusion to this paper, he called for a fresh approach to classifying the neurotic affective disorders. He has gone on (Hallam 1983) to criticize the label 'agoraphobia' from a different stance. He argues that the term is a psychiatric description, which is incompatible with a psychological construction. He asserts that psychological descriptions need

10

psychological explanations and says that the current practice of combining psychiatric and psychological terminology indicates a misplaced eclecticism. Hallam argues that psychiatric diagnoses such as agoraphobia are, in fact, fascinating examples of social stereotyping and of professional appropriation, exercised through naming. He concluded this paper by saying that clinical psychologists should generate new systems of classification. He cited Lang's three response systems (Lang 1971) as being a most useful starting point for this exercise.

Hallam (1985) has developed his argument in a book which criticizes the disorder model and attempts to apply many diverse psychological theories to explain anxiety. He argues against the reification of anxiety and agoraphobia, urging the acceptance of lay constructs as a starting point for understanding these phenomena. Certainly, he describes a range of studies which are very relevant to agoraphobic behaviour, but in contrast to many other authorities who have examined the same evidence, he concludes that the agoraphobic syndrome does not exist. At present, Hallam's view represents a small dissenting minority.

However, as Barlow (1986) has pointed out in a lengthy review of Hallam's (1985) book, Hallam's work helps us view the problem in several novel ways. Barlow also points to Hallam's partial success in challenging several currently fashionable theories, for example, that hyperventilation is central to panic, as well as, *inter alia,* Jeffrey Gray's psychophysiological theories, Richard Lazarus's coping theory, and attribution theory.

While it is difficult to accept Hallam's conclusions, it should be said that his writings have stimulated debate and some of his alternative constructions are certainly open to experimental testing.

Studies comparing agoraphobics with normal controls

There have been only three well-designed studies comparing agoraphobics with matched normal controls. In the first, Solyom *et al.* (1974) compared forty-seven phobic patients with a matched normal control group. They showed that the agoraphobics had significantly more symptoms of depression and hysterical disorder and that the agoraphobics were significantly more hypochondriacal and anxious. There was no significantly greater incidence of sexual problems than in the normal control group. This study in fact contained a mixture of simple phobic and agoraphobic subjects, but these results were very similar to a study conducted by Buglass et al. in 1977. The latter authors investigated a group of agoraphobics with a view to determining aetiological factors. They also compared the husbands from the two groups. The study examined domestic activities, decision making, assertiveness, and affection. The authors also examined the marital situation and in particular sexual behaviour, conflict, and co-operation within the marriage. They also looked at psychiatric symptoms in the children, the nature of social contact, and the husbands' view of their spouses with regard to the agoraphobic syndrome. Contrary to their original hypothesis, the authors found striking similarities between the groups on all measures. The data provided no evidence to support any theory of assortative mating, e.g. Kreitman (1968), or that the illness affected the husband in any significant way. However, there were obvious differences between the two groups in minor behavioural areas such as the amount of shopping done by the spouse. The most significant other differences were that the agoraphobics seemed to have a more disturbed early family life and there was also a loss of erotic drive. However, the loss of erotic drive seemed to be a consequence of the problem rather than pre-dating it. Likewise, any increase in anxiety or depression in a group of agoraphobics can also be viewed as a consequence rather than a cause. The studies of Buglass et al. cannot be assumed to describe typical examples of agoraphobics, but the overall impression is that the group appears far more normal, with regard to general behaviour, than had previously been hypothesized. In particular, the data from these studies indicates that certain variables, such as the marital state of agoraphobic patients, may have been prematurely labelled as aetiologically significant. The control groups highlighted, in this respect, that normal populations consist of fairly large proportions of subjects with marital and sexual dysfunction.

The final study in this area was conducted by Fisher and Wilson (1985). These authors investigated the psychological characteristics of agoraphobics and used a control group. They assessed and compared groups in terms of personality measures, level of arousal, cueing, attributional processes, and marital satisfaction. While the agoraphobics were predictably more anxious, depressed, and less assertive and reported feeling more powerless and helpless than non-agoraphobics, the group of agoraphobic subjects appeared far more 'normal' than the hypothesis of workers such as Chambless and

Goldstein (q.v.) would suggest. Overall, their findings were in accord with those of Buglass and her colleagues. The authors also felt strongly that, in agoraphobia, helplessness was a consequence of severe debilitating panic rather than causative. This view is of course contrary to that of workers with a more psychodynamic stance. Fisher and Wilson felt that this helplessness and the associated fear of fear becomes part of the agoraphobic's self-schema and thus becomes self-perpetuating and recalcitrant to change.

In summary therefore, the controlled evidence points to agoraphobic people being, apart from their agoraphobia, as normal (or abnormal) as the general population. This evidence, together with the data reviewed by Barbara Hudson in Chapter 3 which shows that agoraphobic marriages are in a general way no different from the population at large, tends to confirm the view that many of the psychodynamic theories of agoraphobia are based solely on speculation.

The alcohol–agoraphobia relationship

This issue has become increasingly important as there is a growing body of evidence supporting the view that alcohol abuse and agoraphobia may very frequently overlap. Alcohol is certainly the oldest and most universal anxiolytic drug. However, as Bibb and Chambless (1983) and Chambless *et al.* (1987) point out, just how alcohol reduces anxiety is subject to wide individual differences (Sher and Levenson 1983). In more general terms, a review of animal experiments (Hodgson *et al.* 1979) shows clearly that alcohol does inhibit fear, though probably a feature of the 'craving' characteristic of withdrawal from alcohol is an elevation of anxiety (Rankin *et al.* 1979).

Quitkin *et al.* (1972) estimated that 5-10 per cent of agoraphobics abused alcohol or drugs and were the first to indicate that this was an area which should be further investigated. The first clear evidence of a relationship came with the work of Mullaney and Trippett (1979). They looked at consecutive admissions to an alcohol treatment unit and found that 13 per cent of the men and 33 per cent of the women had clear agoraphobic symptoms, while 28 per cent and 22 per cent respectively were 'borderline agoraphobics'. The authors also found that the mean age of onset of agoraphobia of the sample predated the onset of alcohol abuse. Among other conclusions, Mullaney and Trippett suggested that there was a higher rate of agoraphobia among males than had previously been found in clinical samples, positing that agoraphobic men drank to hide their fears. Unfortunately, the authors did not attempt long follow-up of their subjects. It would have been interesting to see whether withdrawal and successful rehabilitation led to fear reduction or whether the agoraphobic symptomatology had an autonomous character. Mullaney and Trippett's findings were confirmed by a second British study, Smail *et al.* (1984). They found that 18 per cent of their sample of alcoholics had severe phobic states and there was clear evidence that these subjects used alcohol as an anxiolytic. In the same study a control group of phobics also showed this tendency.

One isolated study did not find a higher rate of alcohol intake among a group of agoraphobics. Samarasinghe *et al.* (1984) looked at the use of alcohol and tranquillizers in a sample of neurotic patients attending a psychological treatment unit. The sample of 106 subjects included thirty agoraphobics. The authors used a questionnaire which looked at the amount of alcohol consumed and also whether the alcohol reduced phobic anxiety in those subjects. Contrary to expectation, the authors did not find that the phobic group's drinking behaviour was significantly different to that of the general population. Furthermore, the group did not perceive alcohol as a reliable anxiolytic. In fact the thirty agoraphobics consumed rather less alcohol in quantity and frequency than the other phobics in the rest of the study sample. The findings of this study are rather in contrast to those described by Chambless *et al.* (1987) in a comprehensive review of the area. There are several factors which may explain Samarasinghe *et al.*'s findings. First, over 30 per cent of their sample used tranquillizers in quantities equivalent to more than 10 mg of diazepam daily and this anxiolytic use may have replaced, for some subjects, alcohol use. Second, the sample was rather small and may have been atypical. Third, the treatment unit where the data was collected was at the Maudsley Hospital, which offers a very comprehensive and wide- ranging service. It is possible that many agoraphobics with alcohol abuse may have found their way into alcohol treatment because of the availability of such services and the arguably more competent screening and referral sources.

A far larger study was carried out by Bibb and Chambless (1983, 1986). They looked at 254 agoraphobics using a wide set of measures including the very reliable Michigan Alcohol Screening Test (MAST, Selzer 1971). 21 per cent of the sample scored five or more on the

MAST (i.e. 18 per cent of the women and 36 per cent of the men). On a more conservative cut-off score of ten on the MAST, 10 per cent still scored as alcoholic. The authors compared the alcoholic agoraphobics with a demographically similar non-alcoholic group of agoraphobics and demonstrated that the alcoholic group were more depressed, more socially phobic, more fearful of somatic symptoms when nervous or afraid, and more likely to engage in catastrophic thinking. The authors looked at the hypothesis that pre-existing agoraphobia may lead to problem drinking. Their data was rather complex and suggested that 'mixed alcoholism and agoraphobia does not follow a consistent developmental sequence for either in-patient alcoholics or out-patient agoraphobics'. Bibb and Chambless recommend that 'a corresponding appreciation of the complex contribution of alcohol use and abuse may be necessary for a comprehensive understanding of agoraphobia and its effective treatment'. The authors conclude by recommending the routine screening of agoraphobics for alcohol problems and caution that alcohol use during treatment must surely detract from treatment efficacy.

In summary, the data from a wide range of studies would indicate an important interaction between alcohol and agoraphobia. Furthermore, it seems vital that clinicians involved in the treatment of agoraphobia are vigilant for the signs of alcohol abuse.

CURRENT VIEWS OF THE SYNDROME

Learning theory models

Eysenck and Rachman (1965) advanced an explanation of phobic behaviour based on the work of Mowrer (1947, 1960). This two-factor theory involving the classical conditioning of fear and its maintenance by instrumental conditioning has continued to be held, albeit in modified fashion, by some workers. One important such modification to the theory is that certain phobias are biologically prepared for rapid acquisition (Seligman 1971). In demonstrating this phenomenon convincingly, Ohman et al. (1978) used an aversive conditioning procedure with various stimuli, concluding that certain of these seemed 'pre-programmed' for rapid learning. Latterly, Eysenck (1982) has argued that phobias are produced by classical conditioning and thence are incubated. This theory accommodates three main difficulties of classical conditioning theory, i.e.:

1 that neurotic conditioned responses persist in spite of
  numerous presentations of unreinforced conditioned stimuli;
2 that traumatic unconditioned stimuli are infrequent in the
  development of peacetime neurosis; and
3 that conditioned responses increase in strength with repeated
  presentations of unreinforced stimuli.

Eysenck states that with neurosis we are dealing with Pavlovian B rather than Pavlovian A conditioning, but under these conditions, the conditioned response is essentially identical with the unconditioned response and acts as a positive reinforcement in the absence of an unconditioned response. He used the Napalkov phenomenon (Napalkov 1963) as the laboratory analogue of the process that takes place in neurotic disorders. In this experiment, a single combination of a conditioned stimulus with an unconditioned stimulus, followed by repeated presentations of the conditioned stimulus alone, was followed by an incrementation of the conditioned response. Eysenck (1982) has suggested possible mechanisms which may operate to produce this effect and concludes that it is more likely to occur in neurotic introverts. He goes on to argue that measures of individual differences, such as his personality questionnaire, should be considered when drawing up treatment programmes.

However, many workers in both the theoretical field (e.g. Bersh 1980, 1983) and in the clinical field (Marks 1981, Mathews *et al.* 1981) have criticized the notion that learning theory satisfactorily explains the acquisition, evolution, and maintenance of phobias. The main criticisms are several. First, as previously discussed, there is little evidence to suggest that specific conditioning events are present in clinical cases. Second, although one can explain in learning theory terms why phobias may fail to extinguish (e.g. the Napalkov effect), the fact that phobias vary considerably in their intensity over time suggests a severe shortcoming in a simple conditioning process.

In a series of papers which have addressed both theoretical and clinical issues in agoraphobic avoidance, Rachman (1984) has advanced the argument for introducing properly experimental analyses of agoraphobia. He puts forward, as a first step in effecting such analyses, the suggestion that safety signals be analysed and he sets out a specific set of predictions. He agrees with Hallam (1985) that agoraphobia is not a categorical pathological condition, which is either present or absent, but is rather part of a continuum ranging between severe clinical agoraphobia and as he puts it 'impaired mobility'. He states that there are six arguments which justify the inclusion of the safety signal component into the analysis of agoraphobia, and they are:

1 that the use of the safety signal concept can help to account for the undue persistence of agoraphobic avoidance behaviour;
2 that the safety signal concept can be used to explain fluctuations in the agoraphobic's fears;
3 that safety signal concepts help to explain why fear is limited in space and time;
4 that the theme of a search for safety is prominent in many clinical conditions of the disorder;
5 that the concept helps to make intelligible some puzzling features of agoraphobia, e.g. the onset of the problem after bereavement or loss;
6 that the introduction of the concept of the safety signals is capable of promoting new therapeutic approaches to this disorder.

He goes on to list a full set of hypotheses concerning the determinants of the strength of the safety signal and other, peripheral, related hypotheses. The main questions he puts forward as being worthy of attention are:

1 what conditions promote the development of safety signals?
2 what factors determine the strength of safety signals?
3 what is the relationship between safety signals, avoidance behaviour, and fear?
4 how and to what extent do safety signals moderate fear?
5 are the effects of safety signals specific or general (presumably, internalized safety signals will have more general effect than external ones)?
6 how and to what extent, do safety signals maintain avoidance behaviours?

Rachman and his colleagues have in fact begun to look at these issues by carrying out a number of experimental analyses of panic with patients with panic disorder and analogue subjects with claustrophobic fears (Rachman *et al.* 1988a, 1988b).

Integrated views

There are two commonly accepted integrated models of aetiology which greatly overlap. In these, to a varying extent, biological, cognitive, and behavioural factors are included.

In the first model, Mathews *et al.* (1981) describe two broad, parallel processes which merge to produce a clinical agoraphobic state. The authors suggest that some individuals have high inherited levels of trait anxiety which combine with increased 'non-specific stress' to produce an elevated level of general anxiety. In the second process, these individuals learn, in formative years, an avoidant style of coping and develop an external locus of control. Thus after an acute anxiety attack, which may be triggered by a variety of stimuli, these people begin avoiding various situations. The authors then discuss factors which positively reinforce phobic behaviour. They state that the sympathy and attention gained by adoption of a 'sick role' may lead to a 'behavioural trap', whereby the attitude or concerns of others prevents extrication from avoidance patterns.

The second popular integrated model belongs to Chambless and Goldstein (1982) and Chambless (1978), who have argued that a combination of behavioural and psychodynamic ideas are necessary to understand the nature of agoraphobia. The authors argue that agoraphobia can be divided into two syndromes. The first is simple agoraphobia, which is probably caused by drug experiences or by hypoglycaemia, and amounts to several simple phobias of public places. In this problem, there is no generalization of anxiety to other life areas and general psychological adjustment is normal. Chambless and Goldstein also state that this syndrome is uncommon. The second, and in their view, most prevalent, disorder they call complex agoraphobia. This is characterized by:

1 fear of fear as the central phobic element;
2 low levels of self-sufficiency, due to anxiety or lack of skill, or both these factors;
3 a tendency to misapprehend the cause of antecedents of uncomfortable feelings, e.g. anxiety following interpersonal conflict is interpreted as fear of being on the street alone;
4 the onset of symptoms occurring in a climate of notable conflict. This conflict is generally, but not necessarily, interpersonal in nature.

Chambless and Goldstein based their conclusions on wide clinical and research observations and supported their arguments by data obtained from thirty-two agoraphobic patients and thirty-six patients with phobias of external stimuli. The groups were not matched, but did not differ statistically in age or sex ratio. The authors describe traditional explanations of the syndrome based on classical and operant models, but add two further operant elements which maintain symptoms. First, there is social reinforcement for being sick or dependent, strengthened by punishment for autonomous behaviour, and second, avoidance behaviours are negatively reinforced by reduction of exposure to the 'fear of fear' and by other situations which cause difficulty.

A prerequisite for these conditioning events is therefore a particular 'vulnerable personality'. The authors' work is obviously much influenced by John Bowlby's (1973) concept of separation anxiety and ensuing fear of abandonment.

The main criticisms of theory have been made by Emmelkamp (1979), Thorpe and Burns (1983), and Mathews *et al.* (1981). These criticisms include the fact that the study on which their theory is based was retrospective and that there was considerable emphasis on clinical impression. Second, there is no explanation of the mechanism of how separation anxiety becomes a fear of public situations. Third, as 'conflict' is essential to the definition of complex agoraphobia, a circular definitive process occurs.

While the theory has the appeal of being all-embracing, it does use rather nebulous concepts such as 'dependence' which do not lend themselves readily to experimental testing. Further, there is now some evidence that the rather central concepts of separation anxiety and inassertiveness have a far lesser incidence in populations of agoraphobics than was previously assumed (Thyer *et al.* 1985, Emmelkamp 1982).

CONCLUSION

The very large amount of work on the nature of agoraphobia has increasingly led to the view that this is a disorder of multifactorial aetiology. It is now clear that there can be no single theory which accounts for causation and one has to formulate the problem in not only cognitive, behavioural, and biological ways, but also look at a probable evolutionary context. While this complexity raises problems in trying to provide the patient with a reasonable explanation of the problem, such a task is an absolute prerequisite for an honest and comprehensive approach.

© Kevin Gournay

REFERENCES

Agras, S., Sylvester, D. and Oliveau, D. (1969) 'The epidemiology of common fears and phobias', *Comprehensive Psychiatry* 10: 151–6.

American Psychiatric Association (1980) *Diagnostic and Statistical Manual of Mental Disorders* (3rd edn), Washington DC: APA.

Arrindell, W. A. (1980) 'Dimensional structure and psychopathology correlates of the fear survey schedule (FSS 111) in a phobic population: a factorial definition of agoraphobia', *Behaviour Research and Therapy* 18: 229–42.

Barlow, D. H. (1986) 'Special review of R. S. Hallam's *Anxiety: Psychological Perspectives*', *Beh. Res. and Ther.* 24, 6: 693–6.

Bersh, P. J. (1980) 'Eysenck's theory of incubation: a critical analysis', *Beh. Res. and Ther.* 18: 11–17.

—(1983) 'The theory of incubation: comments on Eysenck's reply', *Beh. Res. and Ther.* 21, 3: 307–8.

Bibb, J. L. and Chambless, D.L. (1983) 'Agoraphobia and Alcoholism', paper to 2nd World Congress of Behaviour Therapy, Washington DC, December.

—(1986) 'Alcohol use and abuse among diagnosed agoraphobics', *Beh. Res. and Ther.* 24: 49–58.

Bowlby, J. (1973) *Separation: Anxiety and Anger*, New York: Basic Books.

Buglass, D., Clarke, J., Henderson, A. S., and Kreitman, N. (1977) 'A study of agoraphobic housewives', *Psych. Med.* 7: 73–86.

Chambless, D. L. (1978) 'The role of anxiety in flooding with agoraphobic clients', unpublished doctoral dissertation, Temple Univ., PA, USA.

—(1982) Chapter in D. L. Chambless and A. J. Goldstein (eds) *Agoraphobia: Multiple Perspectives on Theory and Treatment*, New York: John Wiley.

Chambless, D. L. and Goldstein, A. J. (1982) *Agoraphobia: Multiple Perspectives on Theory and Treatment*, New York: John Wiley.

Chambless, D. L., Cherney, J., Caputo, G. C., and Rheinstein, B. J. G. (1987) 'Anxiety disorders and alcoholism', *Journal of Anxiety Disorders* 1: 29–40.

Di Nardo, P. A., O'Brien, G. T., Barlow, D. H., Waddell, M. T., and Blanchard, E. B. (1983) 'Reliability of DSM III anxiety disorder categories using a new structured interview', *Archives Gen. Psych.* 40: 1070–9.

Emmelkamp, P. M. G. (1979) 'The behavioural study of clinical phobias', in M. Hersen, R. Eisler, and P. M. Miller (eds) *Progress in Behaviour Modification*, vol. 8, New York: Academic Press.

—(1982) '*In vivo* treatment of agoraphobia', in D. L. Chambless and A. J.

Goldstein (eds), *Agoraphobia: Multiple Perspectives on Theory and Treatment*, New York: John Wiley.

Eysenck, H. J. (1982) 'Why do conditioned responses show incrementation, while unconditioned responses show habituation?', *Beh. Psychotherapy* 10: 217–20.

Eysenck, H. J. and Rachman, S. (1965) *Causes and Cures of Neurosis*, London: Routledge & Kegan Paul.

Fisher, L. M. and Wilson, G. T. (1985) 'A study of the psychology of agoraphobia', *Beh. Res. and Ther.* 23, 2: 97–108.

Gournay, K. J. M. (1985) 'Agoraphobia: a study of the syndrome and its treatment', unpublished Ph.D. thesis, University of Leicester.

Hallam, R. S. (1978) 'Agoraphobia: a critical review of the concept', *Brit. J. Psych.* 133: 314–19.

—(1983) 'Agoraphobia: deconstructing a clinical syndrome', *Bulletin of the BPS*, Oct., pp. 337–40.

—(1985) *Anxiety: Psychological Perspectives on Panic and Agoraphobia*, London: Academic Press.

Hodgson, R., Rankin, H., and Stockwell, T. (1979) 'Alcohol dependence and the priming effect', *Beh. Res. and Ther.* 4: 379–88.

Klein, D. F. (1964) 'Delineation of two drug-responsive anxiety syndromes', *Psychopharmacologia* 5: 397–408.

—(1981) 'Anxiety reconceptualized', in D. F. Klein and J. Rabkin (eds) *Anxiety: New Research and Changing Concepts*, New York: Raven Press.

Kreitman, N. (1968) 'Married couples admitted to mental hospital', *Brit. J. Psych.* 114: 699–718.

Lang, P. (1971) 'An application of psychophysiological methods to the study of psychotherapy and behaviour modification', in A. E. Bergin and S. L. Garfield (eds) *Handbook of Psychotherapy and Behavior Change: an Empirical Analysis*, New York: John Wiley.

Marks, I. M. (1981) 'Behavioural concepts of neurosis', *Behavioural Psychotherapy* 9: 137–54.

—(1987a) *Fears, Phobias and Rituals*, London: Oxford University Press.

—(1987b) 'Agoraphobia, panic disorder and related conditions in the DSM IIIR and ICD 10', *J. Psychopharmacology* 1: 6–12.

Marks, I. M. and Herst, E. R. (1970) 'A survey of 1,200 agoraphobics in Britain', *Social Psychiatry* 5: 16–24.

Mathews, A. M., Gelder, M. G. and Johnston, D. W. (1981) *Agoraphobia: Nature and Treatment*, London: Tavistock.

Mowrer, O. H. (1947) 'On the dual nature of learning as a reinterpretation of conditioning and problem solving', *Harvard Educational Review*, 102–48.

—(1960) *Learning Theory and Behaviour*, New York: John Wiley.

Mullaney, J. A. and Trippett, C. J. (1979) 'Alcohol dependence and phobias: clinical description and relevance', *Brit. J. Psych.* 135: 565–73.

Napalkov, S. V. (1963) 'Information process and the brain', in N. Wiener and J. Schadal (eds) *Progress in Brain Research*, vol. 2, Amsterdam: Elsevier.

Ohman, A., Fredrikson, M. and Hudgahal, K. (1978) 'Orienting and defensive responding in the electrodermal system: palmar dorsal differences and recovery rate', *Psychophysiology* 15: 93–101.

Quitkin, F. M., Rifkin, A., Kaplan, J., and Klein, D. F. (1972) 'Phobic anxiety syndrome complicated by drug dependence and addiction: a treatable form of drug abuse', *Arch. Gen. Psych.* 27: 159–62.

Rachman, S. (1978) *Fear and Courage*, San Francisco: Freeman.

—(1984) 'The experimental analysis of agoraphobia', *Beh. Res. and Ther.* 22, 6: 631–40.

Rachman, S., Levitt, K., and Lopatka, C. (1988a) 'Experimental analysis of panic, III: claustrophobic patients', *Beh. Res. and Ther.* 26, 1: 41–7.

Rachman, S., Lopatka, C., and Levitt, K. (1988b) 'Experimental analysis of panic, II: panic patients', *Beh. Res. and Ther.* 26. 1: 33–40.

Rankin, H., Hodgson, R., and Stockwell, T. (1979) 'The concept of craving and its measurement', *Beh. Res. and Ther.* 17: 389–96.

Rapee, R. (1987) 'The psychological treatment of panic attacks', *Clinical Psychology Review,* 7, 4: 427–38.

Samarasinghe, D. S., Tilley, S., and Marks, I. M. (1984) 'Alcohol and sedative drug use in neurotic out-patients', *Brit. J. Psych.* 145, 7: 45–8.

Schapira, K., Kew, T. A., and Roth, M. (1970) 'Phobias and affective illness', *Brit. J. Psych.* 117: 25–32.

Seligman, M. E. P. (1971) 'Phobias and preparedness', *Beh. Ther.* 2: 307–20.

Selzer, M. L. (1971) 'The Michigan alcohol screening test', *American Journal of Psychiatry* 127: 1653–8.

Sher, K. J. and Levenson, R. W. (1983) 'Alcohol and tension reduction', in L. A. Pohorecky and J. Brick (eds) *Stress and Alcohol Use,* New York: Elsevier.

Smail, P., Stockwell, T., Canter, S., and Hodgson, R. (1984) 'Alcohol dependence and phobic anxiety states, 1: a prevalence study', *Brit. J. Psych.* 144: 53–7.

Solyom, L., Beck, P., Solyom, C., and Hugel, R. (1974) 'Some aetiological factors in phobic neurosis', *Canadian Psychiatric Assn. Journal* 19: 69–78.

Thorpe, G. L. and Burns, L. E. (1983) *The Agoraphobic Syndrome,* New York: John Wiley.

Thyer, B. A., Nesse, R. M., Cameron, O. G. and Curtis, G. C. (1985) 'Agoraphobia: a test of the separation anxiety hypothesis', *Beh. Res. and Ther.* 23, 1: 75–8.

Chapter Two

THE BEHAVIOURAL (EXPOSURE) TREATMENT OF AGORAPHOBIA: A REVIEW AND AN OUTCOME STUDY

KEVIN GOURNAY

INTRODUCTION

The behavioural treatment of agoraphobia has become synonymous with exposure in real life. For several years now the major authorities have agreed that regardless of whatever else is used to treat the problem (drugs, cognitive approaches, etc.), the use of exposure is essential. The controversies regarding exposure are many and complex and the purpose of this chapter is to look critically at the evidence.

BACKGROUND

The first report of *in vivo* exposure of modern times was arguably that of Meyer and Gelder (1963). They described a procedure whereby patients were given relaxation training and then exposure to phobic situations in real life. The description of their cases showed that the approach was much more gradual than that used today, taking some four months to train one patient to walk a quarter of a mile to meet the therapist. Further, two of the cases described by Meyer and Gelder were rather complicated, these subjects having multiple psychiatric symptoms in addition to the agoraphobic avoidance. This study was followed by that of Cooper *et al.* (1965) and Marks and Gelder (1965) who described behavioural methods with samples of psychiatric patients. They also included a large control group of agoraphobics who had been in the same hospital but not received behaviour therapy. The patients in the behaviour therapy condition received graded retraining and other treatments, the specific nature of which was not clearly defined. The behaviour therapy group seemed to improve slightly more than the controls, although they needed double the amount of therapist time. As Mathews *et al.* (1981) point out, this method of treating agoraphobia was viewed more than cautiously by the authors who concluded that the results of treatment did not justify the expenditure of effort. Eysenck (1965) criticized the study on a number of grounds, not least that it was entirely inappropriate to include graded retraining under the descriptive umbrella of behaviour therapy.

Boulougouris and Marks (1969) were the first to describe the application of classical flooding to clinically phobic patients. They described the treatment of four patients who were given real-life exposure to the phobic stimulus, following preparatory imaginal sessions. The paper emphasized the work of Baum (1966) on conditioned avoidance responses and the necessity of blocking such an avoidance response so that the extinction of anxiety could occur. One of the two patients who did not improve was a case of free-floating anxiety.

At this point, it is worth clarifying what exposure treatment actually is, as there is some disagreement as to how it is different from flooding. For the purpose of the current discussion, exposure means facing previously feared or avoided situations in gradual stages. It has, to some extent, become synonymous with flooding, although strictly speaking, flooding demands facing the fear stimulus with maximum evocation of anxiety. However, Marks (1972a) pointed out that flooding is not, in clinical practice, a single technique but comprises a wide range of over-lapping procedures. At that time (according to Marks), at least twenty-four different terms had been used to describe flooding and its variants. By 1981 Marks (1981a) was able to cite a total of forty terms describing, as he put it, exposure and allied treatments. Exposure treatment is essentially a pragmatic exercise. Therapist and patient negotiate tasks on the basis of tackling difficult but manageable tasks. Progression to more difficult tasks is indicated when the patient feels he/she is coping with the current situation, albeit with some anxiety. This, of course, is in contrast to systematic desensitization, where moving to the next step of the hierarchy is only allowed when complete extinction of anxiety occurs.

It is now generally accepted that exposure in real life is the optimum treatment for agoraphobia and research has been directed in three main areas. First, and really only in the last few years, workers have begun to look at the theoretical nature of exposure beyond the original classical theory. Second, there has been a limited amount of work regarding the general issues that treatment generates, for example, the social validity of treatment and treatment failure. Third, the bulk of the research has been concentrated on the most effective ways of applying exposure in the clinical situation.

THE THEORY OF EXPOSURE

This area has been much neglected until only recently, a fact pointed out several times by Rachman. Rachman (1983) stated that while results with exposure treatments are good, it is nevertheless the case that many patients, although improved, have considerable residual difficulty. Furthermore, he underlined the fact that there are significant numbers of treatment failures. Rachman went on to argue in a later paper (1984) that only a thorough understanding of the mechanism of agoraphobic avoidance, and then logically of exposure treatments, will refine treatment further and yield a higher rate of treatment success. At least some of the reluctance to research the underlying psychological processes can be traced to the view of empiricists such as Marks. This author has stated (Marks 1981b) 'that experimental psychology was one of the many idols of origin ignored by behavioural practitioners'. Marks has gone on to advocate speaking simply of the ESs or evoking stimuli which trigger the phobic or obsessional reaction, these reactions being ERs or evoked responses which can themselves become further ESs in a vicious circle (e.g. anticipatory fear of fear). Marks then discussed whether there was any need for considering complex conditioning theories, and suggested that the only theory that clinicians need to carry out treatment is the central hypothesis of exposure. This states 'that phobias and rituals are reduced by exposure of the patient to those stimuli which evoke his discomfort or rituals, until these no longer occur' (Marks 1972b, 1977, 1978, 1981a, Greist *et al.* 1980).

Marks considers that the unsuccessful approaches in the treatment of phobias omit exposure. (This latter point has been the subject of further controversy, but this will be reviewed in detail later).

Marks's general view of exposure in agoraphobia is that psychological processes are only part of the picture. He makes it clear that he considers current psychological models to be inadequate. Wilson (1981) has examined Marks's views at length, and while concurring with Marks's expressed dissatisfaction with current conditioning models of neurosis and exposure, argues convincingly for more psychological research in these areas. Wilson considers that Marks's ES–ER paradigm carries the same limitations as the conditioning paradigm, and that a more profitable line of enquiry may be the social learning approach of Bandura. In particular, he argues that this approach, which incorporates cognitive variables within a behavioural framework, has a more comprehensive and heuristic quality.

Exposure – a prerequisite for fear reduction?

Recently, there has been some controversy as to whether exposure is a necessary condition for fear reduction. This is highlighted in the papers of Boyd and Levis (1983) and de Silva and Rachman (1981, 1983). The latter authors take the view that while 'in most of the effective techniques for reducing fear, exposure to the fear-provoking stimulus is a prominent feature' (de Silva and Rachman 1981: 227) and that while exposure treatments were important and significant, there was evidence that 'fear reduction can take place in the absence of exposure to the fear stimulus'. They cited seven types of evidence in support of this likelihood. These were that:

1 common clinical and experimental observations lead us to conclude that imparting information about the harmlessness of the stimulus can lead to a reduction in fear;
2 cognitive therapy can produce fear reduction;
3 there is spontaneous remission of neurotic, including anxiety, reactions in a proportion of patients;
4 improvement is often observed after the administration of placebos;
5 experimental results show improvements in some patients after non-exposure type therapy;
6 improvements are shown by patients in other phobias than the treated one;
7 there is indirect experimental evidence of the success of non-exposure therapy with obsessional neurotics.

The basis of Boyd and Levis's (1983) reply was that the above evidence could be explained because in all of these examples, exposure may have taken place and was thus responsible for extinction. Boyd and Levis were not satisfied by the *post hoc* nature of their own evaluation but urged further investigation of the extinction process and elaboration of the CS model. Following this, de Silva and Rachman (1983) advocated abandoning attempts to extend the exposure model meaninglessly and called for a methodical collection of data concerning non-exposure fear reduction.

One of the central features of the exposure method is that patients should remain in the feared situation until their anxiety level falls. Authoritative texts of agoraphobia and its treatment emphasize the importance of never leaving a situation until the fear decreases. This assertion is very much based on Mowrer's theory of fear and avoidance (Mowrer 1947, 1960). De Silva and Rachman (1984) have argued that such escape behaviour is not necessarily followed by increases in the strength of associated avoidance behaviour. They conducted an experiment with eighteen agoraphobic patients, randomly allocating them to two conditions. The first was a condition of exposure whereby patients were instructed not to leave the situation until their anxiety dropped to at least half of the peak anxiety felt. In the second group, patients were asked to approach fear-provoking situations, but were instructed to leave when their subjectively felt anxiety level reached a pre-set level of 75 per cent of the maximum anxiety estimated before the exposure. In a third wait list condition, patients were taken on for therapy at a later time. Contrary to the results one would expect if a Mowrerian model held true, the patients who were taught to escape did not show increased avoidance behaviour and while cognitive changes were not monitored, they suggest that variables such as self-efficacy could well be crucial in the fear-reduction therapies.

Most clinicians would agree that an important feature of exposure treatment is to make sure that the subject is not avoiding cognitively when confronting the phobic stimuli. Borkovek and Grayson et al. (1980) have pointed out that the events which interfere with the subject's awareness and/or processing during exposure will critically influence the effects of exposure procedure. However, Rachman et al. (1976) has suggested that with regard to exposure with obsessionals that such exposure may well be facilitated by the introduction of competing activities. There is no published investigation of distraction during exposure treatment of agoraphobia. However, Grayson et al. (1982) compared two conditions of exposure in sixteen obsessive compulsives. The first condition was attention focusing, during which the therapist engaged the subject in a conversation about the phobic stimulus. The second condition was exposure with distraction, with the subject being asked to hold the contaminating object, i.e. the phobic stimulus, in one hand while playing video games with the therapist throughout the session. The results clearly indicated that attention focusing led to a greater habituation to anxiety. Further-more, in this connection, there was greater synchrony between physiological and subjective measures of anxiety, such synchrony being a positive indicator of treatment outcome. The authors concluded that treatment by exposure was more effective if attention focusing is promoted. This finding has obvious applicability for the management of agoraphobics but obviously needs more experimental testing. In particular, Baum (1987) has pointed to work with analogue populations and with animals, which does indicate that some conditions of distraction do seem to facilitate exposure.

Marks is arguably the most influential worker in the area of exposure treatments and, as stated before, he has often criticized, e.g. 1981a, 1981b, the theoretical approaches based on laboratory learning theory. In reviewing the literature, his stance does, however, seem in accord with three of the most prominent groups of researchers in the early 1980s (see Mathews *et al.* 1981, Chambless and Goldstein 1982, and Thorpe and Burns 1983). Marks summarizes (Marks 1981b) the main considerations for exposure theory, cited as the most relevant, by himself and the other prominent workers. These considerations summarize comprehensively current questions regarding the theory of exposure.

In his first consideration he asks, just how does exposure that is traumatic differ from exposure that is therapeutic (or in the loosest sense of the term, habituating)? One example of this distinction is the case of the subject who prior to treatment attempts to visit a shopping precinct and despite repeated attempts continues to suffer fear and panic. The same subject, however, benefits from exposure to the same situation during therapist-aided treatment and with repeated expo-sures shows a decrease in anxiety. Marks suggests that our defin itions of exposure and avoidance need to be tightened. The results of de Silva and Rachman's (1984) experiment referred to earlier would seem to reinforce this suggestion. Marks goes on to ask why various modes of exposure (for example, in terms of length of exposure sessions and intervals between sessions) seem more effective. There seems to be very little in the way of experimental evidence to answer this question. This area of research may well help to explain why some subjects fail to habituate to anxiety-evoking stimuli or alcohol. Marks also indicates that the answer to variability in habituation between individuals may well be accounted for by, as yet, unknown biochemical or physiological variables.

In a wider set of questions, Marks asks whether exposure acts by teaching subjects how to cope with unpleasant feelings in general, and suggests that exposure theory could be widened to a general coping theory. Marks, in his ten major considerations for exposure theory, includes other variables, the role of which needs more careful enquiry. These include therapist variables and various cognitive factors.

Perhaps the most important theoretical consideration concerns the lack of a comprehensive explanatory model of aetiology, of not only agoraphobia but also other syndromes where avoidance is central, e.g. obsessive rituals. The current position is that the successful exposure-based treatments are empirically-derived procedures for ill-understood syndromes. Therefore, Rachman's (1984) call for experimental analyses of agoraphobic behaviour probably offers the most helpful line of enquiry for future research.

Comparisons of various modes of exposure

Although the most favoured mode of exposure is a graduated one in real life, controversy regarding the various modes continues (e.g. James 1985). The early studies of agoraphobia treated by systematic desensitization (e.g. Gelder *et al.* 1967) yielded poor results and by 1969 Marks concluded that flooding was a superior procedure (Marks 1969). Crowe *et al.* (1972) also demonstrated, in a crossover design, that flooding in imagination was superior to desensitization in imagination but not as effective as shaping in real life (also called reinforced practice). However, Mathews *et al.* (1976a) compared imaginal flooding and exposure to real phobic situations with a group of thirty-six agoraphobic patients and concluded that provided patients practise confrontation between treatment sessions, there was no long-term difference between treatments. This paper pointed out that the usefulness of imaginal exposure had been overlooked because of the large amount of positive evidence for prolonged *in vivo* exposure. Mathews *et al.* also pointed out that experimental designs used in comparative research ruled out delayed or carry-over effects. This study to some extent confirmed the suggestions of Gelder *et al.* (1973) that real and imaginal exposure were equivalent. Similarly, James *et al.* (1983) questioned the results of studies which indicated a superiority of *in vivo* to imaginal approaches, pointing out that these claims were based on research which has involved flooding or rapid exposure procedures. The authors used a multiple baseline across single subjects' design to compare imaginal and *in vivo* desensitization in agoraphobia. Their measures were those of avoidance, subjective distress, and heart rate, and these were repeated at various follow-up points. Both treatments yielded improvement but no differences were seen. In a recent review, the main author of this study (James 1986) points to the fact that only three studies (his own and those of Crowe *et al.* 1972 and Mathews *et al.* 1976b) have compared imaginal and real-life desensitization. James's critical review points convincingly to the conclusion that the treatments are similar in effect (provided of course that the subject carries out their own exposure between treatment sessions). He also goes on to point out that in clinical practice (and probably in experimental studies) the two processes are inextricably confounded. He recommends the employment of a judicious blend of both imaginal and *in vivo* exposure, which seems in accord with the advice of Mathews *et al.* (1981).

Hecker and Thorpe (1987) were prompted by James's (1986) paper to re-examine the evidence from the perspectives of bio-informational theory (Lang 1985) and the concept of emotional processing (Foa and Kozak 1986). Hecker and Thorpe argue quite convincingly that the fear reduction which occurs during imaginal and *in vivo* exposure can be explained by the same processes of modification of long-term memory. They conclude that while it is important to compare the outcome of the two procedures, it is equally important to carry out theory-based research which will elucidate the treatment process. They themselves are carrying out such research, looking at whether prior training in activation of response information will potentiate the effects of exposure (whether in imagination or *in vivo*) to fear-relevant stimuli.

However, the issue of real-life versus imaginal desensitization versus flooding is being settled in clinical practice by issues such as costeffect-iveness. For example, hourly sessions of desensitization would seem to lend themselves more readily to the private practice settings of the United States, much more than group *in vivo* exposure sessions of unpredictable length. Conversely, in the United Kingdom, brief high-demand exposure treatment is in vogue as a cost-effective treatment, but can be criticized for taking no account of a substantial proportion of treatment refusers who may find such treatment too demanding.

In summary, all of the studies reviewed contain a major element of *in vivo* practice and between-treatment-session exposure carried out without the therapist. Therefore, our central question would seem to be just how this self-initiated exposure can be facilitated. The one major advantage of imaginal exposure would seem that it reduces the possibility of the subject engaging in cognitive avoidance. However, it does seem that the particular balance of technique(s) depends on the result of the individual assessment. If group treatments are used, graded *in vivo* exposure is the obvious treatment of choice. One further treatment possibility is that patients treated *in vivo* within a group could be prepared by imaginal procedures, either alone or in a group setting.

VARIABLES ASSOCIATED WITH EXPOSURE TREATMENT

Over the years there have been a great number of studies which have looked at what variables influence the outcome of exposure programmes. A summary of the most relevant studies follows.

The spacing and duration of sessions

Stern and Marks (1973) compared exposure treatment consisting of long sessions (two hours) with exposure treatment consisting of brief sessions. They found that long sessions were superior and that during the second hour of exposure there was an increase in habituation as measured by heart rate and subjective anxiety. The authors also pointed out that in seventeen analogue studies of exposure there was a distinct relationship between effectiveness and length of session. Foa *et al.* (1980) showed that exposure treatment was more effective if given on consecutive days rather than once a week. Currently, Chambless is carrying out a study looking at massed versus spaced sessions of exposure for agoraphobics (Chambless, personal communication).

In practical terms, the most effective format may be to offer a package of six to eight exposure sessions, each lasting a complete morning or afternoon, over a period of about three weeks. This would give a total of twenty-five hours of treatment. This would be in accord with the sort of investment given by many services and, if given to groups of patients, would compare favourably with the briefer individual programmes such as described by Mathews *et al.* (1981).

Rapid versus slow exposure

There is one study which looks at this issue. Yuksel *et al.* (1984) compared rapid-exposure *in vivo* in a group of phobic patients, including some agoraphobics. Interestingly, they employed a balanced design to treat twelve patients in London and sixteen patients in Istanbul. Rapid exposure was characterized by moving to the next hierarchy item after subjective anxiety had dropped by two points on a nine-point scale and in the slow condition, by four points on a nine-point scale. Prior to the programme commencing, the criterion for termination of treatment was set as toleration of the highest hierarchy item, with minimal discomfort, for a maximum of eight sessions. While both groups improved substantially and equally, the rapid-exposure group achieved termination criterion quicker than the slow-exposure group. Peak anxiety was similar for both groups.

However, in clinical practice, rapid exposure suits only some patients. Therefore, if programmes do not cater for the needs of the patients who prefer a more cautious approach, drop-out rates will obviously be increased.

Anxiety

In early studies (e.g. Marks *et al.* 1971), anxiety evocation was used in treatment, the theoretical basis of this being the experimental work concerning flooding. However, anxiety evocation does not seem to be a necessary addition to treatment sessions. Hafner and Marks (1976) looked at this issue by comparing groups of agoraphobics with high- and low-exposure anxiety. In this experiment, the therapist was responsible for making anxiety-evoking statements. The authors found no difference in outcome. Emmelkamp (1982) points to the evidence of Foa *et al.* (1977) and Mathews and Rezin (1977) that flooding without cues is more effective. Therefore, in clinical practice, most therapists no longer use strategies aimed at increasing anxiety.

Individual and group treatments

Exposure treatments carried out in groups have obvious advantages. Patients feel reassured that they are not alone in experiencing the distressing symptoms of agoraphobia. Further, the modelling of coping behaviour by other group members would seem to be of obvious benefit and in the setting of scarce resources in the NHS, therapists can spread more effectively over more patients.

While two studies (Hafner and Marks 1976 and Emmelkamp and Emmelkamp-Benner 1975) found no difference between group and individual treatments, one study showed the group treatment to have one major advantage. Hand *et al.* (1974) demonstrated that the group patients continued to improve in the treatment follow-up period. Although Teasdale *et al.* (1977) did not replicate these findings, they did suggest that the post-treatment improvement in Hand *et al.*'s study was due to a high level of group cohesion. In clinical practice, there are several ways of fostering such a beneficial condition. One obvious method would be to treat patients from the same neighbourhood.

In this regard, Sinnott *et al.* (1981) conducted an experiment to look at group treatments conducted with subjects either from the same neighbourhood or from differing neighbourhoods, several miles apart. They found that there was evidence to suggest that the 'neighbourhood group' did slightly better than the other group. In particular, the authors felt that the fostering of neighbourhood groups offered the potential for continuing co-operation and maintenance of long-term gains. Unfortunately, their follow-up period was only three months and they do not appear to have conducted any further longer-term assessment.

The important issue of gains occurring only during treatment contact led Mathews *et al.* (1977) to devise a home-based treatment programme, a central feature of which was a treatment manual used by the patient. Evaluation of this programme demonstrated a good treatment response, with further gains occurring in the follow-up period. The continuing improvement was effected presumably by a continuing use of the manual.

In summary, group treatments organized around particular geographical areas seem to be an obvious choice for hard-pressed services, with the proviso that a minority of patients will continue to need individual programmes.

Assertion training and exposure

Various authors (notably Chambless and Goldstein 1980, 1982 and Fodor 1974) have viewed agoraphobics as generally unassertive and have speculated that this characteristic may be reinforcing of, or even partly causative, of the agoraphobic state. Emmelkamp *et al.* (1983) examined this issue in a between-group design comparing exposure *in vivo*, assertive training, and a combination of the two. The authors did not wish to test the hypothesis that agoraphobia was the result of unassertiveness, rather they wished to examine the specificity of the treatments.

In summary, they found that the treatments were indeed specific to unassertiveness and to avoidance, but were unable to reach any conclusions regarding the role of unassertiveness in maintaining agoraphobia. They pointed out that 'while clinical lore suggests that most agoraphobics are unassertive, there is little in the way of empirical evidence to substantiate this notion'.

To emphasize this finding, Buglass *et al.* (1977) found no difference in assertion between agoraphobic females and controls. Emmelkamp *et al.* (1983) pointed to the need for more research to clarify the issue and suggested a large cross-centre study of unassertive agoraphobics.

Communications training and exposure

Chambless *et al.* (1982), in looking at the difference between a drug-aided and non-drug-aided group of agoraphobics receiving exposure treatment, examined the contribution of communications training. They added to a number of sessions of exposure a sixteen week phase of psychotherapy based on the resolution of interpersonal conflict by increasing communication and self-monitoring. The addition of this to the exposure package did not lead to any further change in measures of fear and avoidance, or of anxious mood and panic attacks. The major criticism of this particular study was that communication or, for that matter, any of the other factors involved in the psychotherapy phase, were not measured. This raises the possibility that the mode of communication training in this particular study was ineffective. There are no published accounts of any similar studies, although the issue of interpersonal conflict is stressed throughout in the psychodynamic literature and indeed in some of the more behavioural literature (e.g. Chambless and Goldstein 1982).

Multi-modal approaches including exposure

Burns (1977) investigated multi-modal approaches in the treatment of agoraphobia and compared four matched treatment groups:
1 behavioural counselling;
2 behavioural counselling and systematic desensitization;
3 behavioural counselling and systematic desensitization, and reinforced graded practice;
4 systematic desensitization, reinforced graded practice, and stress inoculation.

Contrary to expectation, all groups showed significant improvement at post-treatment, using a range of outcome measures. Progress was maintained at twelve-month follow-up. Although this is the only such study in this area, the so-called multi-modal approach continues to be widely used.

Interestingly, this study used a fifth group of waiting list controls. This group showed, on some of the outcome measures, as much change as subjects in treatment groups. Burns argued that non-specific effects were largely responsible for this change. One possible explanation for change in the waiting list group was that the considerable number of measures used in this study (including behavioural testing) exposed the group to a considerable amount of therapist time, when compared with waiting list control studies elsewhere. It is possible, therefore, that short trials of exposure, in the form of behavioural testing, encouraged patients in this study to try their own self-exposure. However, Burns did not examine these anomalous findings any further.

Self-exposure and the role of the therapist

Early studies (e.g. Everaerd *et al.* 1973 and Emmelkamp and Ultee 1974) demonstrated that therapist presence is important. However, this assumption was challenged by the work of Mathews *et al.* (1977) who showed that, using treatment manuals, successful exposure treatment could be conducted with only a couple of hours therapist-aided exposure. This mode of treatment is described fully by Mathews *et al.* (1981) in their book and arose from devising exposure treatments for clients who had not responded to earlier trials of behaviour therapy.

The treatment is predominantly an approach based on helping patients to help themselves, and partners (usually, but not necessarily, the spouse) use simple manuals which detail instructions for graded exposure and give additional advice and information about agoraphobia, its nature, and treatment. The therapist helps with advice and/or education and visits the patient's home for about five sessions over a one-month period, and at follow-up points over a period of six months. A total of about seven hours face-to-face time, plus therapist travel time, is used. Therapists do not actively conduct exposure treatment other than accompanying patient and partner during one practice session to demonstrate the principles of exposure. Therapists supply diary forms and help with short- and long-term target selection. This home-based method prevents reliance on the therapist during exposure sessions. This method also tends to prevent the client attributing any therapeutic success entirely to the therapist. Another major advantage of the method is the reduction of therapist time.

In conclusion, one major effect of a self-directed programme may be a radical change in problem-solving skills, which combined with exposure make for lasting behavioural and cognitive change. The method was evaluated by Mathews *et al.* (1977) with twelve newly referred agoraphobics and the results replicated in the context of a controlled study (Jannoun *et al.* 1980). Programmed practice showed not only significant improvement but continuing improvement during the follow-up period to three months, but no further. The control procedure was a general problem-solving procedure emphasizing general stress-reduction strategies but omitting exposure. Problem solving was first introduced by D'Zurilla and Goldfried (1971) who had described the procedure as a practical training in problem definition, brainstorming, evaluation, and decision making. Unexpectedly, with one of the two therapists, the control problem-solving procedure produced a change equal on most parameters to the programmed-practice condition. However, avoidance and time spent out, as reflected by behavioural diaries, was unchanged. The authors put forward three explanations for such change, including the possibility that the therapist inadvertently encouraged exposure, second that a decrease in general anxiety was effected, and finally that the assessor was rating a change in anticipatory anxiety. Cullington *et al.* (1984) very carefully replicated the study. They were unable to find a similar response to problem solving. The authors concluded that the subjects in the first experiment differed on some important attribute that was not measured, for example, motivation. The authors concluded in rather definite terms that problem solving was not an effective treatment for agoraphobia.

McDonald *et al.* (1979) showed that exposure instructions alone were almost as effective as therapist-aided exposure. Since then, there have been several other studies confirming the efficacy of self-exposure. Taylor (1984) reported a variant of this approach using telephone instructions with a single case.

The use of self-exposure in the form of a self-help book (*Living with Fear*, Marks 1980) or a computer program of the same book's instructions was recently evaluated in the form of a controlled study

(Ghosh and Marks 1987). Results demonstrated that treatment outcome was comparable to that obtained by traditional therapist-aided programmes. The authors drew attention to the fact that the agoraphobics in the study had a level of handicap comparable with subjects in other studies but needed only 2.7 hours of clinician's time in the case of the computer program or 1.5 hours of time in the case of the book (this included 1.5 hours for initial assessment!). In a previous study, Carr and Ghosh (1983a, 1983b) reported that computers are not only very accurate in assessing phobics but more than half of their sample found it easier to communicate with the computer than the clinician! Ghosh and Marks did, however, sound one note of caution. They said that it was important not to oversimplify self-exposure. They pointed out that self-exposure does not consist of merely telling patients to expose themselves to the situations that they fear; rather, they are told to do this within an ordered framework. Ghosh and Marks go on to define the crucial components of the instructions given to patients. They are:

1 how to identify targets which have to be dealt with one by one;
2 to practice self-exposure regularly and for hours at a time;
3 to record tasks anticipated and to deal with set- backs;
4 to recruit significant others as co-therapists.

Another alternative is the use of self-help groups. One such group, 'Phobic Action', helps clients by a number of supportive devices (e.g. telephone help lines, drop-in centres) but they also encourage exposure. In the author's area there are strong links between the professional service and this group. Such a liaison does seem to provide a more comprehensive package for the patient. Regarding the training of therapists to plan and execute exposure programmes, there seems little evidence to show that therapists need extensive or deeply theoretical training. Certainly Marks's nurse-therapy programme has demonstrated that the results gained by nurse therapists are at least as good as those of expensively trained psychiatrists or psychologists. Two other studies (Benjamin and Kincey 1981 and Gournay 1985) showed that a very inexperienced therapist with just a few hours training produced results as good as a highly trained therapist. Taking things one stage further, Wilson (1981) suggested that treated [sic] agoraphobics could be successful therapists. The importance of such coping models is obvious, but selection of such individuals needs careful thought.

Table 2.1 Summary of scores on measures used in comparing experimental groups

		Agoraphobic sub-scale	Fear survey	Symptom check-list	Phobic problem severity assessor
All subjects	Pre-tt	28.97 (7.13)	67.81 (19.45)	23.89 (8.60)	5.96 (1.19)
	Post-tt	12.09 (7.14)	36.01 (18.73)	11.63 (7.59)	2.60 (1.73)
n = 100	3 m.f.u.	11.94 (8.14)	34.35 (21.13)	11.02 (7.68)	2.50 (0.92)
	1 yr f.u.	13.42 (9.47)	36.81 (19.67)	11.01 (8.33)	— —
Home-based	Pre-tt	29.70 (7.09)	68.68 (21.13)	22.60 (8.26)	5.71 (1.43)
group	Post-tt	12.89 (7.90)	38.40 (20.94)	11.40 (7.93)	1.90 (1.13)
	3 m.f.u.	13.04 (9.28)	37.08 (24.13)	11.93 (8.21)	2.25 (0.50)
n = 45	1 yr f.u.	13.30 (9.14)	40.06 (20.47)	11.63 (8.64)	— —
Hospital-based	Pre-tt	28.27 (7.38)	66.68 (19.13)	24.92 (9.45)	6.27 (0.78)
group	Post-tt	11.04 (6.83)	33.30 (17.76)	12.32 (7.44)	3.57 (1.98)
	3 m.f.u.	11.02 (7.12)	32.22 (19.51)	10.37 (7.55)	2.33 (1.15)
n = 43	1 yr f.u.	12.33 (9.18)	34.07 (17.92)	11.03 (8.15)	— —
*Third group	Pre-tt	28.29 (6.49)	68.14 (12.02)	25.71 (5.83)	6.00 (1.41)
	Post-tt	11.29 (6.42)	36.75 (12.09)	10.00 (7.08)	3.00 (2.82)
n = 12	3 m.f.u.	10.91 (6.66)	31.16 (12.61)	9.75 (6.04)	4.00 (0.00)
	1 yr f.u.	11.00 (9.27)	31.71 (22.32)	8.00 (8.02)	— —

Notes
( ) standard deviation
* originally allocated to hospital-based treatment, refused, but subsequently treated at home and considered separately

In summary, it seems that there is little need for extensive training to carry out exposure treatments. Therefore, the most useful role for specialist nurses and psychologists seems to be that of consultant, reserving their clinical efforts for complex cases. Indeed, it could be argued that the majority of exposure programmes demand no more than systematic common sense.

The optimum base for treatment

The author, Gournay (1985), working in a district general hospital setting where there was a long-standing philosophy of community care, became interested in whether it was best to carry out exposure treatment from the patient's own home or from the outpatient clinic. At first sight it did seem that home-based treatment would be more effective. In particular, it was thought that treatment in a natural

Table 2.1 continued

Phobic problem severity subject	Phobic problem severity therapist	Leeds depression inventory	Wakefield depression inventory	Work/home social/ private	Behavioural avoidance test no. of items
7.05 (1.13)	6.85 (0.98)	12.19 (3.97)	23.50 (5.54)	19.31 (5.86)	2.16 (1.25)
2.82 (1.48)	2.92 (1.45)	7.20 (3.46)	14.23 (6.79)	9.12 (5.34)	6.08 (1.74)
2.71 (1.71)	2.83 (1.73)	8.04 (4.26)	13.14 (6.46)	9.59 (6.29)	5.95 (2.31)
2.80 (1.79)	3.04 (1.97)	7.30 (4.06)	9.25 (6.45)	8.93 (6.87)	6.14 (2.24)
6.98 (1.18)	6.89 (1.02)	12.69 (3.69)	22.31 (6.41)	19.82 (6.39)	1.79 (1.10)
2.78 (1.60)	3.06 (1.43)	8.51 (3.04)	12.93 (7.03)	8.68 (6.17)	5.41 (1.56)
3.04 (1.87)	3.13 (1.96)	9.27 (3.56)	13.20 (7.31)	9.65 (7.21)	5.10 (2.52)
2.89 (1.67)	3.39 (2.10)	8.87 (3.44)	8.56 (5.76)	10.21 (8.03)	4.83 (2.37)
7.01 (1.11)	6.77 (0.93)	11.16 (3.98)	25.00 (4.53)	19.09 (4.81)	2.60 (1.39)
2.46 (1.23)	2.81 (1.43)	5.82 (3.61)	15.46 (7.25)	9.97 (4.41)	6.42 (1.73)
2.45 (1.53)	2.57 (1.50)	6.60 (4.39)	13.46 (6.51)	9.97 (5.67)	6.75 (1.93)
2.38 (1.50)	2.73 (1.80)	6.23 (4.54)	10.23 (7.30)	8.46 (5.39)	7.75 (0.75)
7.50 (0.76)	6.90 (0.99)	13.80 (4.51)	23.25 (3.40)	17.69 (7.02)	2.10 (0.87)
1.86 (1.06)	2.75 (1.65)	7.25 (2.76)	14.75 (3.59)	7.63 (4.84)	6.25 (1.71)
2.33 (1.55)	2.58 (1.50)	8.12 (5.22)	11.75 (2.87)	8.00 (4.35)	6.50 (1.69)
2.28 (1.79)	2.57 (1.90)	4.50 (2.38)	8.66 (8.08)	4.85 (4.56)	7.00 (2.16)

setting would offer an advantage and furthermore, this approach would get around the issue of psychiatric stigma.

Therefore, a large sample of patients (190) were randomly assigned at referral to exposure treatment carried out either at home or from the outpatient clinic (detail of design and method are shown in Appendix I). Eventually, a total of 132 patients were deemed acceptable and 64 patients were assessed and treated from home and 68 patients were assessed and treated from the outpatient clinic. Fourteen of the patients in the outpatient clinic condition refused treatment. These patients were offered home-based treatment. Twelve of these fourteen patients went on to complete a trial of exposure therapy. Therefore, the results of 45 patients in the home condition, 43 patients in the outpatient clinic condition, and 12 patients in the small sub-group were compared (see Table 2.1).

Extensive statistical analyses revealed no differences between the groups. It was concluded that any benefit derived from having treatment in the natural setting of one's own home is counter-balanced by the beneficial exposure incurred in travelling to the hospital for treatment. A costing exercise also indicated that in time and travelling a complete course of home-based treatment costs about £65 more per patient.

However, for the small group of patients (about 10 per cent) who found hospital treatment unpalatable, there was every indication from the results that such patients should be offered home-based treatment. In accord with these findings, the practice in the author's service is to maintain the necessary flexibility in service to accommodate such individuals.

Breathing retraining

There is now an increasing amount of evidence to link panic attacks with hyperventilation (for a comprehensive review see Rapee 1987). Because panic is an important component of agoraphobia, this issue has assumed some importance. To recap, hyperventilation can be defined simply, as breathing in excess of bodily requirements. Such a respiratory pattern leads to a reduction of arterial carbon dioxide levels. The ensuing change in arterial ph leads to a wide range of physiological symptoms. These have been described in detail by various authors (e.g. Lum 1984). Physiologically, the effect of lowered blood ph is biphasic; i.e. it first stimulates, at less profound levels of hypocarbia, neurone activity. Then, at greater levels, lowered ph depresses neurone activity. There are several studies which show that a significant number of agoraphobics do hyperventilate (e.g. Garssen *et al.* 1983). This causes an array of symptoms such as dizziness, pins and needles, visual disturbances, muscle cramps, etc. Now, a number of influential workers see hyperventilation and its sequelae having considerable cognitive impact (e.g. Clark 1986). Thus the sufferer perceives these symptoms as, for example, proof of an impending collapse. This causes anxiety which, in turn, produces more hyperventilation and so on. Importantly, there is now evidence that breathing retraining given to agoraphobics does produce a reduction in anxiety symptoms (e.g. Bonn *et al.* 1984). This is in accord with the research carried out with non-agoraphobic sufferers of panic disorder (e.g. Salkovskis *et al.* 1986).

In practical terms, it may be difficult to establish a firm diagnosis. In the author's service, all agoraphobics entering the group treatment programme are offered brief sessions of breathing retraining conducted by a physiotherapist. These sessions take place just before exposure trips and seem to be accepted by patients as a very logical treatment component. Of course, the contribution of this method needs further extensive evaluation.

The influence of the spouse on exposure treatment

This area has attracted considerable research endeavour in the last decade and indeed Barbara Hudson has examined many of the issues in Chapter 3. Therefore, discussion in this section is restricted to two particular areas.

In the first area concerning marital adjustment and outcome (see Tables 2.2a and b), the author (Gournay and Davis 1984 and Gournay 1985) looked at a large sample of patients undergoing exposure treatment (see Appendix I for detail of the study). As the data shows, in this group of patients higher levels of initial marital satisfaction correlated with a better outcome. However, it should be added that this correlation was of low order ($r = -0.225$) indicating that only a limited weighting should be placed on this particular variable.

Regarding the change in marital satisfaction, the results are very much in accord with the studies of Cobb *et al.* (1980), Monteiro *et al.* (1985), and Himadi *et al.* (1986). Certainly, the evidence is now very clear that simple exposure programmes generally enhance marital

Table 2.2a Marital adjustment and outcome: correlations with subjects' pre-treatment marital questionnaire scores

Pearson's correlation of subject's pre-treatment marital questionnaire score	n	r	p
with: Initial (pre-treatment) agoraphobic sub-scale score	62	0·006	n.s.
Change in agoraphobic sub-scale score	55	−0·225	< 0·05
Spouse's pre-treatment marital questionnaire score	58	0·811	< 0·0001

Table 2.2b Marital adjustment and outcome: change in marital questionnaire
scores for subjects and their spouses

	Pre-treatment	Post-treatment	1 year follow-up
Subjects	19·25	17·63	13·46
n = 55	(SD 13·25)	(SD 13·44)	(SD 12·05)
Spouses	16·47	13·19	12·23
n = 48	(SD 12·20)	(SD 10.52)	(SD 9·86)

Tests *(t)*
Subject scores   pre-treatment to post treatment   *t* = 1·67 n.s.
                pre-treatment to 1 yr follow-up   *t* = 3·33 *p* <0·005
Spouse scores   pre-treatment to post-treatment   *t* = 1·47 n.s.
                pre-treatment to 1 yr follow-up   *t* = 2.34 *p* <0·025

relationships and the widespread practice (in psychodynamic circles)
of carrying out marital therapy without any exposure treatment with
agoraphobics should be condemned as ineffective if not actually
unethical.

In the second area, the author was interested in findings of Hafner
(1977a, 1977b). To recap, Hafner examined the symptom and
personality profiles of thirty-three agoraphobic women and their
spouses and related these to treatment outcome.

Hafner did not find an overall high level of neuroticism among
spouses but he demonstrated that there was a complementary pattern
in the marriages, supporting the notion of assortative mating. Of
central importance to his subsequent theory was his division of
groups, in terms of scores from *The Hostility and Direction of Hostility
Questionnaire* (Caine *et al.* 1967), which indicated two types of
interaction. Type I interaction was characterized by 'extrapunitive'
women with high levels of hostility who are married to men with
normal total hostility scores and relatively low intrapunitiveness. In
this group, there appeared to be more widespread neurotic disturbance and when treatment changed the level of independence of the
agoraphobe, the consequences were dramatic. In some cases this
involved either relapse of the patient in the post-treatment phase, or
serious breakdown (e.g. suicidal depression and psychosis) in some of
the spouses. In type II interactions, there seemed to be a group of
intrapunitive women with lower hostility scores, who were married to
highly hostile men with high extrapunitive scores. This group seemed

Table 2.3 Hostility and Direction of Hostility scores: Hafner's (1977b) study compared with Gournay's (1983) and Gournay and Davis's (1984) attempt to replicate

| | Most hostile | | | | Least hostile | | | |
| | Subjects (n = 9) | | Spouses | | Subjects (n = 8) | | Spouses | |
	Total	Direction	Total	Direction	Total	Direction	Total	Direction
Pre-treatment	24·78	+8·78	18·00	−3·11	14·00	+6·38	8·00	−3·50
	(28·6)	(−4·2)	(14·1)	(−3·5)	(15·0)	(+0·87)	(17·5)	(−5·6)
Post-treatment	23·67	+5·56	15·25	−1·13	8·00	+7·75	10·25	−4·75
	(27·9)	)−4·6)	(13·2)	(−3·4)	(13·3)	(−0·4)	(12·7)	(−6·1)
Follow-up after	20·76	+6·44	14·88	−1·25	14·50	+6·00	9·00	−4·00
treatment	(26·2)	(−5·3)	(16·1)·	(−4·6)	(14·50)	(−1·80)	(13·2)	(−4·6)

Notes
Data from Hafner's (1977b) study in parentheses
(−) sign denotes extrapunitive direction
(+) sign denotes intrapunitive direction

to exhibit less general disturbance and the marital system was stable enough to accommodate the effects of positive treatment outcome. In these women it seemed that the agoraphobia was an isolated problem, while in type I interactions the agoraphobia was part of complex neurotic symptomatology.

Hafner concurred with the view of Webster (1953) who asserted that a proportion of agoraphobics are unlikely to relinquish their symptoms unless their husbands enter psychiatric treatment. The author (Gournay 1983 and Gournay and Davis 1984) attempted to replicate Hafner's findings in the study described in Appendix I.

Table 2.3 shows the data presented as in Hafner's original 1977b paper. As the data demonstrate, the hostility and direction of hostility questionnaire data are different in many respects. First although the total hostility scores are very similar for the most and least hostile groups, the direction of hostility is very different. Furthermore, in Hafner's groups, treatment seemed to effect little change in the hostility profiles of the most hostile group while in Gournay's sample, treatment produced significant reductions in the scores of this group.

In conclusion, it should be said that although Hafner's theories based on his 1977 studies have found considerable support among some workers, the attempt to replicate his findings leads to the conclusion that caution is demanded in this area.

Social validity

The social validity of treatments for agoraphobia was investigated by Norton *et al.* (1983). The authors pointed to two main reasons why such a study was important. First, therapists are ethically responsible for providing treatment which is not only effective, but acceptable to the consumers of treatment. Second, perceived acceptability of a treatment method may influence the political and legal decisions affecting treatment procedures.

The five treatments for agoraphobia studied were:

1 treatment with minor benzodiazepine tranquillizers;
2 treatment with antidepressants;
3 a therapy based on relationship insights;
4 a cognitive modification treatment;
5 exposure in real life.

The experiment was divided into two parts. In the first part, a group of university students were asked to rate on various scales the concepts of treatment acceptability and perceived effectiveness. In the second experiment, ten female agoraphobic patients were asked (pre-treatment) to use the same rating scale to rate the same two concepts.

The student group consistently rated the psychological treatments as more socially valid than the drug treatments. Further, they also rated the psychological treatments as more effective. The patient group also rated the psychological treatments as more socially valid and effective but differed from the student group in seeing a therapy based on relationship insights as being less socially valid and less effective. The patient group also rated exposure as the most acceptable and effective treatment. However, there was unsolicited anecdotal evidence that the therapy was terrifying in prospect. The authors of the study, in conclusion, argued that views of treatment validity should be considered when planning the programme.

Because of the general importance of this area, this study needs to be replicated. Furthermore, similar studies should be carried out with other treatment procedures to establish definitions of public perception.

Jansson and Ost's summary of controlled studies of behavioural treatment

This study was carried out in 1983. The authors reviewed twenty-four controlled studies of behavioural treatment for agoraphobia carried out between 1976 and 1982. A total of 650 patients were treated and of these, 400 were treated with an extinction-based exposure method which was non-pharmacological. They found that patients treated with direct exposure consistently improved with such treatment. Of importance was the fact that seven of these studies used some kind of control procedure in which a total of fifty-four patients either received no treatment or a placebo intervention. In none of these studies were there any significant changes in the control group reported. This reinforced the view that agoraphobia is a disorder with a very low rate of spontaneous recovery, this being one of the key findings of Marks and Herst (1970). Jansson and Ost also critically examined whether the improvement in clinical status of the patients in all the studies was of real clinical significance, rather than just being a statistical phenomenon. Their criteria for clinical improvement were i) a rating of three or less, post-treatment, on the almost universally used 0–8 scale of anxiety and avoidance, ii) a reduction of the pre-treatment mean of at least 50 per cent shown at follow-up assessment. Regarding the direct exposure methods, they found that 55 per cent of the subjects showed such clinical improvement at post-treatment and 67 per cent showed clinical improvement at a six-month follow-up. However, using this criteria, the study of Munby and Johnston (1980), which followed up the total of sixty-five patients who had been treated in three trials conducted between five and nine years previously, did not show overall significant improvement.

Regarding the problems of design in the studies reviewed and other experimental shortcomings, Jansson and Ost made several observations. First, only eleven of the twenty-four studies reported inclusion criteria and only six of these eleven had criteria of the stringency acceptable to most contemporary researchers. The problem duration of the sample of agoraphobics treated was, in all the studies, greater than five years and in only three studies were there any reports of medication being held constant during the period of the study. Regarding assessment procedures, Jansson and Ost point out that the battery of measures used in outcome studies are less than comprehensive. For example, in only three of the studies were there measures of *in vivo* physiological activity and even then, these measures were not repeated at follow-up. Jansson and Ost also point out that in making assessments of the difficulty, not a single study in the series used any measure of credibility.

Regarding treatment variables, Jansson and Ost make a number of observations. First is the fact that there is little in the way of description of therapist behaviour during *in vivo* exposure sessions and that the exposure method is often confounded by factors such as self-initiated exposure in the form of homework assignments. Also there is the fact that imaginal procedures are used within *in vivo* exposure thus producing a major confound. Jansson and Ost also point to the fact that various studies use very different numbers and lengths of therapy sessions and only two replications of session length and number have been attempted. Another significant criticism is that treatment programmes have been conducted over a variable period of time, from a few days to many weeks, thus making comparison difficult.

Prognostic factors

Jansson *et al.* (1987) reviewed the evidence regarding prognostic factors in the behavioural treatment of agoraphobia and reported data from their own study. They agreed with Marks that initial levels of marital satisfaction and depression were weak predictors of outcome. Further, they reviewed the evidence that other variables such as assertiveness, expectancy, initial response to treatment, and various personality measures may be predictors of outcome. They concluded that none of these was reliable in this regard.

In their own study, which used a multiple linear regression analysis on behavioural, questionnaire, and other data from forty agoraphobic patients, the authors felt that they had found some clear predictors of outcome. In particular, subjective anxiety improved most in subjects who had higher levels of self-rated anxiety at pre-treatment behavioural testing. The authors also found that the lower the score on the autonomic perception questionnaire, the better the behavioural improvement at follow-up. They also found that subjects with lower scores on the fear survey (i.e. purer agoraphobics) had better long-term outcomes.

Although Jansson *et al.*'s data are reasonably clear, the overall picture is that there is no precise definition of what constitutes a patient with a good prognosis. This is borne out over and again in clinical practice, when patients' responses are the source of continual surprise!

Long-term follow-up of exposure treatment

There is no doubt that the last twenty years has seen enormous improvement in the strategies for evaluating treatment outcome. However, as many authors have pointed out, most follow-ups on treatment are of brief duration, studies usually reporting only a three- or six-month follow-up. The area of agoraphobia and exposure is no exception and there are only a handful of studies following up patients beyond two years after exposure treatment. In addition to the paucity of studies, there are obvious shortcomings with the type of assessments used. For example, behavioural testing and independent assessment are usually omitted. Another problem is that during the follow-up period, patients may be subject to other treatments, including drug therapy, and this limits drawing conclusions about the effectiveness of exposure.

The first study which indicated that behavioural treatment had lasting effectiveness was that conducted by Marks (1971). He followed up for four years thirty-six agoraphobic patients who had been treated by imaginal desensitization. These subjects maintained their gains in the follow-up period, and measures included not only data on the phobic problem, but also work, social, and family relationships.

The next study with long follow-up was that of Emmelkamp and Kuipers (1979) who completed a detailed postal follow-up on seventy agoraphobics from an original sample of eighty-one subjects, between 3.5 and 5 years after they had received exposure treatment. They found that subjects maintained improvement, and there was partial augmentation in the areas of depression and anxiety.

Furthermore, they could find no evidence of fresh symptom emergence. This potential problem had been highlighted by a study carried out by Hafner (1976). Hafner had followed up thirty-nine agoraphobic patients who had received exposure *in vivo*. While there was an overall excellent response to treatment, Hafner claimed that twenty-six of the sample showed fresh symptom emergence. On the face of it, this finding was quite disturbing, but closer scrutiny of Hafner's data reveals a less problematic picture. In particular, many cases of 'fresh symptom emergence' are so defined on the basis of an increase in an isolated sub-scale score from the Middlesex Hospital questionnaire from pre-treatment levels. Indeed, it appears that these minor negative changes were more than compensated by many other general and specific positive changes in the agoraphobic state.

In another study which reported stable improvement, McPherson *et al.* (1980) followed up fifty-six patients from 3 to 6.3 years post-treatment with a mean of 4.3 years post-treatment. Rating scale data was collected by post. The authors looked at five variables, i.e. agoraphobic symptoms, other phobias, depression, social relationships, and disruption at work. In addition, they asked questions about the patients' condition since the end of treatment and whether new symptoms had emerged. They found no evidence of new symptoms occurring, and found that improvement was maintained from post-treatment with no further augmentation of treatment gains. While the results of this study were encouraging, the conclusions should be limited in view of the postal method and because the fifty-six subjects represented only 70 per cent of the original sample.

In the same year, another study reported on a follow-up in which sixty-five subjects of an original sample of sixty-six were assessed. Munby and Johnston (1980) reported data on these subjects at 8.6, 6.8, and 5.3 years post-treatment. Significantly, their data included independent assessment; therefore the results can be considered more seriously than McPherson *et al.*'s study. Overall, patients were very much improved, although there was little or no further change from six-months post-treatment. As Burns *et al.* (1986) point out, this study would have been much improved had a behavioural test of phobic avoidance been used.

Indeed, these authors (Burns *et al.* 1986) used such a test in an eight-year follow-up study. They also used rating scale and interview measures. However, they only managed to follow up twenty subjects from an original sample of thirty-two. They concluded that their clients had maintained their status at one-year follow-up to the extended follow-up seven years later. They stated that these results encourage confidence in the resilience of relatively short-term problem-oriented treatment for agoraphobia. However, their study did raise some cause for concern which may be common to other follow-up studies. Apart from the lack of data on twelve of the original sample, the authors also added that many of the clients had received additional booster treatment between the original treatment programme and one-year follow-up, and also during the seven years between one-year follow-up and the final follow-up. In addition, eleven patients took some form of medication and continued to use the same. The issue of medication is obviously a major confound, the area being of general methodological concern. Finally, the authors present individual data on the current status of phobia. Notable is the absence of any statements of cure. Most patients are apparently improved, or much improved, but 'living with' aspects of their problem.

To conclude, there are two further studies involving long follow-up after exposure treatment. Hand *et al.* (1986) provided data on seventy-five subjects at various follow-up intervals from eighteen months to 3.5 years. The original sample was eighty-five patients who completed treatment, of which exposure was the major component. As with the Burns *et al.* study, many patients took some form of psychotropic medication, but the proportion was lower, with nineteen patients continuing to take psychotropic medication. However, there was also a significant number of patients who had received other forms of treatment, the detail of which was not clear from Hand's description.

Hand *et al.*'s study indicated that exposure treatment produced significant phobia reduction and other variables, such as depression, social anxiety, obsessions, compulsions, and functional somatic complaints continued to improve during the follow-up period. Of the total sample, 70 per cent showed marked reduction in phobic anxiety, and overall, visits to GPs were reduced by 75 per cent and visits to psychiatrists and psychotherapists by 50 per cent. Before treatment, 80 per cent of patients had taken psychotropic medication, whereas after treatment the figure had fallen to 25 per cent. Interestingly, 90 per cent of the improved patients attributed improvement to behaviour therapy or behaviour therapy combined with other life events and they also said that they would go back to behaviour therapy if they were again in need of some help.

When Hand and his colleagues looked for particular patterns which differentiated good from poor treatment response, they found that agoraphobics who were not disordered in terms of depression, obsessions, compulsions, and functional somatic complaints, did much better than patients who had disturbance in one or more of those areas. In particular, the authors felt that high levels of depression pre-treatment correlated with poorer outcome. This finding was also evident in a study by Marks (1987) who reported five-year follow-up data on forty subjects of an original sample of forty-five. The original study had compared various additions to self-exposure including imipramine or a placebo.

In conclusion, therefore, the evidence is that exposure treatment produces a significant change which is maintained at long follow-up.

Overall,not only is there little convincing evidence of fresh symptom emergence, but all studies agree that non-phobic problem areas improve as a general effect of behavioural treatment. The one note of caution is that further improvement after treatment is limited and long-term cure of the problem is a rare exception.

CONCLUSION

Exposure treatment has been consistently demonstrated to be a highly effective treatment for agoraphobia. It is not however, a panacea as the chapter on treatment failure indicates. However, for many patients, brief treatment involving very limited contact with professional agencies may well dramatically alter function. Unfortunately, there is ample evidence to suggest that patients are not referred often enough and when they are referred, it is only after many years. In the author's area and over a ten-year period, from 1978–88, all the patients who were referred in this time came from only one-third of all the general practices in his area. Further, in his large outcome study (Gournay 1985), the main duration of problem at initial assessment was 11.35 years (SD 8.51) for the 100 female patients and 9.17 years (SD 7.78) for the male patients.

Perhaps therefore, the education of the medical profession, as well as the general public, remains a priority.

© Kevin Gournay

APPENDIX I

This appendix describes a study which is referred to several times in the text. The bulk of the work was carried out by the author between 1981 and 1985 (some follow-up data was collected after that time).

In all, 190 patients were referred to the study and 132 were deemed suitable. These patients conformed to DSM III criteria for agoraphobia, had been agoraphobic for at least one year, and had had no previous behavioural treatment.

Patients were referred from general practitioners and psychiatrists within the Barnet Health Authority. This is an area of about 380,000 people, covering parts of North London, Barnet, Edgware, and part of suburban and semi-rural Hertfordshire. The area covers the spectrum of socio-economic conditions.

All subjects were screened at home by the study's author and were randomly allocated to one of two treatments: using their own home as the treatment base or the outpatient department of the psychiatric unit in a district general hospital (Barnet General).

Therapists, who treated patients randomly, comprised:

1 two nurse therapists (trained on the English National Board of Nursing course 650: adult behavioural psychotherapy);

2 five clinical psychologists (of widely varying experience);

3 one research psychologist (without clinical training and naive to the use of behavioural methods prior to the commencement of the study).

TREATMENT

Treatment was individual and consisted of six two-hour sessions of exposure *in vivo*. This was carried out in a graduated fashion and involved the patients facing a very wide range of situations (these included: walking; travelling by bus, train, and tube; shopping in quiet and busy shops; visiting local and West End shopping centres; and other tasks such as driving on motorways, using lifts, using escalators).

The therapists assisted the patients to enter these situations and gradually withdrew, as appropriate. Patients were simply told that if they systematically faced the situations that they had previously avoided, their fear levels would gradually fall. All patients were given repeated instructions to carry out 'homework exposure' between sessions.

Treatment for all patients took place over a period of between eighteen and twenty-two days.

Medication

If patients were taking medication at assessment, they were told to keep the dose constant during the treatment period.

Spouse contact

Spouses were seen for two reasons:

1 to give a standard explanation of treatment;
2 to collect questionnaire data.

The spouses were not instructed in any way to act as therapists in treatment.

Measures

All patients were assessed with the following measures:

1 fear survey schedule (Marks and Mathews 1978); this yields a total fear score, an anxiety depression score, and an agoraphobic sub-scale score;
2 phobic severity (after Watson and Marks 1971); this is a nine-point scale and was rated by:
   a) independent assessor,
   b) therapist,
   c) patient;
3 Wakefield depression inventory (Snaith *et al.* 1971) and Leeds scales (Snaith *et al.* 1976);
4 work/home/social/private leisure adjustment (after Marks *et al.* 1977);
5 behavioural avoidance test.

This was a ten-item *in vivo* test, rating success and degree of distress.
In addition, patients were involved in several smaller studies. Some patients, therefore, were assessed with the following measures:

1 Maudsley marital questionnaire (Crowe *et al.* 1981);
2 a repertory grid;

3 the hostility and direction of hostility questionnaire (Caine *et al.* 1967);

4 treatment expectancy questionnaire (Caine *et al.* 1981);

5 behavioural diaries measuring time spent in phobic situations;

6 Bem sex-role stereotyping questionnaire (Bem 1974);

7 two measures of cognition, i.e. subjective probability and value of feared phobic consequences;

8 two questionnaires related to treatment failure (Gournay 1985).

REFERENCES

Bandura, A. (1969) *The Principles of Behaviour Modification*, New York: Holt, Rinehart and Winston.

Baum, M. (1966) 'Rapid extinction of an avoidance response following a period of response prevention in the avoidance apparatus', *Psychological Reports* 18: 59–64.

—(1987) 'Distraction during flooding (exposure): concordance between results in animals and man', *Behaviour Research and Therapy* 25, 3: 227–8.

Bem, S. L. (1974) 'The measurement of psychological androgyny', *Journal of Consulting and Clinical Psychology* 42: 155–62.

Benjamin, S. and Kincey, A. (1981) 'Evaluation of standardised behavioural treatment for agoraphobic in-patients administered by untrained therapists', *British Journal of Psychiatry* 138: 423–8.

Bonn, J. A., Readhead, C. P. A., and Timmons, B. H. (1984) 'Enhanced adaptive behavioural response in agoraphobic patients', *Lancet* 22 September.

Borkovek, T. D., and Grayson, J. B. (1980) 'Consequences of increasing the functional impact of internal emotional stimuli', in P. Blankstein, P. Pliner, and J. Policy (eds) *Advances in the Study of Communication and Affect: Assessment and Modification of Emotional Behaviour*, vol. 6: 117–37, New York: Plenum Press.

Boulougouris, J. C. and Marks, I. M. (1969) 'Implosion (flooding)', *British Medical Journal* 2: 721–3.

Boyd, T. L. and Levis, D. J. (1983) 'Exposure is a necessary condition for fear reductions. A reply to de Silva and Rachman, 1983)', *Behaviour Research and Therapy* 21, 2: 143–9.

Buglass, D., Clarke, J., Henderson, A. S., Kreitman, N. and Presley, A. S. (1977) 'A study of agoraphobic housewives', *Psychological Medicine* 7: 73–86.

Burns, L. E. (1977) 'An investigation into the additive effects of behavioural techniques on the treatment of agoraphobia', unpublished Ph.D. thesis, University of Leeds.

Burns, L. E., Thorpe, G. L., and Cavallaro, L. A. (1986) 'Agoraphobia eight years after behavioural treatment', *Behaviour Therapy* 17, 5: 580–91.

Caine, T. M., Foulds, G. A., and Hope, K. (1967) *The Manual of the Hostility and Direction of Hostility Questionnaire*, London: University of London Press.

Caine, T. M., Wijesinghe, O. B. A., and Winter, D. A. (1981) *Personal Styles in Neurosis: Implications for Small Group Psychotherapy and Behaviour Therapy*, London: Routledge & Kegan Paul.

Carr, A. C., and Ghosh, A. (1983a) 'Response of phobic patients to direct computer assessment', *British Journal of Psychiatry* 142, 1: 60–5.

——(1983b) 'Accuracy of behavioural assessment by computer', *British Journal of Psychiatry* 142, 1: 66–71.

Chambless, D. L., Foa, E. B., Groves, G. A., and Goldstein, A. J. (1982) 'Exposure and communications training in the treatment of agoraphobia', *Behaviour Research and Therapy* 20, 3: 219–32.

Chambless, D. L., and Goldstein, A. (1980) 'The treatment of agoraphobia', in A. Goldstein and E. Foa, (eds), *Handbook of Behavioural Interventions*, New York: John Wiley & Sons, 322–415.

Clark, D. M. (1986) 'A cognitive approach to panic', *Behaviour Research and Therapy* 24: 461–70.

Cobb, J. P., McDonald, D. R., Marks, I., and Stern, R. S. (1980) 'Marital versus exposure therapy: psychological treatment of co-existing marital and phobic-obsessive problems', *Behavioural Analysis and Modification* 4: 3–16.

Cooper, J. E., Gelder, M. G., and Marks, I. M. (1965) 'Results of behaviour therapy in 77 psychiatric patients', *British Medical Journal* 1: 122–5.

Crowe, M. J., Gillan, P., and Golombok, S. (1981) 'Form and content in the conjoint treatment of sexual dysfunction', *Behavioural Research and Therapy* 19: 47–54.

Crowe, M. J., Marks, I. M., Agras, W. S., and Leitenberg, H. (1972) 'Time limited desensitization, implosion and shaping for phobic patients: a crossover study', *Behaviour Research and Therapy* 10: 319–28.

Cullington, A., Butler, G., Hibbert, G., and Gelder, M. (1984) 'Problem solving: not a treatment for agoraphobia', *Behaviour Therapy* 15: 280–6.

de Silva, P. and Rachman, S. (1981) 'Is exposure a necessary condition for fear reduction?', *Behaviour Research and Therapy* 19: 227–32.

——(1983) 'Exposure and fear reduction', *Behaviour Research and Therapy* 21, 2: 151–2.

—— (1984) 'Does escape behaviour strengthen agoraphobic avoidance? A preliminary study', *Behaviour Research and Therapy* 22, 1: 87–91.

D'Zurilla, T. J. and Goldfried, M. R. (1971) 'Problem solving and behaviour modification', *Journal of Abnormal Psychology* 78: 107–26.

Emmelkamp, P. M. G. (1982) *Phobic and Obsessive-Compulsive Disorders: Theory Research and Practice* New York: Plenum.

Emmelkamp, P. M. G. and Emmelkamp-Benner, A. (1975) 'Effects of historically portrayed modelling and group treatment on self observation. A comparison with agoraphobics', *Behaviour Research and Therapy* 13: 135–9.

Emmelkamp, P. M. G. and Kuipers, A. C. M. (1979) 'Agoraphobia: a follow up study four years after treatment', *British Journal of Psychiatry* 134: 352–5.

Emmelkamp, P. M.G. and Ultee, K. A. A. (1974) 'A comparison of "successive approximation" and "self observation" in the treatment of agoraphobia', *Behaviour Therapy* 5: 606–13.

Emmelkamp, P. M.G., van der Hout, A., and de Vries, K. (1983) 'Assertive training for agoraphobics', *Behaviour Research and Therapy* 21, 1: 63–8.

Everaerd, W., Rijken, H. M., and Emmelkamp, P. M. G. (1973) 'A comparison of flooding and successive approximation in the treatment of agoraphobia', *Behaviour Research and Therapy* 11: 105–17.

Eysenck, H. J. (1965) 'Correspondence on behaviour therapy', *British Journal of Psychiatry* 111: 1007–13.

Foa, E., Blau, J., Prout, M., and Latimer, P. (1977) 'Is horror a necessary component of flooding?', *Behaviour Research and Therapy* 16: 391–9.

Foa, E. B., Jameson, J. S., Turner, R. M., and Payne, L. L. (1980) 'Massed versus spaced exposure sessions in the treatment of agoraphobia', *Behaviour Research and Therapy* 18: 333–8.

Foa, E. B. and Kozak, M. J. (1986) 'Emotional processing of fear: exposure to corrective information', *Psychological Bulletin* 99: 20–35.

Fodor, I. G. (1974) 'The phobic syndrome in women', in V. Franks and V. Burtle (eds) *Women in Therapy*, New York: Brunner/Mazel.

Garssen, N., van Veenendaal, W., and Bloemink, R. (1983) 'Agoraphobia and the hyperventilation syndrome', *Behaviour Research and Therapy* 6: 643–9

Gelder, M. G., Bancroft, J. H. J., Gath, D. H., Johnston, D. W., Mathews, A. M., and Shaw, P. M. (1973) 'Specific and non- specific factors in behaviour therapy', *British Journal of Psychiatry* 123: 445–62.

Gelder, M. G., Marks, I. M., and Wolfe, H. H. (1967) 'Desensitization and psychotherapy in the treatment of phobic states: a controlled inquiry', *British Journal of Psychiatry* 113: 53–75.

Ghosh, A. and Marks, I. M. (1987) 'Self treatment of agoraphobia by exposure', *Behaviour Therapy* 18, 1: 3–16.

Gournay, K. J. M. (1983) 'Agoraphobia: a study of some treatment variables', M.Phil. thesis, University of Leicester.

—(1985) 'Agoraphobia: a study of the syndrome and its treatment', unpublished Ph.D. thesis, University of Leicester.

Gournay, K. J. M. and Davis, J. (1984) 'Marital interaction and the exposure treatment of agoraphobia', paper to BABP annual conference, University of Nottingham.

Grayson, J. B., Foa, E. B. and Stcketee, G. (1982) 'Habituation during exposure treatment: distraction versus attention focusing', *Behaviour Research and Therapy* 20: 323–8.

Greist, J. H., Marks, I. M., Berlin, F., Gournay, K., and Noshivrani, H. (1980) 'Avoidance versus confrontation of fear', *Behaviour Therapy* 11: 1–14.

Hafner, R. J. (1976) 'Fresh symptom emergence after behavior therapy', *British Journal of Psychiatry* 129: 378–83.

——(1977a) 'The husbands of agoraphobic women: assortative mating or pathogenic interaction?', *British Journal of Psychiatry* 130: 233–9.

——(1977b) 'The husbands of agoraphobic women and their influence on treatment outcome', *British Journal of Psychiatry* 13: 280–94.

Hafner, R. J. and Marks, I. M. (1976) 'Exposure *in vivo* of agoraphobics: contributions of Diazepam, group exposure and anxiety evocation', *Psychological Medicine* 6: 71–88.

Hand, I., Angenendt, J., Fischer, M., and Wilke, C. (1986) Chapter in I. Hand and H. U. Wittchen (eds) *Panic and Phobias*, Berlin: Springer.

Hand, I., Lamontagne, Y., and Marks, I. M. (1974) 'Group exposure (flooding) *in vivo* for agoraphobia', *British Journal of Psychiatry* 124: 588–602.

Hecker, J. E. and Thorpe, G. L. (1987) 'Fear reduction processes in imaginal and *in vivo* flooding', *Behaviour Psychotherapy* 15: 215–23.

Himadi, W., Cerny, J., Barlow, D., Cohen, S., and O'Brien, G. (1986) 'The relationship of marital adjustment to agoraphobia treatment outcome', *Behaviour Research and Therapy* 24, 2: 107–15.

James, J. E. (1985) 'Desensitisation treatment of agoraphobia', *British Journal of Clinical Psychology* 24: 133–4.

——(1986) 'Review of the relative efficacy of imaginal and *in vivo* flooding in the treatment of clinical fear', *Behavioural Psychotherapy* 14, 3: 183–91.

James, J. E., Mayhampton, B. A, and Larsen, S. A. (1983) 'The relative efficacy of imaginal and *in vivo* desensitisation in the treatment of agoraphobia', *Journal of Behaviour Therapy and Experimental Psychology* 14, 3: 203–8.

Jannoun, L., Munby, M., Catalan, J., and Gelder, R. M. (1980) 'A home based treatment for agoraphobia. Replication and controlled evaluation', *Behaviour Therapy* 11: 294–305.

Jansson, I. and Ost, L.-G. (1983) 'Behavioural treatments for agoraphobia: an evaluative review', *Clinical Psychology Review* 2: 311–37.

Jansson, I., Ost, L., and Jerremalm, A. (1987) 'Prognostic factors in the behavioural treatment of agoraphobia', *Behavioural Psychotherapy* 15, 1: 31–44.

Lang, P. J., (1985) 'The cognitive psychophysiology of emotion, concept and action', in C. Izard, J. Kagan, and R. Zajonc (eds) *Emotion, Cognition and Behaviour*, New York: Cambridge University Press.

Lum, H. (1984) 'Hyperventilation: nature and treatment', paper to the College of Speech Therapists, Hampstead, September.

McDonald, R., Sartory, G., Grey, S., Cobb, J., Stern, R., and Marks, I. M. (1979) 'The effects of self exposure instructions on agoraphobic out-patients', *Behaviour Research and Therapy* 17: 883–5.

McPherson, F. M., Brougham, L., and McLaren, S. (1980) 'Maintenance of improvement in agoraphobic patients treated by behavioural methods: a four year follow up', *Behaviour Research and Therapy* 18: 150–2.

Marks, I. M. (1969) *Fears and Phobias*, London: Heinemann.

—(1971) 'Phobic disorders four years after treatment: a prospective follow up', *British Journal of Psychiatry* 118: 683–8.
—(1972a) 'Perspective on flooding', *Seminars Psychiatry* 4: 129–38.
—(1972b) 'Flooding (implosion) and allied treatments', in W. S. Agras (ed.) *Learning Theory and Psychiatry*, Boston: Little, Brown & Co.
—(1977) 'Exposure treatments', in S. Agras (ed.) *Behaviour Modification*, 2nd edition, New York: Little, Brown & Co.
—(1978) 'Behavioural psychotherapy of adult neurosis', in S. L. Garfield and A. E. Bergin (eds) *Handbook of Psychotherapy and Behaviour Change*, New York: John Wiley.
—(1980) *Living with Fear*, New York: McGraw-Hill.
—(1981a) *Cure and Care of Neurosis*, New York: John Wiley.
—(1981b) 'Behavioural concepts of neurosis', *Behavioural Psychotherapy* 9: 137–54.
—(1987) *Fears, Phobias and Rituals*, New York: Oxford University Press.
Marks, I. M., Connoly, J., Hallam, R., and Phillpot, R. (1977) *Nursing in Behavioural Psychotherapy*, London: RCN.
Marks, I. M. and Gelder, M. G. (1965) 'A controlled retrospective study of behaviour therapy in phobic patients', *British Journal of Psychiatry* 111: 561.
Marks, I. M. and Herst, E. R. (1970) 'A survey of 1,200 agoraphobics in Britain', *Social Psychiatry* 5: 16–24.
Marks, I. M., Marset, P., Boulougoris, J. and Huson, J. (1971) 'Flooding versus desensitization in phobic patients', *British Journal of Psychiatry* 119: 353–75.
Marks, I. M. and Mathews, A. M. (1978) 'A brief standard self-rating for phobic patients', *Behaviour Research and Therapy* 17, 3: 263–7.
Mathews, A. M., Gelder, M. G., and Johnston, D. W. (1981) *Agoraphobia: Nature and Treatment*, London: Tavistock.
Mathews, A. M., Johnston, D. W., Lancashire, M., Munby, M., Shaw, P. M., and Gelder, M. G. (1976a) 'Imaginal flooding and exposure to real phobic situations: treatment outcome with agoraphobic patients', *British Journal of Psychiatry* 129: 362–71.
—(1976b) 'Imaginal flooding and exposure to real phobic situations: changes during treatment', *British Journal of Psychiatry* 129: 372–7.
Mathews, A. M. and Rezin, V. (1977) 'Treatment of dental fears by imaginal flooding and rehearsal of coping behaviour', *Behaviour Research and Therapy* 15: 321–8.
Mathews, A. M., Teasdale, J., Munby, M., Johnston, D., and Shaw, P. (1977) 'A home-based treatment program for agoraphobia', *Behaviour Therapy* 8: 915–24.
Meyer, V. and Gelder, M. G. (1963) 'Behaviour therapy and phobic disorders', *British Journal of Psychiatry* 109: 19–28.
Monteiro, W., Marks, I. M., and Ramm, E. (1985) 'Marital adjustment and treatment outcome in agoraphobia', *British Journal of Psychiatry* 146: 383–90.

Mowrer, O. H. (1947) 'On the dual nature of learning as a reinterpretation of conditioning and problem solving', *Harvard Educational Review*, 102–48.
—(1960) *Learning Theory and Behaviour*, New York: John Wiley.
Munby, M. and Johnston, D. W. (1980) 'Agoraphobia: the long term follow up of behavioural treatment', *British Journal of Psychiatry* 137: 418–27.
Norton, G. R., Allen, G. E., and Hilton, J. (1983) 'The social validity of treatments for agoraphobia', *Behaviour Research and Therapy* 21, 4: 393–9.
Rachman, S. (1983) 'The modification of agoraphobic avoidance behaviour: some fresh possibilities', *Behaviour Research and Therapy* 21, 5: 567–74.
—(1984) 'The experimental analysis of agoraphobia', *Behaviour Research and Therapy* 22, 6: 631–40.
Rachman, S., de Silva, P., and Roper, G. (1976) 'The spontaneous decay of compulsive urges', *Behaviour Research and Therapy* 14: 445–53.
Rapee, R. (1987) 'The psychological treatment of panic attacks: theoretical conceptualization and review of evidence', *Clinical Psychology Review* 7, 4: 427–38.
Salkovskis, P. M., Jones, D. R. O., and Clark, D. M. (1986) 'Respiratory control in the treatment of panic attacks', *British Journal of Psychiatry* 148: 526–32.
Sinnot, A., Jones, R. B., Scott-Fordham, A., and Woodward, R. (1981) 'Augmentation of *in vivo* exposure treatment for agoraphobia by the formulation of neighbourhood self help groups', *Behaviour Research and Therapy* 19: 339–48.
Snaith, R. P., Ahmed, S. N., Mehta, S., and Hamilton, M. (1971) 'Assessment of the severity of primary depressive illness, Wakefield self assessment depression inventory', *Psychological Medicine*, 1 February: 143–9.
Snaith, R. P., Bridge, G. W. K., and Hamilton, M. (1976) 'The Leeds scales for the self assessment of anxiety and depression', *British Journal of Psychiatry* 128: 156–65.
Stern, R. S. and Marks, I. M. (1973) 'Brief and prolonged flooding: a comparison in agoraphobic patients', *Archives of General Psychiatry* 28: 270–6.
Taylor, I. (1984) 'Self-instructions by telephone with a secret agoraphobic', *Behavioural Psychotherapy* 12: 68–72.
Teasdale, J. D., Walsh, P. A., Lancashire, M., and Mathews, A. M. (1977) 'Group exposure for agoraphobics: a replication study', *British Journal of Psychiatry* 130: 186–93.
Thorpe, G. L. and Burns, L. E. (1983) *The Agoraphobic Syndrome*, New York: John Wiley.
Watson, J. P. and Marks, I. M. (1971) 'Relevant and irrelevant fear in flooding. A crossover study in phobic patients', *Behaviour Therapy* 2: 275–93.
Webster, A. (1953) 'The development of phobias in married women', *Psychological Monographs* 67: no. 367.

Wilson, G. T. (1981) 'Behavioural concepts and treatment of neuroses: comments on Marks', *Behavioural Psychotherapy* 9: 155–6.

Yuksel, S., Marks, I. M., Ramm, E., and Ghosh, A. (1984) 'Slow versus rapid exposure *in vivo* of phobics', *Behavioural Psychotherapy* 12, 3: 249–56.

Chapter Three

SOCIAL FACTORS AND THE ROLE OF SOCIAL WORKERS

BARBARA L. HUDSON

This chapter will describe some of the social consequences of agoraphobia; consider the influence of social factors on its course; and, in the final section, discuss the role of social workers. A useful starting point is the integrated model put forward by Mathews *et al.* (1981). These authors suggest that in addition to a (possible) genetic loading for high trait anxiety, a variety of non-specific stresses combine to produce a high level of general anxiety which leads on to an acute anxiety attack and thence to agoraphobia. Extending this narrative, one might suggest that the consequences of agoraphobia form a feedback loop bringing even greater stress; thus instituting a vicious circle of stress–anxiety–phobia–and more stress. An extended model along these lines might help us to accommodate some of the conflicting accounts of the role of social factors, seen as consequences by some authorities, as causes by others, and as unrelated by yet others.

Another point to be made at the outset is that research on social factors in agoraphobia has typically aimed at getting valid generalizations about what is certainly a very varied population. The practitioner who 'knows' that agoraphobia is caused by bad marriages and the practitioner who 'knows' that it is not are *both* at a disadvantage if they neglect to do a careful analysis of the individual case. One of these hypothetical workers is probably more accurate than the other in terms of making a generalized statement about the agoraphobic population; but neither of them has the makings of a very good therapist! Social consequences and social causes of agoraphobia can be detected in some cases and not in others.

SOCIAL CONSEQUENCES OF AGORAPHOBIA

The consequences of agoraphobia have received little research attention. Consequences can easily be mistaken for causes. For example, among the respondents in Marks and Herst's study (1970), the proportion of housewives who went out to work was lower than in the general population and most said they were unhappy with this; but it is not possible to decide whether agoraphobia caused or was caused/exacerbated by their lack of outside employment. There is not yet sufficient evidence to help us satisfactorily to unravel cause–effect sequences.

Burns and Thorpe's survey of agoraphobics (1977a) provides an account of the individual sufferer's viewpoint. The respondents said the worst consequences of agoraphobia were lack of social contact (28 per cent), personal psychological effects (21 per cent), inability to work (17 per cent), effect on marital relationship (13 per cent), travel restrictions (10 per cent), and guilt about children (5 per cent). Mathews *et al.* (1981) and Thyer (1987) note the possibility, in a minority of patients, of alcohol and drug problems, in which we should include dependence on benzodiazepines; and Edwards (1985) remarked on the surprisingly large number of agoraphobics encountered at a council for alcoholism. Nevertheless, the picture is not one of unrelieved gloom: for instance, students of the Open University who suffer from agoraphobia tend to perform better than students with other kinds of illness or disability and better than students with none (Palmer 1982).

There is no clear evidence of seriously adverse effects on the marital relationship. While it is true that some agoraphobia sufferers become extremely – and perhaps irritatingly – dependent on their relatives, studies comparing agoraphobics' marriages (at pre-treatment) with those of other psychiatric patients and of the general population have found marital problems to be no more severe among this patient group than among non-agoraphobic women: indeed, as far as their marital relationships are concerned, these patients resemble a non-patient population more closely than they resemble other types of psychiatric patient (Buglass *et al.* 1977, Arrindell and Emmelkamp, 1986).

Husbands of agoraphobics have been found to be no more defensive or disturbed than husbands of controls (Arrindell and Emmelkamp, 1985, Buglass *et al.* 1977) and children of agoraphobics have not been found to suffer from more symptoms than children of controls (Buglass *et al.* 1977).

Mathews *et al.* (1981) conclude that 'there is no good evidence for any substantial detrimental effect of agoraphobia on family life, if we exclude those routines, such as shopping, that are directly affected by the patient's avoidance behaviour' (p. 17). This seems somewhat dismissive of the importance of routines in family life, and there can be little doubt that some burden is imposed by having a parent and spouse disabled in regard to numerous ordinary tasks, such as shopping, taking the children to school, going on trips, and visiting friends and relatives. The husbands in the study by Buglass *et al* (1977) said they did the shopping and other chores more often and spent less time working than did the control husbands. Like the families of other disabled people, these families do seem to accommodate to the problems. In some cases it is only when a crisis occurs, for example a child gets into trouble for not attending school, or a husband changes jobs and has less time to help, that the difficulties surface and the sufferer feels constrained to seek professional help.

Improvement in other areas of functioning usually follows improvement in agoraphobic symptoms. For example, Cobb *et al* (1984) found that marital relationships tended to improve as agoraphobic symptoms were overcome, whether or not the spouse was involved in treatment. Sexual problems, which seem often to accompany agoraphobia, starting at the same time or after the anxiety symptoms, usually decrease when the anxiety symptoms subside (Buglass *et al* 1977). Most relevant studies have found that reduction in phobic symptoms is accompanied by stable or improved marital, sexual, social, and work adjustment (for a concise review, see Arrindell *et al* 1986).

These findings do not prove that the agoraphobia had caused the other problems, but such a causal link is a possibility. (We shall return to some of these studies in discussion of the reverse cause–effect narrative: from social problems to agoraphobia.)

INFLUENCE OF SOCIAL FACTORS ON THE AETIOLOGY AND COURSE OF AGORAPHOBIA

Cause–effect relationships between the social environment (family, neighbourhood, social networks, and cultural influences) and personal psychological dysfunction are very difficult to unravel. The intervening processes are likely to be complex: the actual or objective environment interacts with the individual's perceptions and the individual's own particular ways of reacting. This makes research findings hard to interpret; and in any case, with a few outstanding exceptions (notably in the area of marital relationships), little research of high quality is available with respect to agoraphobia. Some studies have looked chiefly at onset, others at relapse, and yet others at the social sequelae of successful treatment. From the evidence available, it seems likely that social factors may play an indirect and contributory role in the onset and prognosis of agoraphobia; and that their importance varies according to the circumstances of the individual case.

Life events and social stresses

Social factors may set the scene for onset of agoraphobia – the initial panic attack and its aftermath when the person develops the anxiety and avoidance that make up the agoraphobic syndrome. Patients often describe a background of social and emotional problems (Buglass *et al.* 1977). Against this background, a more acute stressor may supervene. For example, a substantial number of respondents in the surveys by Marks and Herst (1970) and Shafar (1976) reported that onset followed a significant life event: for example, serious illness in themselves or a relative, bereavement or separation, engagement, marriage, miscarriage, or childbirth; and Solyom *et al.* (1974) found that agoraphobics were more likely to report such events than people suffering from specific phobias. Moving house is often suggested as a possible precipitant of agoraphobia, but such impressions can often be explained in terms of 'bringing to light' pre-existing problems, as, indeed, can the apparent involvement of other kinds of life events. Nevertheless, there is strong evidence that life events can play a significant role in the onset and relapse of many kinds of psychiatric disorder (see, for example, Dohrenwend and Dohrenwend 1974), and although the relevant research has not yet been done, there is no reason why agoraphobia should be an exception to the general rule.

During treatment and during maintenance programmes, stress can distract patients from making the continuing effort to practise that is needed in order to consolidate treatment gains; and the sheer emotional exhaustion brought about by, say, a row with the boss or a financial crisis, can reduce their ability to cope with anything else. Thus, social factors continue to exert an influence after agoraphobia has developed, whether or not the sufferer receives treatment. Social factors can weaken the sufferer's resistance or help her to overcome her symptoms; and hinder or aid treatment and maintenance of improvement.

Probably the person who succumbs to agoraphobia after an initial panic attack is the person with the fewer resources to draw upon, both personal and social-environmental (Vines 1987). And although there is no evidence to suggest that – generally speaking – this is a sole determinant of outcome, the better the individual's social/interpersonal environment the more likely she is to benefit from treatment. Good long-term outcome is related to good initial general (i.e. work and social) adjustment (Arrindell *et al* 1986, Monteiro *et al* 1985) and also, according to some studies, to good initial marital relationships (Milton and Hafner 1979, Bland and Hallam 1981, Emmelkamp and van der Hout, 1983). Some of these correlations are probably mediated by 'coping skills'; that is, the person with the 'good' environment may have personal qualities that both act to make that environment 'good' and also facilitate recovery.

We turn now to a more detailed consideration of clusters of social factors that are often implicated by clinicians, theorists, or researchers in the onset and course of agoraphobia.

Social class and neighbourhood

Sufferers come from all socio-economic backgrounds (Buglass *et al* 1977), but social class may partly determine where a person lives and this in turn can be important in some cases of agoraphobia.

Many anecdotal accounts link agoraphobia with aspects of the person's living situation: housing, crime rates (real or imagined), and transport difficulties. For example, a client of mine improved greatly while an in-patient, relapsed on return home to an inner-city area where she went in fear of being mugged, and responded satisfactorily to a second course of exposure after she had been rehoused in a safer neighbourhood. Elderly patients with marked agoraphobic features seen by geriatricians may well have fears of getting lost, or of meeting with hostility of one kind or another (J. Grimley-Evans, personal communication, 8 September 1987). (How often such 'irrational' fears could be diagnosed as true agoraphobia it is impossible to estimate without formal investigation.)

A further feature of neighbourhoods is 'integration', the presence of multiple and caring relationships between residents; a feature which does not depend upon material prosperity, but may depend on physical environment and the composition and stability of the community. Toynbee (1982) quotes a woman whose symptoms abated when she became involved in a local action group. Quite a common account of the development of agoraphobia is the case of the young working-class housewife who moves from a close-knit community to a large new housing estate where she does not meet anyone she knows and has to travel to distant shops by herself.

But there is no evidence that neighbourhood features regularly play a role in the onset or maintenance of agoraphobia. It is more likely that they sometimes combine with other stress factors to make up a general background of anxiety, against which agoraphobia might develop; or else add to the obstacles facing the person trying to overcome her agoraphobia.

Social role: the young mother at home

Since the most common age of onset is the twenties or thirties, the likelihood of the patient having young children is high. Research by Brown and Harris (1978) has indicated that the presence of young children and lack of outside employment (along with loss of mother in childhood and lack of a confiding relationship) may act as predisposing factors in depression. They propose that such factors operate by way of depriving the woman of role identities that are highly valued in our society, thus causing low self-esteem. Parry (1987) found that dissatisfaction with the 'home-maker' role correlates with higher levels of psychiatric symptoms, psychological distress, and self-depreciation.

As yet there have been no studies on agoraphobia comparable to those on depression, but similar mechanisms might well be operating. This social role approach is closely linked to the feminist perspectives discussed next.

Feminist perspectives: 'the woman's place is in the home'

About two thirds of *known* agoraphobics are women (Mathews *et al.* 1981), a figure that appears to be inflated even higher by writers of the feminist therapy school (e.g. 95 per cent according to Eichenbaum and Orbach 1983). Feminist writers such as Fodor (1974) cite agoraphobia as one phenomenon that demonstrates the continuing oppression of women by men and by modern western institutions.

'It is largely a women's disease with, many researchers believe, deep roots in women's role in society. Because they are made dependent, they become obsessively so. Because they are confined to the house, they develop fears of leaving it' (Toynbee 1982). Over-protected from childhood, their 'nerves' indulged by their parents and then by their husbands, and not encouraged to go out and about, women find it all too easy to stay at home after the symptoms of agoraphobia appear. The latter part of this analysis fits well with the behaviour therapist's emphasis on the role of other people in maintaining or helping to modify avoidance behaviour.

The feminist psychotherapists Eichenbaum and Orbach (1983) propose more complex explanations. They suggest that the agoraphobic woman has constructed 'false boundaries' for herself because she has been deprived of the possibility of true personal separateness and needs these 'false boundaries' in order to preserve a sense of identity or individuality. Yet this defensive manoeuvre is counterproductive: she is also trapped by the boundaries she has erected. To this they add explanations of the recently married woman becoming phobic as an unconscious 'cry for help' upon finding (at an unconscious level) that her husband cannot fulfil her unmet needs 'at last to be understood, met, and cherished' (p. 165). No evidence for these claims is provided, but presumably they are based on experience of psychotherapy with agoraphobic women; they would appear to consist of untestable hypotheses. I am not aware of any empirical support for the suggested association between a weak sense of personal identity or separateness, nor between recently married status and agoraphobia. A study of the personality characteristics of agoraphobic women found no indication of greater dependency than among controls (Arrindell and Emmelkamp 1987).

Feminist analyses contrast with the view of the founder of the Phobic Trust (Vanna Gothard quoted by Samstag 1985) 'women are simply more willing to admit their weakness' (p. 1). If this is more likely, then helping men to admit to their problems and seek treatment would be as appropriate a course of action as concentrating on women's consciousness raising. However, sex ratios are different in other phobias, so that differential consulting rates for men and women can only be part of the explanation. Further, there is some evidence that differences between men's and women's rates of non-psychotic psychiatric disturbance are indeed the result of their dissimilar life situations: Jenkins (1985), comparing women and men in the same jobs and in a similar social situation, found their rates of illness were equivalent and she suggests that the large differences found in other studies are probably due not to constitutional but to environmental factors. These have variously been construed as differences in amount of stress experienced, differences in satisfaction with one's role, and the woman's exclusive reliance on husband and children for a sense of being valued or 'self-esteem'.

Social support

Social support appears to mediate between stress and illness (Cobb 1976). In this context, 'support' refers to confirmation that one is valued, constructive feedback, encouragement, and help in solving problems. People who live in 'unintegrated' neighbourhoods, who are socially isolated (for example, many housewives with young children), and people with difficult personal relationships will lack social support. Some may not have the skills to elicit support from those around them (although lack of social skills is not a typical feature of the agoraphobia sufferer).

Before considering the central topic of family support, it is worth recalling that effective support can come from other sources and from less intimate friends as well as people who are closely attached (Miller and Ingham 1976). Hand *et al.* (1974) found that agoraphobic patients treated in a 'cohesive' group improved more than those in an 'uncohesive' group, although this finding was not replicated by Teasdale *et al.* (1977). Sinnott *et al.* (1981) found a neighbourhood-based treatment, in which patients used each other's homes as target destinations, was more effective than a clinic-based group.

The family: help or hindrance

In the complex area of family interaction, the very relationships that can provide the most valuable protection against stress can themselves be a source of stress rather than support. Arguments with husbands are among the varied forms of stress which may make the symptoms worse (Mathews *et al.* 1981). 'Domestic arguments and stress' were mentioned as factors provoking anxiety by 87 per cent of agoraphobics responding to the survey by Burns and Thorpe (1977b). Conflict with other people is commonly cited as a major high-risk situation for relapse (see, for example, Jansson *et al.* 1984). In general terms, then, family conflict must be considered a possible contributor to onset and relapse in the way that other life difficulties are contributors.

Going beyond the broad and ill-defined categories of stress and support, it is possible to decipher a variety of possible mechanisms whereby family members (particularly husbands) and the family system as a whole can hinder or help recovery of the individual sufferer. I have chosen to look at two contrasting theoretical frameworks: the behavioural approach and the family-systems approach.

Behavioural analysis

Lazarus (1966) maintains that it is not possible to be agoraphobic without the co-operation of another person. By accompanying the patient and undertaking tasks she cannot do herself, family members can make agoraphobia easier to tolerate; and they can help to maintain the symptoms before, during, and after treatment. For example, they might unintentionally 'reward' avoidance behaviour or 'punish' the patient's efforts to conquer her phobia. There is no evidence to suggest that this is true of every, or even many agoraphobics' families: only a detailed analysis of antecedents and consequences of the individual patient's behaviours can elucidate these mechanisms.

A 'good' partner or son or daughter is not necessarily a good therapist or mediator. Thomas-Peter et al. (1983) sought to identify factors predicting outcome, and found that the 'management potential' of the significant other (usually the spouse) was one of the only two predictive variables (the other being the patient's high score on a measure of aggression). It may be this 'management potential' that was enhanced in the programme evaluated by Arnow et al. (1985): on a number of measures of severity of agoraphobia, partner-assisted exposure was found to be significantly more effective when followed by communication training for couples than when followed by a couples relaxation programme. Arnow et al. (1985) suggest that communication training helps couples to recognize and modify interaction patterns which may impede progress or maintenance of improvement. Such patterns might involve mutual hostility, causing emotional stress and detracting from the spouse's potency as a source of support or reinforcement.

However, unhelpful patterns of interaction take many and varied forms. For example, there can be positively reinforcing consequences of agoraphobic symptoms: control of other people ('If I stay home, then you will do x'), punishment of other people ('If I stay home, then you will be hurt'), or social rewards ('If I stay home, then you will pay attention to me'). This takes us into the 'constructional' analysis of behaviour (Goldiamond 1974). In this view, the person is paying a price (remaining phobic) for some pay-off. The price may be too high, and the person unaware of the mechanism. Hudson's (1974) small-scale study of agoraphobics and their family relationships suggested that for a *minority* of the patients there appeared to be patterns of family interaction of this kind that seemed likely to hinder successful treatment or maintenance of improvement. For example, one woman gained a great deal of attention from parents and professionals as a result of staying at home and her symptoms had the effect of controlling others. In some families, a pay-off may be received by the patient's relatives: the child who gets to stay away from school, the elderly parent who is glad to have her daughter at home with her, and the stereotypical jealous husband whose wife is safely indoors rather than out meeting potential lovers.

A negative reinforcement scenario may fit certain cases. For example, the wife of an ambitious and domineering man avoided having to accompany him to social functions which she admitted she hated. Edwards (1985) mentions a woman who, prior to onset of the disorder, spent most of her day with her mother-in-law. Edwards seems to suggest that conflict between obligation to the mother-in-law and the wish not to see her was a cause of the agoraphobia. While this appears to be going beyond the evidence, nevertheless, a situation like this might need sorting out before treatment could be expected to show lasting effects.

On the positive side, family members can play a crucial role in helping the person recover and maintain recovery. Being accompanied by the spouse was mentioned by the highest number of the respondents in the Burns and Thorpe study (1977a) as a situation that relieved their anxiety. This ability to 'help' can, of course, make the sufferer less likely to seek treatment (Emmelkamp and van der Hout, 1983); but harnessed in a programme of behavioural treatment it can be an asset. A typical programme requires the spouse to help plan a series of exposure tasks, prompt and reinforce each step, and provide a reassuring presence during exposure. The most sophisticated approach is the programme devised by Mathews *et al.* (1981) which includes manuals for the patient and the partner with information on the disorder and how to plan and carry out graded exposure.

Mathews *et al.* (1977) found that involving the patient's spouse in planning and treatment led to better results than hospital-based exposure treatment. Barlow *et al.* (1984) found that agoraphobic women in group treatment who were accompanied by their husbands improved significantly more than women treated similarly but without their husbands, and the former group improved more quickly on social, work, and family functioning ratings (although this latter advantage disappeared at post-test). Cobb *et al* (1984), on the other hand, found no such advantage, so this remains to some extent an open question, although as Cobb *et al* (1984) point out, much may depend on the quality of the relationship and the husband's ability to offer appropriate help.

Although the literature on what makes for effective maintenance programmes is thin, the involvement of a 'significant other' is frequently suggested; and this follows naturally from a spouse-as-therapist treatment programme. In their maintenance programme, Jansson *et al* (1984) have patients make a commitment to a significant other about the importance of continuing practice.

Behaviour therapy exponents have suggested a variety of ways in which the family may be involved in the maintenance or the removal of agoraphobic symptoms. Some propose a detailed behavioural analysis of the patient and her living group prior to treatment, and a programme of intervention that goes beyond therapist-directed exposure; others recommend a more conservative approach, only attending to family variables in the event of treatment failure or relapse. The latter group emphasize their high success rates and demonstrate a realistic (economic) adherence to the principle of least intervention.

Systems approach

A different view of the role of the family, and a popular one in the clinical literature, sees the family and/or the marital system as operating in altogether more subtle and complicated ways to produce and maintain agoraphobia in one of its members. Agoraphobia is seen as the result of conflict, the symptoms reflecting the conflict. One source of these ideas is family-systems theory, which states that any symptom functions as a homeostatic mechanism to keep the family system in balance. This theory indicts a troubled family system as the cause of agoraphobia, and predicts that the patient will change only if the family system itself changes. Family-systems theorists seem to look for an agoraphobogenic family as a matter of course and in particular they believe that agoraphobics' marriages are typically problematic, with the symptom taking the place of overt communication or else being used by the husband to divert attention from inadequacies of his own.

What is operating here may be a 'self-perpetuating myth': clinicians tend to see what other clinicians have seen before them! (Hafner 1982, himself one of the advocates of the 'myth', makes this suggestion). Certainly family-systems proponents have been extremely influential among practitioners, particularly social workers. Their claims are difficult either to confirm or to refute by research. However, the theory does generate several key hypotheses, which have been examined in a number of studies.

Marital conflict Mathews *et al.* (1981) propose that the widespread belief that all or most agoraphobics' marriages are troubled is due to the vividness with which we remember cases where severe marital problems were a major factor. There is very little empirical support for the view that marital conflict plays more than an occasional contributory and minor role in causation. Arrindell (1987) and his colleagues have undertaken extensive literature reviews and conducted several research studies in an effort to clarify this matter. They have examined the key hypothesis that unhappy marital relationships are typical of agoraphobics. In fact, the bulk of the evidence suggests that unhappy marriages are not common in this population; though it is fair to note that a family-systems proponent would reply that marital problems do not show up if the symptom is doing its work properly and therefore would be hard to uncover in untreated cases. It is impossible to determine whether or not systems theory receives confirmation from these findings: an insuperable problem in investigating this theory is that 'no sign of marital problems' and 'evidence of marital problems' can both be cited as confirmation, 'no sign' being taken to mean that the problems have been hidden or dealt with by the symptom. It is worth noting, however, that Arrindell and Emmelkamp (1985) took considerable trouble to prevent respondents from 'faking happy' on their tests of marital satisfaction.

A related hypothesis deriving from systems theory is that the more severe the marital problems, the less likely it is that treatment directed at the phobia would prove successful. Milton and Hafner (1979) and Bland and Hallam (1981) suggest that marital satisfaction is indeed a key prognostic factor in behavioural treatment of agoraphobia. Reviewing the literature, Jansson *et al.* (1987) conclude that the relationship between long-term outcome of treatment and initial level of marital satisfaction remains an open question. Their own investigation found no correlation between initial marital satisfaction and behavioural, subjective, or overall improvement up to fifteen months after treatment. Similar findings have been reported by Emmelkamp (1980), Barlow *et al.* (1983), Cobb *et al.* (1984), Arrindell *et al.* (1986), and Himadi *et al.* (1986).

Reviewing these contradictory studies, Emmelkamp (1986) suggests that the pre-treatment picture obtained may be inaccurate in some studies, and that a more accurate rating of marriage satisfaction is likely to be given after the patient has come to trust the therapist more. Indeed, Emmelkamp and van der Hout (1983) found that patients' complaints about the marital partner reported *during* treatment did predict failure of treatment.

A few studies have reported marital difficulties apparently arising or coming to light after successful treatment (e.g. Hand and Lamontagne 1976, Milton and Hafner 1979, Barlow *et al.* 1981): these findings may be taken as evidence of poor marital relationships all along, or of 'symptom substitution' (see paragraph after next). However, these reports have been criticized on the grounds that they are based on clinical case material and they are contradicted by the more general finding from controlled studies that, overall, marriages tend to improve after symptom removal (e.g. Cobb *et al.* 1984, Himadi *et al.* 1986, Arrindell 1987).

Disturbed husbands Related to the marital conflict hypothesis is another widely held belief: that the husband of the agoraphobic woman is himself disturbed and therefore causes in some subtle manner the symptoms which his wife displays; but Arrindell and Emmelkamp (1985) and Cobb *et al.* (1984) found that husbands of agoraphobics were no more defensive or disturbed than controls. However, one study has found husbands showing increased neurotic symptomatology and self-dissatisfaction after their wife's recovery from agoraphobia (Hafner 1977). Cobb *et al.* (1984) and Himadi *et al.* (1986) found the reverse to be the case. Barlow *et al.* (1983) suggest Hafner's findings might be due to the use, in his study, of very rapid intensive exposure treatment without spouse involvement, causing the spouse to face sudden and major role change without preparation or a sense of control. Husbands' problems coming to light after the phobia has gone, like marital problems appearing at this stage, are cited as examples of 'symptom substitution'.

'Symptom substitution' Systems theory proposes that disappearance of the symptom carried by one family member (i.e. agoraphobia) will

'unbalance the system', possibly leading to overt family conflict, until the return of the old symptom or the arrival of a new symptom, perhaps carried by someone else (a somewhat more complex version of the Freudian notion of 'symptom substitution'). As we have seen, studies by Hand and Lamontagne (1976) and Milton and Hafner (1979) do support the view that improvement in agoraphobic symptoms is followed by the emergence of marital problems; but other, and better controlled, studies come to the opposite conclusion (Arrindell *et al* 1986, Bland and Hallam 1981, Cobb *et al* 1984, Himadi *et al* 1986). Further, disappearance of agoraphobic symptoms does not result in emergence of new symptoms (Emmelkamp and Kuipers 1979, Monteiro *et al* 1985, Himadi *et al* 1986). Nor have fresh problems of any other kind been discovered: rather, as noted above, good functioning remains good, and if there is change, it takes the form of improvement spreading to other aspects of the person's life (e.g. Cobb *et al* 1980, 1984).

Nevertheless, when their 'symptom substitution' predictions are not fulfilled, family-systems proponents can still explain this outcome away: in the words of Hudson (1974), agoraphobia in these particular cases is re-defined as 'a remnant symptom, no longer fulfilling its original purpose'.

If a systems view is accepted, then direct treatment of agoraphobic symptoms will not be appropriate; rather, the theory requires a family or marital therapy approach directed at uncovering the presumed root causes and helping families or couples deal with or communicate their difficulties in more direct and less damaging ways. While this is not the place to review treatment outcome research, it should be noted that the systems approach to agoraphobia lacks the empirical support that the behavioural approach has received.

This said, it is fair to observe that clinicians have reported individual cases where family-systems theory seems to fit like a glove. No doubt the jealous husband sometimes has his suspicions confirmed! No doubt some marriages do break up once the wife is no longer so dependent on her husband. And behaviour therapists nowadays are on the lookout, not for 'symptom substitution', but for problems in re-adapting: for example, social anxiety or inadequacy may come to light, or worry about getting or holding a job; and difficulties can occasionally arise in the redistribution of family responsibilities and changes in family interaction patterns. Examples from my own caseload include the teacher whose parents resented her leaving home to pursue her interrupted career, the mother whose children rebelled against returning to regular school attendance, the woman who became angrily dissatisfied with her neighbourhood once she was able to go out and about, and the politician's wife who still avoided public engagements after her agoraphobic symptoms had disappeared. We have already noted that there is some research indicating that husbands may have difficulties after successful treatment, and the point made by Barlow *et al* (1983) is well taken: recovery from agoraphobia might bring new problems if the family is not prepared for the change, and has not been involved in any meaningful way in the process of change. It seems appropriate to accept that the family is a complex system, in which one person's behaviour inevitably affects and is affected by the behaviour of others, but not a 'System' in which the disorder is a symptom of group pathology (Orford 1987: 4).

Attention to the social outcome as well as to the role of family members in treatment and maintenance programmes are common features of modern behavioural approaches to agoraphobia. Within this broader arena social workers can sometimes play a significant part.

SOCIAL WORKER ROLES

There are potential roles for social workers throughout the patient's career. These roles include case finding, assessment, direct treatment, 'support', and help with problems other than the agoraphobia. Social workers can be helpful or counterproductive in cases of agoraphobia. This will depend partly on the social worker's level of competence and partly on features of the agency, whether social services or multi-disciplinary.

Case finding

The first point of contact is sometimes a social worker, perhaps a member of a local authority social services area team. He or she may have a duty to assess the family situation and offer help or consider some form of statutory action. For example, in cases where non-school attendance has led to threats from the education authority, the social worker may find a housebound mother who permits or even encourages her child to miss school as a way of getting company or help with her shopping; or a phobic child whose agoraphobic mother sympathizes all too readily with the child's fears. The social worker may liaise with the family doctor to try to obtain treatment for the mother, while holding off more punitive intervention.

Edwards (1985) writes of the unexpectedly large number of clients with agoraphobic symptoms she encountered in a social services department. It is probable that agoraphobia is greatly underreported (Marks 1969); and Vines (1987), reviewing estimates of average time lapse between onset and beginning treatment, found a range between seventeen months and six-and-a half years. There is a growing body of evidence concerning the extent of minor mental illness among social services clients (Huxley and Fitzpatrick 1984, Cohen and Fisher 1987). Edwards (1985) comments: 'How many of us [social workers] have dismissed the comments "I don't go out much", or "I feel a bit frightened going to the shops", and moved on unwittingly to the next item?' (p. 7).

Social workers attached to a general medical practice are even more likely to come across the condition (especially in those practices where the doctor regularly refers 'emotional' problems to the social worker). It is estimated that about 10 per cent of the population consult a doctor about 'tension' at some time (France and Robson 1986). Of these, an unknown number doubtless suffer from agoraphobia.

Another setting where social workers have a high profile and where there appear to be 'unreported agoraphobics' is the geriatric department of the general hospital. Elderly people who 'do not go out' include a number who do not go out because of irrational fears, rather than because of physical disability, and these cases may not readily be identified by busy geriatricians (Grimley-Evans, personal communication, 8 September 1987).

Assessment

A common task of the social worker in the multidisciplinary setting is to produce a 'social history'. This rather traditional document is based on interviews with both the patient and the family and attempts to provide useful information from a 'non-psychiatric' point of view. In reality, much of it may be not relevant, or will simply confirm what others have already learned from interviews, tests, and questionnaires. At its best, however, the social history will explore the social factors that may have formed the backdrop to the onset of symptoms, the social consequences of the disorder, and the social resources the patient has (or lacks) that could be important in treatment and maintenance programmes. These resources might include financial means, family support, and community networks.

Direct treatment

According to the large-scale survey by Marks and Herst in 1970, at least one-third of agoraphobics in Britain never entered psychiatric or psychological treatment. While the proportion may have changed since then, in my experience, social workers sometimes find that their agoraphobic client refuses contact with psychiatric services or has already been relegated to the category of 'treatment failure'.

In such circumstances, a social worker will sometimes attempt treatment without medical or psychologist backup apart from the courtesy of informing the client's doctor. There are a few social workers in the community who have the knowledge and skills to engage agoraphobic clients in programmed practice. Like the general practitioner in the book by France and Robson (1986), they undertake assessment of the agoraphobia and other areas of difficulty, analyse the problem in behavioural terms, take baseline measures, and carry out and evaluate a treatment package.

A major disadvantage of this solo work is that social workers are not qualified to detect physical conditions or reassure regarding worries about health (which often accompany agoraphobia). While it is sometimes held that medical involvement is necessary only for screening before interventions likely to precipitate severe anxiety, authorities such as Thyer (1987) consider it necessary to have 'a good knowledge of contemporary psychopharmacological management practices relevant to the anxiety disorders' (p. 7). Indeed, social workers outside of medical settings are likely to fight shy of a direct treatment role. They take to heart such warnings as that from Mathews et al. (1981), who 'strongly advise against ... unsupervised application [of their client's manual] and assume no responsibility for the effects resulting from such use' (p. 160). Yet Mathews and his colleagues have been willing to share their expertise with general practitioners, whose training is not, generally speaking, markedly superior to that of social workers in respect of agoraphobia and its treatment; and experts such as Marks (1978) and Vines (1987) offer behaviour therapy techniques direct to the agoraphobia sufferer.

I believe that social workers can readily be taught to use behaviour therapy techniques. They have skills in interviewing, forming relationships, and assessing client and environment which provide the necessary base on which to build; they are used to home visiting and working with relatives. Particularly in cases where they already know the family and are familiar with the local community and the resources it offers, they seem eminently suitable as 'key worker'. This said, few social work training courses at present provide social workers with the full range of skills required for direct treatment of agoraphobia and there are few references to such work in the social work literature (exceptions include textbooks by Sheldon 1981 and Hudson and Macdonald 1986, and the detailed guide by Thyer 1987). I do not endorse Edwards's (1985) apparent belief that one 'practical guide' such as her own is sufficient preparation for social workers who have no other training in behavioural principles and methods. Fortunately, an increasing (but still small) number of social workers are obtaining this training.

Competence is one of two key issues in considering the possibility of social workers undertaking direct treatment of agoraphobia. The other is 'permission': from the other professions involved in this field and from the hierarchies in which most social workers have to function.

Permission from the other professions is not necessarily a problem when the client is not formally in their care and when the social worker has the necessary competence. Psychiatrists' territorialism appears to be relaxing to allow not only the clinical psychologist but also the general practitioner, the nurse, and the occupational therapist to undertake behavioural treatments (see, for example, France and Robson 1986, Edwards 1985). The social worker too has some claim to be counted as a mental health professional.

However, the social services social worker must operate within time constraints and a departmental policy of priorities. The latter has been shown by many researchers to disadvantage mentally ill clients. Howe (1979) describes them as 'a lost group' and Corney (1982) has shown that intake teams in social services departments tend to offer only re-referral or brief help in the form of information or advocacy unless the problems presented involve a priority category such as child care, urgent physical need, or risk to personal safety or freedom. Such a service may not even recognize, let alone attempt to modify a problem such as agoraphobia. Even if agoraphobia is recognized, it is necessary to convince the social services hierarchy that the problem can be helped *and* is worth helping in terms of both reduction of the sufferer's distress and also additional benefits to the family, especially to children.

In fact, research on social workers' involvement with clients who suffer from some form of mental disorder suggests that at present the position is not encouraging. For example, Fisher *et al* (1984) found that little in the way of 'therapeutic' work was being undertaken. They detail the case of an agoraphobic woman who later developed both alcohol and drug problems and with whom social services were involved for twenty years: her problems were handled exclusively as 'child care'. The authors comment: 'this case appears to show a dramatic misapplication of skills and resources. The problems presented at referral were of a type amenable to therapeutic intervention. This was not provided.' They conclude: 'The lesson to be drawn from this example is that the tragic process could start again today, within another family, unless social work develops a more therapeutic orientation.' We can infer their preferred approach from a further comment about 'present understanding of the significance of family dynamics in agoraphobia' (p. 155). Edwards (1985) seems the lone advocate of behavioural treatment of agoraphobia in a social services setting, but this situation may change as more social workers become interested and competent in behavioural approaches.

Another form of direct treatment that a social worker might offer is family therapy based on a family-systems view of the disorder. Social workers are more likely to have had training in this than in behaviour therapy. This approach, as noted before, leads to erroneous predictions. It is an inappropriate starting point for work with these patients because it lacks empirical support as an effective intervention for agoraphobia and it devalues and undermines the approach more likely to be effective, behaviour therapy. A similar problem arises with psychodynamic approaches, which were the mainstay of social work education until fairly recently. Psychodynamically-oriented workers see agoraphobia as a reflection of some conflict deriving from early experience and being re-enacted in present relationships. This theory indicates a need for insight-giving or 'working through' in terms of family relationships past or present.

The possibility that one's social work colleague may hold a family-systems or psychodynamic view of the disorder, and welcome the opportunity to do some 'real' family therapy or psychodynamic casework is a potential drawback of the otherwise splendid 'multidisciplinary team'.

Multi-faceted intervention

When a social worker remains involved beyond the assessment and planning stage, this is usually as an ancillary, either providing 'support' (where support from the patient's own environment is not available), or intervening with problems additional to the agoraphobic symptoms.

Whatever the answers to theoretical and empirical debates about cause and effect in agoraphobia, we may need to address other areas of concern to the individual and her family, whether they predate, result from, or simply happen to co-exist with the agoraphobic symptoms. Help with these concerns may reduce the likelihood of relapse by removing a backdrop of worry against which the disorder originally developed, may free the patient from emotional and practical constraints so that she can undertake the hard work required of her in therapy, and help her family and friends to provide the loving but firm support she needs. In offering help with other problems, social work with agoraphobics differs not at all from social work with other kinds of clients.

A key question, as yet unanswered in the literature, is to do with timing. Should the agoraphobia treatment programme be interrupted by, say, a major effort to work on welfare rights or housing needs, or child behaviour problems, or marital difficulties? Should this help precede treatment for the agoraphobia, should it be provided in parallel, or should it be undertaken afterwards? Or, indeed, should it be seen as something totally separate like going to the dentist while under treatment for arthritis?

One general indication is best summed up in a paraphrase from another field of behavioural intervention (with apologies to Griest and Forehand 1982): 'How can I get any exposure treatment done with all these other problems going on?' But perhaps this question of timing can be answered in terms of the reasons why help with other problems might be important in selected cases of agoraphobia. If 'lack of motivation' is hindering co-operation, then attempts to find ways of making effort worthwhile, and to change a 'helplessness' mental set may be a prerequisite. If family relationships are so strained that support will not be forthcoming, then some effort to improve relationships or to link the patient up with alternative sources of social support will be required. On the other hand, we should note the finding of Cobb et al (1980) that whereas exposure treatment benefited the patients' marital relationships, marital therapy did not improve their agoraphobia. This suggests that if at all possible it may be wise to start with direct treatment of agoraphobia, then see if other serious problems remain. If it seems likely that stress contributed to onset and stress remains, then a relapse prevention plan must include efforts to remove that pre-existing stress as well as to ward off new forms of stress. And, crucially, the patient's own selection of priority goals ought to inform the planning of intervention at any point in time.

Agoraphobia is a crippling disorder, and conquering it requires energy, optimism, and a supportive environment. The clients with whom the social work profession is most closely identified tend to lack these advantages, and social work involvement might improve the chances of success with people who have previously been unable to benefit from effective treatments.

© Barbara L. Hudson

REFERENCES

Arnow, B. A., Taylor, C. B., Agras, W. S., and Telch, M. J. (1985) 'Enhancing agoraphobia treatment by changing couple communication patterns', *Behavior Therapy* 16, 5: 452–67.

Arrindell, W. A. (1987) *Marital Conflict and Agoraphobia: Fact or Fantasy?*, Delft: Eburon.

Arrindell, W. A. and Emmelkamp, P. M. G. (1985) 'Psychological profile of the spouse of the female agoraphobic patient: personality and symptoms', *British Journal of Psychiatry* 146: 405–14.

——(1986) 'Marital adjustment, intimacy and needs in female agoraphobics and their partners', *British Journal of Psychiatry* 149: 592–602.

——(1987) 'Psychological states and traits in female agoraphobics: a controlled study', *Journal of Psychopathology and Behavioral Assessment* 9: 237–53.

Arrindell, W. A., Emmelkamp, P. M. G., and Sanderman, R. (1986) 'Marital quality and general life adjustment in relation to treatment outcome in agoraphobia', *Advances in Behaviour Research and Therapy* 8, 3: 139–85.

Barlow, D. H., Mavissakalian, M., and Hay, L. R. (1981) 'Couples treatment of agoraphobia: changes in marital satisfaction', *Behaviour Research and Therapy* 19: 245–55.

Barlow, D. H., O'Brien, G. T., and Last, C. G. (1984) 'Couples treatment of agoraphobia', *Behavior Therapy* 15, 1: 41–58.

Barlow, D. H., O'Brien, G. T., Last, C. G., and Holden, A. C. (1983) 'Couples treatment of agoraphobia: initial outcome', in K. D. Craig and R. J. McMahon (eds) *Advances in Clinical Behavior Therapy*, New York: Brunner/Mazel.

Bland, K. and Hallam, R. (1981) 'Relationship between response to graded exposure and marital satisfaction in agoraphobics', *Behavior Therapy* 19: 335–8.

Brown, G. W. and Harris, T. (1978) *Social Origins of Depression*, London: Tavistock.

Buglass, D., Clarke, J., Henderson, A. S., Kreitman, N., and Presley, A. S. (1977) 'A study of agoraphobic housewives', *Psychological Medicine* 7: 73–86.

Burns, L. E. and Thorpe, G. B. (1977a) 'The epidemiology of fears and phobias with particular reference to the national survey of agoraphobics', *Journal of International Medical Research* 5, supplement 5: 1–7.

—(1977b) 'Fears and clinical phobias', *Journal of International Medical Research* 5, supplement, 1: 132–9.

Cobb, J. P., McDonald, R., Marks, I. M., and Stern, R. S. (1980) 'Marital versus exposure therapy', *European Journal of Behavioral Analysis and Modification* 4: 3–17.

Cobb, J. P., Mathews, A. M., Childs-Clarke, A., and Blowers, C. M. (1984) 'The spouse as co-therapist in the treatment of agoraphobia', *British Journal of Psychiatry* 144: 282–7.

Cobb, S. (1976) 'Social support as a moderator of life stress', *Psychosomatic Medicine* 38: 300–14.

Cohen, J. and Fisher, M. (1987) 'Recognition of mental health problems by doctors and social workers', *Practice* 1, 3: 225–40.

Corney, R. H. (1982) 'Social workers' interventions: a comparative study of a local authority intake team with a general practice attachment scheme', in A. W. Clare and R. H. Corney, (eds) *Social Work and Primary Health Care*, 151–61, London: Academic Press.

Dohrenwend, B. P. and Dohrenwend, B. S. (1974) *Stressful Life Events: Their Nature and Effects*, New York: John Wiley.

Edwards, Liz (1985) *Anxiety Management of Agoraphobia: a Practical Guide for Social Workers*, Social Work Monograph 38, Norwich: University of East Anglia.

Eichenbaum, L. and Orbach, S. (1983) *Understanding Women*, Harmondsworth: Penguin.

Emmelkamp, P. M. G. (1980) 'Agoraphobics' interpersonal problems: their role in the effects of exposure *in vivo* therapy, *Archives of General Psychiatry* 37: 1303–6.

—(1986) 'Behavior therapy with adults', in A. E. Bergin and S. L. Garfield (eds) *Handbook of Psychotherapy and Behavior Change*, 3rd edition, 391–3, New York: John Wiley.

Emmelkamp, P. M. G. and Kuipers, A. (1979) 'Agoraphobia: a followup study four years after treatment', *British Journal of Psychiatry* 134: 352–5.

Emmelkamp, P. M. G. and van der Hout, A. (1983) 'Failure in treating agoraphobia', in E. Foa and P. M. G. Emmelkamp (eds) *Failures in Behavior Therapy*, 58–81, New York: John Wiley.

Fisher, M., Newton, C., and Sainsbury, E. (1984) *Mental Health Social Work Observed*, London: George Allen & Unwin.

Fodor, Iris Goldstein (1974) 'The phobic syndrome in women', in V. Franks and V. Burke (eds) *Women in Therapy*, New York: Brunner/Mazel.

France, R. and Robson, M. (1986) *Behaviour Therapy in Primary Care*, London: Croom Helm.

Goldiamond, I. (1974) 'Towards a constructional approach to social problems', *Behaviorism* 2: 1–84.

Griest, D. and Forehand, R. (1982) 'How can I get any parent training done with all these other problems going on?', *Child and Family Behavior Therapy* 4, 1: 73–80.

Hafner, R. J. (1977) 'The husbands of agoraphobic women and their influence on treatment outcome', *British Journal of Psychiatry* 131: 1537–63.

—(1982) 'The marital context of the agoraphobic syndrome', in D. L. Chambless and A. J. Goldstein (eds) *Agoraphobia: Multiple Perspectives on Theory and Treatment*, New York: John Wiley.

Hand, I. and Lamontagne, Y. (1976) 'The exacerbation of interpersonal problems after rapid phobia removal', *Psychotherapy: Theory, Research and Practice* 13: 405–11.

Hand, I., Lamontagne, Y., and Marks, I. M. (1974) 'Group exposure (flooding) *in vivo* for agoraphobics', *British Journal of Psychiatry* 124: 588–602.

Himadi, W. G., Cerny, J. A., Barlow, D. H., Cohen, S., and O'Brien, G. T. (1986) 'The relationship of marital adjustment to agoraphobia treatment outcome', *Behaviour Research and Therapy* 24, 2: 107–16.

Howe, D. (1979) 'A preliminary report on the nature of area social workers' caseloads', unpublished paper, University of East Anglia, quoted in D. Goldberg and P. Huxley *Mental Illness in the Community*, London: Tavistock.

Hudson, B. L. (1974) 'The families of agoraphobics treated by behaviour therapy', *British Journal of Social Work* 4, 1: 51–60.

Hudson, B. L. and Macdonald, G. M. (1986) *Behavioural Social Work: an Introduction*, London: Macmillan.

Huxley, P. and Fitzpatrick, R. (1984) 'The probable extent of minor mental illness in the adult clients of social workers: a research note', *British Journal of Social Work* 14: 67–73.

Jansson, L., Jerremalm, A., and Ost, L.-G. (1984) 'Maintenance procedures in the behavioral treatment of agoraphobia: a program and some data', *Behavioural Psychotherapy* 12: 109–16.

Jansson, L., Ost, L.-G., and Jerremalm, A. (1987) 'Prognostic factors in the behavioral treatment of agoraphobia', *Behavioural Psychotherapy*, 15: 31–44.

Jenkins, R. (1985) 'Sex differences in minor psychiatric morbidity', *Psychological Medicine*, supplement 7.

Lazarus, A. A. (1966) 'Broad-spectrum behaviour therapy and the treatment of agoraphobia', *Behaviour Research and Therapy* 4: 95–7.

Marks, I. M. (1969, repr. 1975) *Fears and Phobias*, London: Heinemann.
—(1978) *Living with Fear*, New York: McGraw-Hill.
Marks, I. and Herst, E. R. (1970) 'A survey of 1,200 agoraphobics in Britain', *Social Psychiatry* 5, 1: 16–24.
Mathews, A. M., Gelder, M. G., and Johnston, D. W. (1981) *Agoraphobia: Nature and Treatment*, London: Tavistock.
Mathews, A. M., Teasdale, J., Munby, M., Johnston, D., and Shaw, P. (1977) 'A home-based treatment program for agoraphobia', *Behavior Therapy* 8: 915–24.
Miller, P. and Ingham, J. G. (1976) 'Friends, confidants and symptoms', *Social Psychiatry* 11: 51–8.
Milton, F. and Hafner, J. (1979) 'The outcome of behaviour therapy for agoraphobia in relation to marital adjustment', *Archives of General Psychiatry* 36: 807–11.
Monteiro, W., Marks, I. M., and Ramm, E. (1985) 'Marital adjustment and treatment outcome in agoraphobia', *British Journal of Psychiatry* 146: 383–90.
Orford, J. (1987) (ed.) *Coping with Disorder in the Family*, London: Croom Helm.
Palmer, F. (1982) 'Seriously stressed students', *Teaching at a Distance*, November, pp. 77–81.
Parry, G. (1987) 'Sex-role beliefs, work attitudes and mental health in employed and non-employed mothers', *British Journal of Social Psychology* 24: 47–58.
Samstag, T. (1985) 'Phobics come forward to take the stress out of fear', *The Times*, 31 August, p. 5.
Shafar, S. (1976) 'Aspects of phobic illness: a study of 90 personal cases', *British Journal of Medical Psychology* 49: 221–36.
Sheldon, B. (1981) *Behaviour Modification*, London: Tavistock.
Sinnott, A., Jones, R. B., Fordham, A. S., and Woodward, R. (1981) 'Augmentation of exposure treatment of agoraphobia by formation of neighbourhood self-help groups', *Behaviour Research and Therapy* 19: 338–47.
Solyom, L., Beck, P., Solyom, C., and Hugel, R. (1974) 'Some etiological factors in phobic neuroses', *Canadian Psychiatric Association Journal* 19: 69–77.
Teasdale, J., Walsh, P. A., Lancashire, M., and Mathews, A. M. (1977) 'Group exposure for agoraphobia: a replication study', *British Journal of Psychiatry* 130: 186–93.
Thomas-Peter, B. A., Jones, R. B., Sinnott, A., and Fordham, A. S. (1983) 'Prediction of outcome in the treatment of agoraphobia', *Behavioural Psychotherapy* 11: 320–8.
Thyer, B. A. (1987) *Treating Anxiety Disorders*, Newbury Park: Sage Publications.
Toynbee, Polly (1982) 'Agoraphobia', *Guardian*, 23 April, p. 5.
Vines, Robyn (1987) *Agoraphobia: the Fear of Panic*, London: Fontana.

Chapter Four

THE ROLE OF MEDICATION IN THE MANAGEMENT OF AGORAPHOBIA: A REVIEW

CHERRIE A. COGHLAN

As anxiety symptoms are a central feature of the agoraphobic syndrome, it is hardly surprising that drugs with anxiolytic and antidepressant properties have been used in an attempt to treat this condition. In most studies, drug treatment is used in conjunction with behavioural or supportive psychotherapy. The two principal classes of drugs used have been the antidepressants and the benzodiazepines. Beta blockers have also been studied, but these are less widely prescribed.

ANTIDEPRESSANTS

There are two main types of antidepressants, the tricyclics and the mono amine oxidase inhibitors (MAOIs). Tricyclic antidepressants act by inhibiting the re-uptake from the neuronal synapse of monoamine neurotransmitters such as noradrenaline and 5HT (serotonin). These neurotransmitters are believed to be involved in the aetiology of affective disorders. MAOIs inhibit the enzyme involved in the breakdown of monoamines in the presynaptic neurone.

Tricyclics

Of the tricyclics, the principal representative compound studied in agoraphobia has been imipramine. Its use in the treatment of agoraphobia was first described by Klein and Fink (1962). In this uncontrolled study of treatment of resistant cases, imipramine apparently reduced panic attacks. However, the patients continued to avoid the feared situation. A further controlled study (Klein 1967) showed imipramine to be superior to placebo, which in turn was superior to chlorpromazine in the management of agoraphobics who had not responded to psychotherapeutic measures alone. In this study, imipramine seemed not only to reduce panic attacks, but also phobic avoidance. Zitrin *et al.* (1978) showed that more generalized phobias such as agoraphobia benefited from imipramine, in contrast to simple phobias. In a later study (Zitrin *et al.* 1980), they carried out a more detailed examination of the effect of imipramine on phobias. In this study, all the subjects were agoraphobic, and the behaviour therapy involved was exposure *in vivo* rather than imaginal desensitization, the former having been found to be more effective (Marks *et al.* 1971, Stern and Marks 1973). In a study with fifty-seven chronic agoraphobics, Sheenan *et al.* (1980) showed imipramine to be superior to placebo on a wide range of measures except on a measure of phobic avoidance. Telch *et al.* (1985) looked at twenty-nine agoraphobics and compared imipramine alone, *in vivo* exposure alone , and a combination of these treatments with placebo and supportive psychotherapy. The most effective treatment was the combination of imipramine and *in vivo* exposure. However, the only benefit over exposure alone was a reduction in general anxiety. The imipramine seemed, therefore, to facilitate the exposure, which was considered to be the main therapeutic agent.

In 1983, there were two major studies with conflicting results. Zitrin *et al.* (1983), in a large study of over two hundred subjects, showed that the effects of imipramine were significantly superior to placebo in phobic patients with spontaneous panic attacks, but not in simple phobics in whom panic attacks did not occur. Marks *et al.* (1985) in contrast, in a similar study, found only a minimal benefit of imipramine compared to placebo. At two-years follow-up of these subjects, there was no significant difference (Cohen *et al.* 1984). In reviewing the conflicting studies, Matuzas and Glass (1983) highlighted three methodological differences between them. First, different patterns of prescribing were used. Second, the dosage levels were very different, and third, the timing of the ratings relative to treatment were different. These factors would, therefore, tend to exaggerate a difference in outcome.

Telch *et al.* (1985) found in comparing imipramine, with and without exposure, with placebo plus exposure, that the combined treatment was superior and this group was the only one to show a reduction in panic attacks. Mavissakalian and Pezel (1985) showed that imipramine was superior to placebo. They highlighted the importance of the dosage used in evaluating different studies, and suggested that the therapeutic response is dose related, with optimal response in a range of over 150 mg daily. Similar high dosages have been used in the studies by Zitrin and her colleagues.

In addition to the studies on imipramine, there has been increasing interest in another tricyclic compound, i.e. clomipramine. However, most of the studies have been uncontrolled. Doses used have been large and the route of administration used has been intravenous as well as oral. These studies have been reviewed by Telch *et al.* (1985) and all report a favourable outcome comparable with imipramine.

Mono amine oxidase inhibitors

With mono amine oxidase inhibitors (MAOIs) there were initially good results from uncontrolled studies (Sargent and Dally 1962, Kelly *et al.* 1970). The two representative compounds studied have been phenelzine and iproniazid. The subsequent controlled studies can be divided into two groups: 1. those which show no difference between phenelzine and placebo (Mountjoy *et al.* 1977, Solyom *et al.* 1981) and 2. those which show some improvement in phobic symptoms which is not sustained after the cessation of treatment (Tyrer *et al.* 1973, Solyom *et al.* 1973, Lipsedge *et al.* 1973). One positive exception is Sheehan's study (1980) in which three groups were compared, i.e. imipramine, phenelzine, and placebo, each combined with supportive group therapy. Those subjects on active treatment had a reduction in general disability and avoidance behaviour. However, the benefit did not accrue until after six weeks of treatment and phenelzine was marginally superior to imipramine.

MECHANISM OF ACTION OF ANTIDEPRESSANTS IN AGORAPHOBIA

There are three basic theories to explain the mechanism of action of antidepressants in agoraphobia and the lack of consensus reflects the varied outcome of the studies. Zitrin *et al.* 1980 and 1983) suggest that efficacy depends on the antipanic activity of the drug. The authors relate this to an aetiological theory, whereby the panic attack is primary and this leads in turn to avoidance behaviour. They found imipramine to be of benefit in those phobic patients who exhibited spontaneous panic attacks, but not in the simple phobics who did not. They also found that patients who were clinically depressed had a poorer outcome. This would argue against an antidepressant mechanism of action and suggest that these drugs have antipanic activity. This may be reflected by their ability to block lactate-induced panic attacks (Kelly *et al.* 1971). However, Marks *et al.* (1983) attributes the efficacy of antidepressants in phobic states to antidepressant action. He explains the poorer outcome with imipramine in his own study in terms of the low scores on measures of depression at the outset. Telch *et al.* (1985) also relates the benefit of imipramine to antidepressant activity, but suggests that this may be mediated through the relief of dysphoria, in turn improving the subject's cognitive self-appraisal during behaviour therapy. This would account for the superiority of combined treatment with drugs plus exposure, over treatment with drugs alone. McNair and Kahn (1981) have postulated a dual mechanism whereby the antipanic effect is independent of the antidepressant action, but the relief of phobic symptoms is related to it.

Although antidepressants have been shown to be beneficial in agoraphobia, there are some problems with their use. Dosages required are high and side-effects distressing. This leads to a very high drop-out rate from treatment. Zitrin *et al.* (1980) found this to be in the order of 30 per cent. This problem is compounded by the fact that agoraphobics as a group are known to be reluctant to take drugs (Telch *et al.* 1985). Therapeutic benefit from antidepressants may take as long as six weeks to be evident and there is a high relapse rate after cessation of the drug. Studies are essentially in agreement that there is a place for antidepressants in the treatment of agoraphobia, but that the most important element of treatment is exposure to the feared situation (Matuzas and Glass 1983). Thus it would seem that the most appropriate use of these drugs is as an adjunct to behaviour therapy and in particular, to facilitate the process of exposure. For the majority of patients with agoraphobia, behaviour therapy alone is effective (Mavissakalian *et al.* 1983) and therefore, the use of these drugs might well be reserved for those patients who are either clinically depressed, or whose anxiety is at such a level as to preclude their engagement in behaviour therapy without them.

BENZODIAZEPINES

This group of drugs, otherwise known as the minor tranquillizers, have been widely used as anxiolytics in the last twenty years. Their mechanism of action is believed to involve potentiating the effect of the inhibitory neurotransmitter GABA (gamma amine butyric acid) and specific benzodiazepine receptors have been found in the CNS in close proximity to GABA receptors. The efficacy of benzodiazepines in the treatment of generalized anxiety is not in doubt (Hallstrom 1985). There is evidence, however, to suggest that most benzodiazepines are not effective in reducing panic attacks (Sheehan 1982). There have, however, been studies which suggest that the triazalobenzodiazepine, alprazolam, has antipanic properties in common with the antidepressants (Charney and Heninger 1985, Feighner *et al.* 1983, Rickels *et al.* 1983). Charney and Heninger (1985) suggest that this may be attributable to an additional effect of the drug on the noradrenergic neurotransmitter system.

In recent years, the popularity of the benzodiazepines has declined (Tyrer 1984) as reports of dependency have increased. Reports of the incidence of the withdrawal syndrome vary between 5–45 per cent of users (Hallstrom 1985). The size of this incidence range reflects differences in whether the studies were prospective or retrospective, the definition of the withdrawal state, and the populations studied. Hallstrom points to various factors which make a patient more likely to develop a withdrawal syndrome. For example, patients attending a psychiatric clinic as opposed to their general practitioner, those who expect adverse effects on cessation of treatment, and patients with a 'passive, dependent personality'. In this regard, there is said to be an association between agoraphobia and passive dependent pre-morbid personality traits (Freeman 1983). Additionally, there is an increased incidence of a withdrawal syndrome occurring with short-acting benzodiazepines such as lorazepam and alprazolam (Hallstrom 1985, Noyes *et al.* 1985).

The benzodiazepam withdrawal syndrome consists of symptoms which may be difficult to distinguish from the original anxiety symptoms and may also include perceptual disturbances and more major effects such as convulsions or psychosis. The perceptual changes are characteristic and consist of hypersensitivity to stimuli such as noise and abnormal sensations of movement. The acute withdrawal syndrome tends to subside over a period of about two weeks. It is not apparently dose related, but has been related to the duration of treatment. It has not been described with treatment duration of less than one month (Hallstrom 1985). Of course, there are now numerous accounts of the more chronic withdrawal problems.

In summary, therefore, the benzodiazepines can be considered less effective than antidepressant medication in the treatment of agoraphobia. Alprazolam, the particular benzodiazepine which may be effective, is also a short-acting compound and these tend to be associated with a withdrawal syndrome. The evidence would, therefore, suggest that the benzodiazepines would not be drugs of choice in the treatment for agoraphobia and if used at all, should be used for short periods of less than a month.

Beta blockers, or more correctly the beta-adrenoceptor blocking drugs, have been used by some clinicians to reduce the physiological arousal of agoraphobics. They have been studied in three controlled trials. In the first study, Hafner and Milton (1977) looked at two groups of subjects who received exposure therapy. The first group received a single dose of propranolol prior to treatment sessions and the second group received a placebo. At follow-up, the results showed that the placebo group did better. In a second study, Noyes *et al.* (1984) compared propranolol with diazepam and again subjects in the propranolol group had an inferior outcome. In a third small study (Ullrich *et al.* 1975), alprenolol seemed to confer some advantage over a placebo (both were combined with exposure homework). However, there was no follow-up reported and the general methodology of the study could be criticized. In summary, therefore, there is very little evidence to suggest that beta blockers are helpful for agoraphobics.

(The reader is referred to Chapter 6 of this book, in which Gournay describes a comparison of exposure treatment in two groups of subjects, i.e., those taking and those not taking benzodiazepines.)

CONCLUSION

Pharmacotherapy is the usual physical treatment for agoraphobia. Telch *et al.* (1985) and Marks (1987) in extensive reviews, point to the considerable methodological problems of assessing the effectiveness of drugs in treatment and also to problems with side-effects and compliance. Research findings indicate an adjuvant role for drugs in a minority of patients, and drugs may also be offered when the patient refuses exposure treatment.

© Cherrie A. Coghlan

REFERENCES

Charney, S. and Heninger, G. (1985) 'Noradrenergic function and the mechanism of action of antianxiety treatment', *Arch. Gen. Psychiatry* 42: 458–67.

Cohen, S., Monteiro, W., and Marks, I. M. (1984) 'Two year follow-up of agoraphobics after exposure and imipramine', *Brit. J. Psychiatry* 144: 276–81.

Feighner, J., Aden, G., Fabre, L., Rickels, K., and Smith, W. (1983) 'Comparison of alprazolam, imipramine and placebo in the treatment of depression', *JAMA* 249: 3057–64.

Freeman, C. P. (1983) 'Neurotic disorders', in R. Kendell and A. Zeally, (eds) *Companion to Psychiatric Studies*, 330–54, Edinburgh: Churchill Livingstone.

Hafner, R. J., and Milton, F. (1977) 'The influence of propranolol on the exposure *in vivo* of agoraphobics', *Psychological Medicine* 7: 419–25.

Hallstrom, C. (1985) 'Benzodiazepines: clinical practice and control mechanisms', in K. Granville-Grossman (ed.) *Recent Advances in Clinical Psychiatry*, vol. 5: 143–59, Edinburgh: Churchill Livingstone.

Kelly, D., Guirguis, W., Frommer, E., Mitchell-Heggs, N., and Sargent, W., (1970) 'Treatment of phobic states with antidepressants', *Brit. J. Psychiat.* 116: 387–98.

Kelly, D., Mitchell-Heggs, N. and Sherman, D. (1971) 'Anxiety and lactate effects assessed clinically and physiologically', *British Journal of Psychiatry* 119: 129–41.

Klein, D. F. (1967) 'Importance of psychiatric diagnosis in prediction of clinical drug effects', *Arch. Gen. Psychiat.* 16: 118–26.

Klein, D. and Fink, M. (1962) 'Psychiatric reaction patterns to imipramine', *Amer. J. Psychiat.* 119: 432–8.

Lipsedge, M., Hajiott, P., Huggins, P., Napior, L., Pearce, J., Pike, D., and Rich, M. (1973) 'The management of severe agoraphobia: a comparison of iproniazid and systematic desensitisation', *Psychopharmacologia* 32: 67–80.

McNair, D. and Khan, R. (1981) 'Imipramine compared with a benzodiazepine for agoraphobia', in D. Klein and J. Rabkin (eds) *Anxiety – New Research and Changing Concepts*, 69–79, New York: Raven Press.

Marks, I. M. (1987) *Fears, Phobias and Rituals*, New York: Oxford University Press.

Marks, I., Boulougouris, J., and Marset, P. (1971) 'Flooding versus desensitisation in the treatment of phobic patients: a crossover study', *Brit. J. Psychiat.* 119: 353–5.

Marks, I., Grey, S., Cohen, S., Hill, R., Mawson, D., Ramm, L., and Stern, R. (1983) 'Imipramine and brief therapist-aided exposure in agoraphobics having self exposure homework: a controlled trial', *Arch. Gen. Psychiat.* 40: 153–62.

Matuzas, W. and Glass, R. (1983) 'Treatment of agoraphobia and panic attacks', *Arch. Gen. Psychiat.* 40: 220–2.

Mavissakalian, M., Michelson, L., and Dealy, R. (1983) 'Pharmacological treatment of agoraphobia: imipramine versus imipramine with practice', *Brit. J. Psychiat.* 143: 348–55.

Mavissakalian, M., and Pezel, J. (1985) 'Imipramine in the treatment of agoraphobia: dose response relationships', *Amer. J. Psychiat.* 142: 1032–7.

Mountjoy, C., Roth, M., Garside, R., and Leitch, I. (1977) 'A clinical trial of phenelzine in anxiety, depression and phobic neurosis', *Brit. J. Psychiat.* 131: 486–92.

Noyes, R., Anderson, D. J., and Clancy, J. (1984) 'Diazepam and propranolol in panic disorder and agoraphobia', *Arch. Gen. Psychiat.* 41: 287–92.

Noyes, R., Clancy, J., Conyell, W., Crowe, R., Chaudhry, D., and Doningo, D. (1985) 'A withdrawal syndrome after abrupt discontinuation of alprazolam', *Amer. J. Psychiat.* 124: 114–16.

Rickels, K., Csanalosi, I., Greisman, P., Cohen, D., Werblowosky, J., Ross, H., and Harris, H. (1983) 'A controlled clinical trial of alprazolam for the treatment of anxiety', *Amer. J. Psychiat.* 140: 82–4.

Sargent, W. and Dally, P. (1962) 'Treatment of anxiety state by antidepressant drugs', *Brit. Med. J.* 1: 6–9.

Sheehan, D., Ballager, J., and Jacobson, G. (1980) 'Treatment of endogenous anxiety with phobic, hysterical and hypochondriacal symptoms', *Arch. Gen. Psychiat.* 37: 51–9.

Sheehan, D. V. (1982) 'Panic attacks and phobias', *N. Eng. J. Med.* 307: 156–8.

Solyom, C., Heseltine, G., McClure, D., Solyom, C., Ledwidge, B., and Steinberg, G. (1973) 'Behaviour therapy versus drug therapy in the treatment of phobic neurosis', *Can. Psychiat. Ass. J.* 18: 25–31.

Solyom, C., Solyom, L., La Pierre, Y., Pecknold, J., and Merton, L. (1981) 'Phenelzine and exposure – the treatment of phobias', *Biol. Psychiat.* 3: 239–47.

Stern, R. and Marks, I. (1973) 'Brief and prolonged flooding: a comparison with agoraphobic patients', *Arch. Gen. Psychiat.* 28: 270–6.

Telch, M., Agras, W., Barr Taylor, C., Roth, W., and Gallen, C. (1985) 'Combined pharmacological and behavioural treatment for agoraphobia', *Behav. Res. Ther.* 23: 325–35.

Telch, M., Tearnon, B., and Barr Taylor, C. (1983) 'Antidepressant medication in the treatment of agoraphobia: a critical review', *Behav. Res. Ther.* 2: 505–17.

Tyrer, P., Candy, J., and Kelly, D. (1973) 'A study of the clinical effects of phenelzine and placebo in the treatment of phobic anxiety', *Psychopharmacologia* 32: 237–54.

Tyrer, P. J. (1984) 'Benzodiazepines on trial', *Brit. Med. J.* 288: 1101-2.

Ullrich, R., Crombach, G., and Peikert, V. (1975) 'Three flooding procedures for agoraphobia', in J. C. Brengelmann, (ed.) *Progress in Behaviour Therapy*, New York: Springer.

Zitrin, C., Klein, D., and Woerner, M. (1978) 'Behaviour therapy, supportive psychotherapy, imipramine and phobias', *Arch. Gen. Psychiat.* 35: 307–16.
—(1980) 'Treatment of agoraphobia with group exposure *in vivo* and imipramine', *Arch. Gen. Psychiat.* 37: 63–72.
Zitrin, C., Klein, D., Woerner, M.,, and Ross, D. (1983) 'Treatment of phobias', *Arch. Gen. Psychiat.* 40: 125–38.

Chapter Five

AN ALTERNATIVE CONSTRUCTION OF AGORAPHOBIA

DAVID A. WINTER

THEORETICAL FORMULATION

Personal construct theory: central concepts

George Kelly's (1955) personal construct theory views people as scientists who are constantly formulating hypotheses about their world and testing out, and if necessary revising, the predictions thus derived. These predictions have their basis in the system of hierarchically interrelated, bipolar, personal constructs which each individual develops in order to discriminate between, and to anticipate, events. A person may, for example, discriminate between others largely in terms of those who give him support and those who do not. This construct may be related to another construct in his system, distinguishing between people who never get angry and those who do, such that supportive people are viewed as likely never to get angry. If he then encounters a number of angry, supportive people or people who are neither angry nor supportive, this prediction will be invalidated and reconstruing will be called for. The individual's response may be to loosen the linkage between the two constructs, supportiveness no longer being seen as carrying any implications for the degree to which a person expresses anger; the relationship between them may be reversed, supportiveness now implying the likelihood of anger rather than its absence; or a new construct (e.g. 'passionately involved–uninvolved') may be developed which encompasses the possibility of being both supportive and angry.

People are not always good scientists, however, in that they do not always revise their hypotheses in order to accommodate the results of their experimentation, or they may virtually abandon the experimental enterprise altogether. Indeed, Kelly (1955: 831) regarded a psychological disorder as 'any personal construction which is used repeatedly in spite of consistent invalidation'. It is also clear that some constructs in an individual's system are more resistant to revision following invalidation than are others. The former tend to be 'superordinate' constructs, which carry many implications for other constructs in the system and any change in which will therefore reverberate throughout the system more than will a change in a 'subordinate' construct. Particularly threatening, and therefore likely to be resisted, is a change in that subset of superordinate constructs, central to a person's identity, which Kelly termed 'core' constructs. Some of these core constructions will concern the individual's role in relation to others, and Kelly viewed guilt, another factor militating against change, as the experience of finding oneself acting in a way inconsistent with one's core role. It should be noted that this need not involve behaving 'badly' in a conventional moral sense: the agoraphobic who has habitually seen herself as reliant on her husband may find the increasing independence which accompanies symptom loss to be a guilt-provoking prospect, particularly if, as we shall consider later, independence carries other undesirable implications for her.

A further type of change which is likely to be resisted is one that reduces the predictability of the individual's world. Kelly regarded anxiety as the experience of finding some aspect of one's world largely unconstruable, and it may be, for example, that loss of a symptom will be resisted because this would reduce the certainty of the person's world and would therefore be anxiety-provoking. Indeed, any revision of their view of world is likely to cause an individual to experience a certain amount of anxiety. Nevertheless, most people, as noted earlier, do constantly revise their constructions without suffering intolerable anxiety, and are able to do this because their superordinate constructs are 'permeable', in that they can encompass the apparent inconsistencies in construing which may be encountered in the process of reconstruction. Kelly's view was that this is not the case with the neurotic person since their superordinate constructs are impermeable, and there is now a certain amount of research evidence for this formulation in that neurotics have been found to display 'a characteristic pattern of tight, polarised construing and intolerance of ambiguity . . . particularly apparent in the construct subsystems concerning the symptoms and the self' (Winter 1985a: 122). Other features of construing have also been found to characterize the neurotic, namely that he is

94

someone who sees himself as unlike others in general and unlike his parents in particular, who is dissatisfied with himself, who tends to extreme judgements and operates with a less complex construct system than do normals, and who tends to construe others in ways which depart from consensual values in respect of certain attributes.

(Ryle and Breen 1972: 488)

As well as these general neurotic characteristics, certain specific ways of construing might be expected to be observed in the agoraphobic, as we shall now consider.

A personal construct theory model of agoraphobia

Applying the concepts previously outlined to the predicament of the agoraphobic, it is apparent that as a 'personal scientist' such an individual limits their experimentation within fairly narrow confines. Agoraphobia might therefore be considered to reflect an expression at the behavioural level of the process which Kelly termed constriction, in which a person draws in the outer boundaries of their perceptual field to exclude from awareness material which their constructs are ill-equipped to predict and which therefore generates anxiety and confusion. Such an explanation would regard the agoraphobic as behaving in an essentially similar manner to the culture-shocked tourist, whose response to the largely unpredictable events with which they are confronted is to spend their holiday within the safely predictable confines of the hotel swimming pool. As Lorenzini and Sassaroli (1988:333) have put it, agoraphobic avoidance behaviour 'aims at defending the predictive skills of the subject who gives up predicting any further because he runs the risk of not successfully predicting anything at all'.

If agoraphobia is indeed a strategy whereby the person constricts their perceptual field in order to avoid events which they find unpredictable, what are these anxiety-provoking events? Some clues are provided by the work of authors of alternative theoretical persuasions which has indicated the agoraphobic's difficulties in situations of interpersonal conflict and intense emotion, linking the onset of agoraphobia to such situations (Goldstein and Chambless 1978, Guidano and Liotti 1983). Goldstein (1982: 185), for example, states that agoraphobics 'go to great lengths to avoid such feelings as anger and frustration', while the view of Guidano and Liotti (1983: 225) is

95

that such clients 'do not possess articulate cognitive structures capable of dealing with emotions' and that their 'theories of emotion do not allow them to recognize the affective nature of certain inner states, so that they are incapable of relating them to their life's events' (212). Drawing on attribution theory, these formulations go on to suggest that in such individuals the autonomic arousal generated by conflict situations is inappropriately labelled as anxiety or fear rather than, for example, anger. As Rachman (1984) has noted, if the agoraphobic does express anger, particularly with their partner in a dependent relationship, the effect is often 'a temporary reduction in the fear and immobility that characterise agoraphobia' (69).

Rephrased in personal construct theory terms, these observations would suggest that the agoraphobic has a poorly elaborated subsystem of constructs concerning emotions, particularly those relating to interpersonal conflict, the relative unconstruability of which leads the client to experience anxiety in, and to adopt a constrictive response to, such situations. If, as some writers on agoraphobia have noted, the outside world is construed as consisting of hostile strangers (Guidano and Liotti 1983) or of situations, such as the risk of marital infidelity (Abraham 1955, Hafner 1979), which carry the potential for conflict, it will be avoided. The vicious circle which then develops has been indicated by Fransella's (1972) observation that the more the client centres their life around not leaving home, the more meaningful the agoraphobic way of life will become and the less structured, and therefore more anxiety-provoking, the prospect of venturing into the outside world will appear. It should be noted, however, that the 'homeostatic model', in which symptoms such as those of the agoraphobic are assumed to provide the client with some structure, has been criticized by Semerari and Mancini (1987) for its lack of correspondence with the client's description of the suffering which they experience. They propose instead a model of 'recursive self-invalidation' which draws on a formulation of agoraphobia put forward by Lorenzini and Sassaroli (1987, 1988), who have emphasized the mother's role in inhibiting the exploratory, hypothesis-testing, behaviour of their pre-agoraphobic child. Lorenzini and Sassaroli suggest that the future agoraphobic comes to view exploration and attachment as incompatible and, in the pre-pathological phase, often chooses the former option and construes himself or herself as strong and independent. The situation which precipitates agoraphobic symptoms in such an individual is, according to these authors, one, such as a marriage or a loss, that invalidates the construction of the self as autonomous and strong. As Semerari and Mancini point out, this invalidation produces anxiety and threat, which in turn invalidate even further the previous self-construction. Such a vicious circle is most likely to occur when the client does not have available constructs to make sense of the experience of anxiety and threat other than those, such as strong/weak, whose invalidation was responsible for the anxiety and threat in the first place. To quote Semerari and Mancini,

> the tighter . . . the implicative connections, the less the agoraphobic will have at his disposal autonomous subsystems from those defined as strong/autonomous for construing his emotional experiences, the more probable will be the establishment of a vicious cycle of recursive self-invalidation. In other words, the findings of experimental research on neurosis can be read as favourable preconditions for the establishment of the vicious cycle. The same self-established process of validation and invalidation produces a retightening of the symptomatic area. The neurosis is, in essence, a self-perpetuating process.
>
> (Semerari and Mancini 1987)

Dunnett (1988) also regards phobias as involving invalidation, but he emphasizes that the phobic object poses the threat of invalidation of a superordinate core role construct which is applicable in virtually every area of the phobic's life: 'Avoidance becomes understandable as an attempt to preserve the core constructs under threat' (326).

That difficulties in the recognition and expression of emotions are not confined to the agoraphobic has been suggested by Liotti and Guidano (1976: 161), who have observed that the wives of agoraphobic men 'showed a fear of any expression of aggressive behaviour. For the majority this fear amounted to a phobia of violence.' Similarly, Hafner (1977a), who has made use of such psychodynamic concepts as repression and denial in exploring the agoraphobic's marital situation, concluded that 'any study aimed at understanding phobic disorders in married females which fails to acknowledge the importance of denial in their husbands seems unlikely to be fully successful' (294). Carrying as it does the implication that an individual is not accepting the 'correct' view of events, denial is a concept which does not rest easily with the basic philosophical assumption of personal construct theory that numerous alternative constructions of reality are possible.

Nevertheless, although Kelly himself did not employ such notions as denial and the unconscious, he did acknowledge that a person may have a low level of cognitive awareness of some of their constructions. For example, the person's construing will be at a low level of cognitive awareness 'when he deals with elements which lie at the outer extremities of the ranges of convenience of his available constructs' (Kelly 1955: 476). Denial of negative feelings, as described by Hafner, may therefore reflect a low cognitive awareness of an area in which the individual's construing is poorly elaborated. A further example which Kelly provided of low cognitive awareness is what he termed submergence, in which one pole of a particular construct is relatively unavailable. The individual who is regarded as denying hostile feelings may, therefore, exhibit submergence of those poles of their constructs which imply conflict with others.

These formulations of agoraphobia, from different perspectives, would therefore suggest that low cognitive awareness of construing in the area of interpersonal conflict characterizes at least some agoraphobics and at least some of their spouses (for the analyses of Goldstein and Chambless and Hafner both include the qualification that the pattern of denial of conflict is only apparent in a subgroup of agoraphobics). Hafner's research also indicated that, rather than there necessarily being a similarity in the pattern displayed by the agoraphobic and their spouse, complementarity was apparent in the expression or denial of hostility, and in the self-esteem, of the more severely disabled members of his female agoraphobic sample and their husbands (Hafner 1977b). For example, symptom loss and recovery of self-esteem in his agoraphobics during behaviour therapy were accompanied by changes in the reverse direction in their husbands, who recovered when the phobics relapsed. Such observations, coupled with reports of marriages characterized by phobia in one partner and 'counterphobia' in the other (Holmes 1982), may be accommodated by the notion of a 'family construct system' shared by both partners and defining the 'slots' which they may occupy (Procter 1981). If, for example, the family construct system of an agoraphobic and her husband contrasts the role of weak, anxious invalid with that of strong, confident care-giver, the husband may be able to occupy the latter position only as long as his wife is disabled by her phobic symptoms: when she loses these, a reversal of positions on this construct may occur such that he now becomes the weak, anxious member of the dyad. As mentioned on p. 96 a further report by Hafner

(1979) also suggests that marital infidelity may be a superordinate construct in the family construct system of some agoraphobics and their spouses. Thus, he describes how 'agoraphobia exercised a protective function for these women, helping to reassure them that they could not in reality act upon their sexual fantasies or impulses' (103).

To summarize the above discussion, it has been proposed that agoraphobia is a manifestation of a constrictive strategy, and that each of the following features of construing in the client and their spouse may be conducive to the development and maintenance of agoraphobic symptoms, although this is not to suggest that they will all be relevant in every such case:

1 poorly elaborated construct subsystems concerning emotions and interpersonal conflict, such that there is low cognitive awareness of construing in these areas;
2 construal of the ability to go out as carrying implications, such as the risk of marital infidelity, which may be inconsistent with the client's core role;
3 a superordinate construct relating to marital infidelity;
4 a family construct system in which the client and their spouse occupy opposite poles of constructs concerning weakness and strength, such that, for example, the agoraphobic exhibits low, and their spouse high, self-esteem;
5 construal of exploration and attachment as incompatible, perhaps as a result of a family background which discouraged experimentation;
6 serial invalidation of the client's initial construction of the self as strong.

PERSONAL CONSTRUCT THEORY INVESTIGATIONS OF AGORAPHOBIA

Features of construing in agoraphobics and their spouses: research evidence

Considerable methodological problems have been faced in testing the formulations of agoraphobia discussed in the previous section concerning limited awareness of interpersonal conflict. Hafner (1983: 380), for example, states that 'Since psychological defence mechanisms such as repression and denial are, by definition, unconscious processes, the technical problems of their systematic measurement are enormous.' Such problems are evident in the numerous analyses which he has published of the results of a single study of the response of agoraphobics to behaviour therapy, in which repression and denial are assumed to be variously indicated by low scores on questionnaire measures of hostility, symptomatology, and marital dissatisfaction, high scores on a friendliness scale, and inconsistency of responses on a mood state questionnaire (Hafner 1977a, 1977b, 1983, 1984, Milton and Hafner 1979). He therefore makes the assumption, which contrasts markedly with the 'credulous approach' to clients advocated by Kelly, that those of his subjects who do not report negative feelings on a questionnaire must be denying such feelings. A study of spouses of agoraphobics by Arrindell and Emmelkamp (1985) displayed similar problems in that it tested the seemingly contradictory hypotheses that such individuals would obtain high scores on measures of psychopathology but also on measures of defensive denial of psychological problems. One of the instruments used by these workers, and also by Turner *et al.* (1983) in studying agoraphobics, was the Repression–Sensitization scale, but such a gross measure of the extent to which an individual reports psychological distress seems of little relevance to the expression or denial of interpersonal conflict. Of greater relevance has been the more direct examination by some workers of clients' perception of, or response to, marital conflict and criticism. Fisher and Wilson (1985), for example, demonstrated that agoraphobics show little emotional reaction to scenes of marital conflict, a finding which supports the denial component of the Goldstein and Chambless formulation but not the mislabelling of anger as anxiety. Peter and Hand (1987), while providing no evidence that agoraphobics deny critical feelings, did find that the spouses of such clients displayed little criticism of their partners and were unable to perceive their partners' criticism of them.

A major problem with some of the above studies is the use of measuring instruments with different theoretical roots to the concepts which they are attempting to measure. By contrast, a personal construct theory formulation of agoraphobia may be appropriately tested with the major assessment method derived from the theory, repertory grid technique (Fransella and Bannister 1977). In a grid, the subject sorts (for example, using a rating scale) a number of elements, such as significant people in their lives, in terms of constructs which have either been elicited from, or supplied to, him or her. Analysis of the resulting matrix, commonly by a computer program such as Slater's (1972) INGRID, provides measures of how important, or superordinate, particular constructs are in the subject's system; of the interrelationships between constructs, the statistical relationship between two constructs being assumed to reflect their psychological relationship for the subject; of the degree of structure in the system; and of the perceived dissimilarity of, or psychological distance between, particular elements for the subject. Using such measures, it is possible to provide operational definitions of some of the features of construing which it has been suggested on p. 99 may characterize the agoraphobic and their spouse. Thus:

1. low cognitive awareness of constructs concerning interpersonal conflict (e.g. angry–not angry') may be reflected in a low degree of discrimination between grid elements on these constructs, such that they account for a low percentage of the variation in the grid; a tendency to allocate elements primarily to the pole of the construct which implies lack of conflict; and very favourable perceptions of such significant others as parents;
2. the construal of the ability to go out as implying the possibility of marital infidelity may be reflected in the tendency to construe people who are able to go out as likely to be unfaithful, such that a high correlation is obtained between the ratings of grid elements on these two constructs;
3. the superordinacy of a construct concerning marital infidelity may be indicated by such a construct differentiating highly between grid elements and accounting for a high percentage of the variation in the grid;
4. the low self-esteem of the agoraphobic may be revealed by a high psychological distance between the grid elements 'self' and 'ideal self', and their spouse's high self-esteem by a low distance between these elements in the spouse's grid.

A study employing a grid with supplied constructs, several of these selected from constructs elicited from agoraphobics in previous pilot studies, did find that the above patterns tended to differentiate the grids of agoraphobics from those of non-agoraphobic neurotics and normal subjects (Winter and Gournay 1987). Agoraphobics perceived less anger and selfishness than did other subjects, and less jealousy than other neurotics. They also construed their parents significantly more favourably than did normal subjects. They were more likely than other neurotics to construe independent people, and people who are able to go out, as likely to be unfaithful, although normal subjects displayed this tendency to an even greater degree. In addition, as with other neurotics, they showed lower self-esteem than did normals. Differences between the spouses of the three groups of subjects were less marked, but the spouses of agoraphobics did perceive less anger, lack of caring, and selfishness than the control groups. Within the agoraphobic sample, severity of symptomatology was associated with clients and their spouses discriminating between grid elements significantly less in terms of selfishness and jealousy and clients showing greater discrimination in terms of possible infidelity. High symptom levels in the agoraphobics were also, as predicted, associated with their showing low, and their spouses high, self-esteem.

A considerable degree of similarity was apparent in this study between the construing of agoraphobics and their spouses, and the greater this similarity, as reflected in an index of correlation (Slater 1977) between the grid of a client and that of his or her spouse, the fewer hours per week did the agoraphobic spend out of the house. It appeared, then, that these clients' phobic symptoms allowed them to delimit their social world to spouses whose construing was similar to their own, with the result that the relationship between agoraphobic and spouse would be likely to be characterized by mutual validation of constructions. One area of unexpected similarity between the grids of agoraphobic and spouse was that they idealized the ability to go out, imagining that if the agoraphobic lost his or her symptoms they would each become more similar to their ideal selves than they were even before the commencement of the phobic difficulties. Further, the more intense the agoraphobic's symptoms the more favourable was the construction of the ability go out by both phobic and spouse. This may reflect what Fransella (1972) has termed the 'if only syndrome': the person who has a fantasy that they could attain all their ideals if only they were able to go out is only able to maintain this fantasy as long as they retain their agoraphobic symptoms. An explanation may thus also be provided for the observation by Guidano and Liotti (1983: 218) that 'even in advanced cases of agoraphobia, it is quite usual to hear statements such as "When I recover from this damned illness, I'll be the freest and most enterprising person in the world."'

Some of the relationships demonstrated in this study between agoraphobic symptomatology and the construing of interpersonal conflict and infidelity have now been replicated in two further samples. These have provided further indications that agoraphobic symptoms are associated with low cognitive awareness of selfishness and jealousy, with idealization of the mother and of the ability to go out, and with agoraphobic and spouse differentiating highly between others in terms of possible infidelity, suggesting that this is a superordinate construct for them. Other recent studies carried out from a personal construct theory perspective have also provided evidence of the agoraphobic's difficulties in construing interpersonal conflict and in the expression of negative feelings, as well as revealing further aspects of construing which characterize such clients. For example, the use of a questionnaire concerning subjects' perceptions of their parents allowed Frazer (1980) to suggest that the agoraphobic's family background was characterized by strict rules concerning emotional expression and by protection from invalidation of construing, so that invalidating events later in life come to generate considerable anxiety. He also employed a repertory grid, the results of which indicated lower self-esteem, and less identification with their fathers and with other males, in agoraphobics than in non-agoraphobic neurotics and normal subjects. O'Sullivan (1985), comparing the grids of agoraphobics, clients suffering from anxiety states, and normal subjects, concluded that agoraphobics construed assertion and the expression of negative feelings more unfavourably than did the other groups but did not identify more strongly with feminine stereotypes. She also found that agoraphobics used fewer constructs relating to change, and showed few strong relationships between their self-constructs and other constructs, a finding which she takes to indicate a rigid core structure which is impermeable in Kelly's (1955) sense that it cannot easily accommodate new events. She therefore suggests that 'agoraphobia occurs as a response of definition or constriction (because of a lack of relevant superordinate permeable constructs) to novel events implying core-structure change' (O'Sullivan 1984: 251). Lorenzini and Sassaroli (1987, 1988), as we have seen, have based their research on a more elaborate theoretical formulation of agoraphobia and its aetiology. Using repertory grids, they found that, compared to non-phobic neurotic clients, phobics employed fewer constructs concerning emotions and differentiated between these constructs less, construed situations of exploration and change as more likely to provoke anxiety and less likely to be associated with attachment, and perceived themselves, particularly themselves when alone, less favourably.

Construing and response to therapy

If agoraphobia reflects a constrictive process in the individual who, perhaps in common with their spouse, shows little cognitive awareness of interpersonal conflict, undifferentiated construing of emotions, but a superordinate construct of infidelity, the more marked this pattern the more resistant to therapy the agoraphobic might be expected to be. Support for this view has been provided by an investigation of the response of agoraphobics to behaviour therapy, which demonstrated that those clients who differentiated highly between others in terms of possible infidelity, but showed little differentiation in terms of anger, at pre-treatment assessment were less likely to display symptomatic improvement during therapy (Winter and Gournay 1987). In addition, the more superordinate the construct of infidelity for their spouses, in that it differentiated highly between people for them, the less symptomatic improvement the agoraphobics showed at three-month follow-up. Another feature of construing predictive of poor outcome, in terms of the extent of increase in the number of hours which clients spent out of the house, was its tightness of organization, as reflected in a large first, and a small second, component from principal component analysis of the grid. In other words, the more unidimensional a client's view of the world the less likely were they to respond to therapy, a finding which has also been obtained with other client groups (Fransella 1972, Button 1983). As such unidimensionality of construing has been regarded as an index of constriction (Sheehan 1981, Ashworth *et al.* 1982), it may be concluded that the more constricted clients showed a less favourable therapeutic outcome. However, the grid measure most highly predictive of outcome post-treatment, and more so than any non-grid variable, was the perceived similarity of the ideal self to the self before the onset of phobic symptoms. Clients showing greatest improvement during therapy were those who had available to them a well-elaborated positive construction of their non- phobic role based on a previous experience of such a state rather than an idealistic fantasy.

Some of these findings concerning response to behaviour therapy have now been replicated in a further sample. Once again, different-iation between others in terms of anger was highly predictive of positive therapeutic outcome, while those clients who perceived most infidelity, and differentiated between others more in terms of this construct, showed significantly less reduction in depression during treatment. Furthermore, separate analyses of their ratings of family members and of people outside the family indicated that these relationships held constant regardless of whom the client was construing. With constructs concerning selfishness and jealousy, however, this was not the case in that clients who made greater use of these constructs in differentiating between their family members were more responsive to therapy whereas the opposite trend was apparent in their construing of people outside the family. Clients were therefore less likely to venture into the outside world if they saw it as highly characterized by selfishness and jealousy but more likely if they used such constructs to describe their family members. This is consistent with the observation that

> agoraphobics believe that only members of the family or people that they know very well are willing to help them in case of danger or indisposition. Strangers are considered indifferent, more prone to criticism or actually hostile, than to giving assistance.

> (Guidano and Liotti 1983: 217)

It might follow that agoraphobic symptoms are less likely to persist if family members are construed as selfish, and therefore presumably less likely to be helpful, while people outside the family are construed as unselfish.

Two further studies have examined the relationship between phobics' construing and their response to behaviour therapy. One, by Wright (1969), demonstrated that clients who were least likely to change during therapy were those for whom change in phobic symptomatology implied many other changes, particularly in their interpersonal world. Another, by Oatley and Hodgson (1987), has employed a repertory grid to examine the relationship between agoraphobics' construing of their husbands and their response to behaviour therapy, testing hypotheses deriving from the work of Hafner. Some evidence was provided that those clients who perceived their husbands as controlling were less likely to respond to therapy if their husbands became depressed. Clients' hostility, as indicated by grid measures of the extent to which they blamed, and felt irritated by, their husbands, was not significantly predictive of response to therapy. This study is not informed by personal construct theory and, perhaps as a result, makes only limited use of the grid, although the authors note that they will report elsewhere further analyses of their grid data.

Therapeutic reconstruction

The assumption that particular features of construing underlie phobic symptoms would suggest that the loss of these symptoms would necessitate reconstruing. It is conceivable that a behavioural intervention, by increasing the client's opportunities for experimentation, may facilitate such reconstruing, a possibility which was explored in a study of spider phobics by Watts and Sharrock (1985), who found that such individuals were characterized by their lack of differentiation between constructs applied to spiders but that this was not significantly modified by desensitization. However, in one of the studies discussed on p. 104, some significant changes in construing were apparent in the grid scores of agoraphobics over the course of behaviour therapy (Winter and Gournay 1987). Clients not only increased in self-esteem, construing themselves as more similar to their ideal selves, but they also came to differentiate more between others in terms of selfishness and caring or its lack. Reduction in their phobic symptoms was associated with reduction in the tightness of their construing and with an increase in the positive implications of confidence, which became more strongly associated with being caring and unselfish. Symptom reduction was also related to the ability to go out becoming a less superordinate construct for clients, but one which they saw as more highly characterizing the spouse's ideal partner; as well as to a reduction in their construal of independent people as likely to be unfaithful. However, at three-month follow-up there was an increasing concern with infidelity, particularly in those clients who were spending more time out of the house, and reduction in agoraphobic symptoms at this time was also associated with a greater tendency to construe independent people as uncaring. It appeared, therefore, that these clients were becoming increasingly aware of the possible negative implications of their growing independence; further assessments will indicate whether this may presage a return of agoraphobic symptoms to forestall such anticipated risks as infidelity.

Some reconstruing was also apparent in their spouses during the clients' therapy. They came to construe the agoraphobic more favourably, and the ability to go out and confidence as less highly associated with possible infidelity, this tendency, and the tendency to associate going out with being caring, being most apparent at follow-up in the spouses of those clients who had shown the greatest symptom loss. For these latter spouses, the ability to go out became a less salient construct, although, unexpectedly, so did selfishness both for them and for their partners. More in line with predictions was the finding that at follow-up spouses were less likely to see selfishness as an implication of independence. Finally, reduction in the agoraphobics' symptoms was correlated with a loosening in their spouses' construing, just as it had been in the agoraphobics themselves, suggesting that recovery from agoraphobia is associated with phobic and spouse developing a less constricted view of the world and one more conducive to experimentation.

Before concluding this discussion of empirical work on construing and reconstruction in agoraphobics and their spouses, it may be of interest to consider an alternative approach, adopted by Schwartz and Michelson (1987). Although cognitive-behavioural in orientation, these workers have drawn on a body of research with links to personal construct theory (Benjafield and Adams-Webber 1976) to propose that the optimal state of mind for coping with stress is one in which there is an internal dialogue between positive and negative cognitions balanced in the 'golden section' ratio, conducive to most effective processing of threatening information, of 0.62:0.38. They have provided some evidence that the cognitive balance of agoraphobics during therapy moved towards this ratio from an initial position which tended to be the complete opposite of it. At three-month follow-up, positive cognitions predominated to an even greater degree, and although according to the model this would suggest less optimal functioning, the authors propose that it reflects a 'protective buffer' while the client is coping with extreme threat. Changes in cognitive balance were found to relate to those observed on independent measures, but the changes characterizing the particular types of treatment studied (relaxation training, paradoxical intention, and exposure) were somewhat different.

IMPLICATIONS FOR CLINICAL PRACTICE

A personal construct theory approach to assessment

In attempting to arrive at an understanding of a client's predicament, the personal construct theorist will essentially try to view the world through the client's eyes and, at least initially, will take this view at face value. In the case of the phobic client, the initial approach may be to explore their construing of their phobic object, perhaps with the aid of repertory grid technique. The simplest application of the grid with such individuals is to employ it similarly to a fear thermometer, with phobic objects as elements and, for example, emotional reactions to these objects as constructs. Used in this way, it has been found to be less than impressive as a predictor of phobic behaviour (Griffiths and Joy 1971). Generally, however, the concern of the personal construct theorist will be less with assessing the client's degree of avoidance of the phobic object than with the features of construing which might underlie this avoidance.

If constructs are elicited from the client, rather than supplied to them as in the Griffiths and Joy study, the personal meaning of, and something of the threat posed by, the phobic object may be revealed. Dunnett (1988:326), for example, describes a spider phobic who construed spiders as 'behaving as though I was a bit of the furniture', while Huber and Altmaier (1983) examined the constructs provided by snake phobic and non-phobic subjects in describing their experience of a behavioural avoidance test involving a boa constrictor. Phobics' constructs were found to be more likely to indicate a negative view of the past, and those constructs which they judged most salient were more likely to imply threat in both their poles. The authors conclude that these latter constructs, contrasting threat with its negation, have a more limited predictive range than the threat-related constructs of non-phobics, which tended to contrast threat with a more elaborated contrast pole.

The relationships between constructs concerning a client's phobic symptoms and other constructs in their system may be examined by the procedure of 'laddering', in which, taking one of the client's constructs, they are asked to which of its poles they would prefer to be allocated and why. The latter question elicits a construct more superordinate than the first, and the procedure may then be repeated with this new construct and continued until the client is unable to provide any further constructs. Using this method with an agoraphobic client, Wright (1970) was able to demonstrate that one of her phobic situations, being enclosed, was associated with 'doing something that I'm made to do', but that this had the positive implication of taking responsibility. By contrast, feeling relaxed was associated by her with 'doing as I please' and shirking responsibility. Laddering therefore revealed a major dilemma underlying the client's phobic symptoms and one which, although Wright does not report its use in this way, could form the focus of psychotherapy.

A client, like Wright's, whose agoraphobic symptoms carry some positive implications may be expected to resist the loss of these symptoms. The inclusion of various different self-elements in a repertory grid may also reveal other reasons for the client's resistance to therapy, as in the case of Crispin, an aging hippy whose agoraphobic symptoms commenced at the end of the 'sixties' (Winter 1988). At first sight the very unfavourable self-construction revealed by his grid, contrasting with a very positive construal of himself without phobic symptoms, suggested that he might be highly motivated to lose his symptoms and therefore likely to be responsive to a behavioural treatment programme. However, closer examination of the grid results indicated that he construed himself as he was prior to the onset of his agoraphobic symptoms in a highly negative light: as someone who 'did not accept responsibilities', 'did not take relationships seriously', and was 'cocky', 'only interested in himself', and an 'I'm all right Jack type'. Like many of the clients in the research study discussed on p. 102, he therefore anticipated that recovery from his agoraphobia would transform him into a much more ideal person than he had ever been, and in fact imagined that if he lost his symptoms he would rapidly achieve fame and fortune as a guitarist. His failure to complete behavioural homework assignments, and eventual dropping out of therapy, may perhaps be seen as allowing him to preserve the unrealistic fantasy that his life would be perfect if only he were not shackled by agoraphobic symptoms.

Sylvia, like Crispin, construed herself as very distant from her ideal self, and as 'unable to go anywhere', 'unable to stand up for herself', 'losing control easily', 'weak', 'backward', and 'quiet'. By contrast, she viewed herself before her agoraphobic symptoms commenced and herself if she were to lose these symptoms during therapy as close to her ideal: 'able to go anywhere with confidence', 'able to stand up for herself', 'in control of herself', 'never giving in to anything', 'clever', and 'extroverted'. Her resistance to behaviour therapy could therefore not be explained in terms of an unfavourable construal of herself before the onset of her agoraphobia, but the probable reasons for it were clearly apparent in the further finding from her grid that her perception of how her husband would like her to be was even more distant from her ideal self than was her present self-perception. This suggested that she anticipated that if she were to lose her phobic symptoms and to become a less phobic, stronger, more confident person, a marital conflict would be the likely result. Attempts to persuade her husband to attend conjoint therapy sessions failed, but it later transpired that he was having an incestuous relationship with two of their daughters. On his imprisonment for incest Sylvia lost her agoraphobic symptoms.

As we have seen, consideration of the construct system of the client's spouse may be as pertinent to an understanding of the maintenance of the client's agoraphobic symptoms as is assessment of their own construing. Of particular relevance may be shared constructions in their 'family construct system', as in the case of Joan and Jack, whose repertory grids indicated that they both associated the ability to go out with the likelihood of marital infidelity (Winter 1988). A further grid assessment at the end of Joan's behaviour therapy, during which her agoraphobic symptoms reduced in intensity, revealed that infidelity had become a much more superordinate construct for Jack over this period and that his self-esteem had also reduced markedly. Not unpredictably, the increase in Joan's self-esteem during therapy was found not to be maintained at three-month follow-up grid assessment, and as she once again construed herself in a negative light Jack recovered his self-esteem and his concern with infidelity lessened.

Therapeutic implications

It will be apparent from the above that assessment of the client's construct system, perhaps with the aid of repertory grid or laddering techniques, is likely to elucidate the contrast for them to being agoraphobic. Also apparent is that the implications of this alternative may not be altogether favourable: the ability to go out may imply for the client and/or their spouse the possibility of marital infidelity or some other threatening or guilt-provoking prospect; it may present the risk of testing out cherished, but unrealistic, fantasies; or it may confront the client with largely unconstruable events, and hence with considerable anxiety. As we have seen, such clients are likely to be resistant to therapeutic approaches which do not take their constructions into account, but from the personal construct theory viewpoint 'are behaving perfectly reasonably *from their own perspective.* It is the therapist who is doing a poor job of subsuming the client's construing if they merely see the client's behaviour as resistance – and therefore something to be overcome' (Fransella 1985: 300).

A personal construct psychotherapy approach in such cases would focus on the elaboration of a viable alternative construction of the self as non-agoraphobic: one which neither carries negative implications nor is so idealistic as to be unattainable; and one which offers at least as much structure and meaning as does the agoraphobic self-construction. It would not involve extensive discussion of symptoms because this might only serve to make more meaningful the agoraphobic way of life (as, incidentally, may societies for agoraphobics unless carefully organized). Rather, the implications of being a person who can go out would be likely to be considered at some length, such discussion perhaps being facilitated by assignments similar to those employed by a behaviour therapist, by role-playing, or by asking the client to write a characterization of the self as they would be without their agoraphobic symptoms (Fransella 1981). Whilst a range of therapeutic techniques and strategies may be employed, underlying all of them would be an emphasis on experimentation, on encouraging the client to test out constructions relating to their agoraphobic complaints and to revise these constructions if they are found wanting.

If, as in clients studied in the research investigations discussed earlier, their agoraphobic symptoms seem to have a basis in low cognitive awareness of construing in the area of interpersonal conflict, therapy might also usefully focus on the elaboration of this sub-system of constructs. The aims of such an approach may not be dissimilar to some of those underlying the psychotherapeutic strategy employed by Guidano and Liotti (1983) with agoraphobic clients, for example 'Appropriate relabeling of emotional experiences' and 'Elucidation of the relationship between emotions and ongoing thoughts' (231). The findings of the Winter and Gournay (1987) study would suggest that in many cases it may be advisable to include the agoraphobic's spouse in such therapeutic ventures in that the spouse may share many aspects of the agoraphobic's view of the world and would therefore be likely to invalidate any revised constructions which the client develops during therapy. Personal construct psychotherapy with such couples would therefore focus on the reconstruction of their 'family construct system'. It may be, for example, that this system has 'very few within-boundary constructs – everyone in the family is kind and considerate and helps each other' but that 'this identity is maintained by its contrast – people outside the family boundary are inconsiderate, selfish and mean' (Procter 1981: 361). Therapy in this instance 'will consist of elaborating the main construct, differentiating the people in the family and in the external social network' (362). In other couples, the focus of therapy may be on the invalidation of constructs which appear to be contributing to the maintenance of the client's symptoms and on the elaboration and validation of alternative constructions. If agoraphobic and spouse occupy opposite poles of family constructs concerning weakness and strength, with the result that there is a tendency towards homeostasis, interventions may focus on lessening this dichotomy, for example by discussing ways in which each partner combines weakness and strength and by developing superordinate constructs which can subsume both weakness and strength.

Personal construct and alternative approaches to the understanding and treatment of agoraphobia

Various similarities and contrasts between the personal construct and other perspectives on agoraphobia have been touched upon in this chapter, and these will now be further elaborated in relation to the behavioural, cognitive, psychodynamic, and systems theory perspectives.

Kelly's view of learning theory models of neurosis was that it was their lack of attention to the client's constructions which led them to find the persistence of self-destructive behaviour by the client so paradoxical (Mowrer 1950). 'Within the client's own limited construction system he may be faced with a dilemma but not with a paradox' (Kelly 1969: 85), as is evident in several of the case examples earlier discussed. Nonetheless, despite his criticisms of their theoretical basis, Kelly was not averse to the use of such behavioural techniques as graduated exposure to a phobic object, viewing them as procedures which 'enable the patient to become his own experimenter' (Kelly 1970: 268). As we have seen, methods such as these may allow the client to elaborate his or her construing of a non-phobic self and therefore might well form part of the armamentarium of the personal construct therapist in their treatment of agoraphobic clients. Furthermore, research findings would suggest that the treatment expectancies of phobic clients may be particularly favourable towards, and therefore predictive of positive response to, behavioural approaches (Caine et al. 1981, Norton et al. 1983), such clients' presentation of symptoms with an external locus and their preference for a directive, structured form of treatment both reflecting their characteristic view of the world, their 'personal style' (Winter 1985b), and agoraphobics with a more external locus of control being more likely to respond to behaviour therapy (Michelson *et al.* 1983). Wright (1970: 222) regards the symptom as 'a part of a person's experience of himself which he has singled out and circumscribed as in some way incongruous with the rest of his experience of himself', and this certainly appears to be the case with many phobics. Bannister (1965), for example, describes an agoraphobic client whose repertory grid indicated that the construct 'can go anywhere with confidence' was orthogonal to all her other constructs, suggesting that she saw her symptom as an isolated problem independent of other aspects of her view of herself and of the world. A client such as this might be expected to be particularly responsive to an approach, such as behaviour therapy, which also treats her symptom as an isolated problem. However, although Bannister observed a loosening in her construct relationships, and fluctuations in her phobic symptoms, during intensive psychotherapy and behaviour therapy, post-treatment assessment revealed a re-establishment of her original pattern of construing and the return of her symptoms to their original level of intensity. He relates the absence of any substantial reconstruing in this client to the fact that her psychotherapy was non-directive.

This discussion of behaviour therapy would suggest that intervention at the behavioural level may be the most meaningful initial treatment approach for many agoraphobic clients, but that the clients' behavioural experiments may best be seen as opportunities for them to test out their constructions and for the therapist actively to encourage the elaboration of new constructions. Behaviour therapists such as Rachman (1983) now also view the active ingredients of behavioural approaches for agoraphobics as including the disconfirmation of the client's expectancies, and in particular, following Bandura (1977), those concerning self-efficacy. Goldfried (1987) regards Bandura's theory as essentially compatible with Kelly's, and other writers have labelled personal construct psychotherapy a cognitive therapy (Dryden and Golden 1986). However, as Neimeyer and Neimeyer (1981) have argued, the cognitive and personal construct approach may be contrasted in terms of what Sarason (1978) refers to as the 'three lacunae of cognitive therapy', namely the client's cognitive history, the different levels of accessibility of their cognitions, and interactions between these cognitions. Thus, while the cognitive or cognitive-behavioural model of agoraphobia may be concerned with particular expectancies or internal statements concerning the self or personal danger, it would generally show little concern with how these cognitions develop or with the organization of the client's constructs in a system in which different levels of cognitive awareness are apparent (although this is not true of those cognitive approaches, such as that of Guidano and Liotti (1983), which draw on psychoanalytic ideas, while the approach of Schwartz and Michelson (1987), discussed on p. 107, also considers the structure of the client's cognitions to some extent). As Huber and Altmaier (1983) point out, the cognitive therapist's strategy is often to encourage the client to use 'opposite pole' self-statements (e.g. replacing a negative by a corresponding positive self-statement), but as this does not offer the client an alternative construction of the phobic situation, but only reallocates the situation on the client's existing constructs, the personal construct psychotherapist would not expect it to lead to any fundamental change. A further basic difference of approach is that, while the cognitive therapist would tend to see the client's phobia as irrational (Emmelkamp *et al.* 1978, Ellis 1979), the personal construct psychotherapist would proceed from the assumption that, viewed in the context of the client's construing, it is 'understandable and reasonable, even if unpleasant' (Dunnett 1988:323).

As we have seen, the agoraphobic's behaviour may, for example, appear perfectly reasonable if the ability to go out carries negative implications for them, and such negative implications have also been central to psychodynamic formulations of agoraphobia (Snaith 1968). The personal construct psychotherapist will not, however, assume that going out necessarily carries a particular symbolic significance for the agoraphobic, nor will they view the client's problems in terms of a 'hydraulic' model and libidinal energies. Although not employing a concept of the unconscious, they may well be concerned with elaborating areas of the client's construing which are at a low level of cognitive awareness. Constructions underlying the client's symptoms may also be viewed as having some basis in aspects of their past experience, such as parental restrictions on exploratory behaviour or construing of strangers as hostile, but personal construct psychotherapy will not be likely to focus on the past to any great extent and if it does so it may only be in an attempt to 'bind' some construction to the past events from which it derived, and to suggest that it is no longer applicable to present events (Kelly 1955: 1075-6). Such an approach is similar to that employed by Guidano and Liotti (1983: 237) in making their agoraphobic clients 'aware that the source of their *global* view of the world is nothing but a sequence of episodes (however important) that took place when they were children'.

Finally, it is clear that, although originally largely concerned with the intrapsychic domain, personal construct psychology has much to contribute to attempts to explain the predicament of some agoraphobic clients in the context of their marital situation. Of particular relevance in this regard are the commonalities which have recently been elaborated between the personal construct and systems theory approaches (Procter 1981, Feixas *et al.* 1987), and the growing body of work on personal construct assessment and therapeutic techniques applicable to relationships (Neimeyer and Neimeyer 1985).

A personal construct theory perspective on agoraphobia can therefore be seen to combine some features of other models, although also contrasting with these models in so many important respects that it can with justification be considered to provide an alternative construction on the disorder. Therapy derived from this perspective is likely to be technically eclectic, including methods developed from other approaches, but nevertheless offers an alternative to these approaches in that techniques are selected in order to promote particular changes in construing rather than on the basis of the theoretical concepts from which they were developed. Regardless of what techniques it might incorporate, personal construct psychotherapy with an individual agoraphobic client will therefore involve a consistent application of Kelly's theory based on the therapist's construction of the client's construct system. Its encouragement of experimentation will also be coupled with an awareness that the client's ventures as a personal scientist in territory which may previously have been largely unexplored is likely to raise new questions for client and therapist to address, as a final example may illustrate:

> The young man had a phobia about telephones and travelling. About a year of desensitisation treatment enabled him to travel and use the telephone. He commented on the utter pointlessness of such an achievement since he had no one to ring up and no one to travel to. He had formed no relationships with his fellows. After two years of psychotherapeutic exploration and experimentation, the young man was going to social gatherings, visiting his newly found friends, was a member of this or that hobbies group. He then pointed out that no one could care less than he did for the kind of superficial social chit-chat

relationships, mainly with men, which he now formed in great numbers. What he wanted was a deep, passionate, intense, sexual and exclusive relationship with a woman. And so he began. . .

(Bannister and Fransella 1986: 161)

© David A. Winter

REFERENCES

Abraham, K. (1955) *Clinical Papers and Essays on Psychoanalysis*, London: Hogarth.

Arrindell, W. A. and Emmelkamp, P. M. G. (1985) 'Psychological profile of the spouse of the female agoraphobic patient: personality and symptoms', *Brit. J. Psychiat.* 146: 405–14.

Ashworth, C. M., Blackburn, I. M., and McPherson, F. M. (1982) 'The performance of depressed and manic patients on some repertory grid measures: a cross-sectional study', *Brit. J. Med. Psychol.* 55: 247–55.

Bandura, A. (1977) 'Self-efficacy: toward a unifying theory of behavioral change', *Psychol. Rev.* 84: 191–215.

Bannister, D. (1965) 'The rationale and clinical relevance of repertory grid testing', *Brit. J. Psychiat.* 11: 977–82.

Bannister, D. and Fransella, F. (1986) *Inquiring Man: the Psychology of Personal Constructs*, London: Croom Helm.

Benjafield, J. and Adams-Webber, J. R. (1976) 'The golden section hypothesis', *Brit. J. Psychol.* 67: 11–15.

Button, E. (1983) 'Construing the anorexic', in J. Adams-Webber, and J. C. Mancuso (eds) *Applications of Personal Construct Theory*, 305–16, Toronto: Academic Press.

Caine, T. M., Wijesinghe, O. B. A., and Winter, D. A. (1981) *Personal Styles in Neurosis: Implications for Small Group Psychotherapy and Behaviour Therapy*, London: Routledge & Kegan Paul.

Dryden, W. and Golden, W. (eds) (1986) *Cognitive-Behavioural Approaches to Psychotherapy*, London: Harper & Row.

Dunnett, G. (1988) 'Phobias: a journey beyond neurosis', in F. Fransella and L. Thomas (eds) *Experimenting with Personal Construct Psychology*, London: Routledge & Kegan Paul.

Ellis, A. (1979) 'A note on the treatment of agoraphobics with cognitive modification versus prolonged exposure *in vivo*', *Behav. Res. Ther.* 17: 162–4.

Emmelkamp, P. M. G., Kuipers, A. C. M., and Eggeraat, J. B. (1978) 'Cognitive modification versus prolonged exposure *in vivo*: a comparison with agoraphobics as subjects', *Behav. Res. Ther* 16: 33–41.

Feixas, G., Cunillera, C., and Villegas, M. (1987) 'PCT and the systems approach: a theoretical and methodological proposal for integration', paper presented at 7th International Congress on Personal Construct Psychology, Memphis.

116

Fisher, L. M. and Wilson, G. T. (1985) 'A study of the psychology of agoraphobia', *Behav. Res. Ther.* 23: 97–108.

Fransella, F. (1972) *Personal Change and Reconstruction: Research on a Treatment of Stuttering*, London: Academic Press.

—(1981) 'Nature babbling to herself: the self characterisation as a therapeutic tool', in H. Bonarius, R. Holland, and S. Rosenberg (eds) *Personal Construct Psychology: Recent Advances in Theory and Practice*, 219–30, London: Macmillan.

—(1985) 'Individual psychotherapy', in E. Button (ed.) *Personal Construct Theory and Mental Health*, 277–301, London: Croom Helm.

Fransella, F. and Bannister, D. (1977) *A Manual for Repertory Grid Technique*, London: Academic Press.

Frazer, H. M. (1980) 'Agoraphobia: parental influences and cognitive structures', unpublished Ph.D. thesis, University of Toronto.

Goldfried, M. R. (1987) 'Personal construct therapy and other theoretical orientations', paper presented at 7th International Congress on Personal Construct Psychology, Memphis.

Goldstein, A. J. (1982) 'Agoraphobia: treatment successes, treatment failures and theoretical implications', in D. L. Chambless and A. J. Goldstein (eds) *Agoraphobia: Multiple Perspectives on Theory and Treatment*, 182–214, New York: Wiley.

Goldstein, A. J. and Chambless, D. L. (1978) 'A reanalysis of agoraphobia', *Behav. Ther.* 9: 47–59.

Griffiths, R. D. and Joy, M. (1971) 'The prediction of phobic behaviour', *Behav. Res. Ther.* 9: 109–18.

Guidano, V. F. and Liotti, G. (1983) *Cognitive Processes and Emotional Disorders*, New York: Guilford.

Hafner, R. J. (1977a) 'The husbands or agoraphobic women and their influence on treatment outcome', *Brit. J. Psychiat.* 131: 289–94.

— (1977b) 'The husbands of agoraphobic women: assortative mating or pathogenic interaction', *Brit. J. Psychiat.* 130: 233–9.

— (1979) 'Agoraphobic women married to abnormally jealous men', *Brit. J. Med. Psychol.* 52: 99–104.

—(1983) 'Marital systems of agoraphobic women: contributions of husbands' denial and projection', *J. Fam. Ther.* 5: 379–96.

—(1984) 'Predicting the effects on husbands of behaviour therapy for wives' agoraphobia', *Behav. Res. Ther.* 22: 217–26.

Holmes, J. (1982) 'Phobia and counterphobia: family aspects of agoraphobia', *J. Fam. Ther.* 4: 133–52.

Huber, J. W. and Altmaier, E. M. (1983) 'An investigation of the self-statement systems of phobic and nonphobic individuals', *Cog. Ther. Res.* 7: 355–62.

Kelly, G. A. (1955) *The Psychology of Personal Constructs*, New York: Norton.

—(1969) 'Man's construction of his alternatives', in B. Maher (ed.) *Clinical Psychology and Personality: the Selected Papers of George Kelly*, 66–93, New York: Wiley.

—(

1970) 'Behaviour is an experiment', in D. Bannister (ed.) *Perspectives in Personal Construct Theory*, 255–69, London: Academic Press.

Liotti, G. and Guidano, V. F. (1976) 'Behavioral analysis of marital interaction in agoraphobic male patients', *Behav. Res. Ther.* 14: 161–2.

Lorenzini, R. and Sassaroli, S. (1987) *La Paura della Paura: un Modello Clinico delle Fobie* (English translation in preparation) Rome: Nuova Italia Scientifica.

—(1988) 'The construction of change in agoraphobia', in F. Fransella and L. Thomas (eds) *Experimenting with Personal Construct Psychology*, London: Routledge & Kegan Paul.

Michelson, L., Mavissakalian, M., and Meminger, S. (1983) 'Prognostic utility of locus of control in treatment of agoraphobia', *Behav. Res. Ther.* 21: 309–13.

Milton, F. and Hafner, R. J. (1979) 'The outcome of behaviour therapy for agoraphobia in relation to marital adjustment', *Arch. Gen. Psychiat.* 36: 807–11.

Mowrer, O. H., (1950) *Learning Theory and Personality Dynamics*, New York: Ronald.

Neimeyer, G. J. and Neimeyer, R. A. (1981) 'Personal construct perspectives on cognitive assessment', in T. Merluzzi, C. Glass, and M. Genest (eds) *Cognitive Assessment*, 188–232, New York: Guilford.

Neimeyer, R. and Neimeyer, G. (1985) 'Disturbed relationships: a personal construct view', in E. Button (ed.) *Personal Construct Theory and Mental Health*, 195–223, London: Croom Helm.

Norton, G. R., Allen, G. E., and Hilton, J. (1983) 'The social validity of treatments for agoraphobia', *Behav. Res. Ther.* 21: 393–9.

Oatley, K. and Hodgson, D. (1987) 'Influence of husbands on the outcome of their agoraphobic wives' therapy', *Brit. J. Psychiat.* 150: 380–6.

O'Sullivan, B. (1984) 'Understanding the experience of agoraphobia', unpublished Ph.D. thesis, University of Dublin.

—(1985) 'The experiment of agoraphobia', in N. Beail (ed.) *Repertory Grid Technique and Personal Constructs: Applications in Clinical and Educational Settings*, 75–86, London: Croom Helm.

Peter, H. and Hand, I. (1987) 'Expressed emotion and agoraphobia in the Camberwell family interview', paper presented at 18th annual meeting, Society for Psychotherapy Research, Ulm.

Procter, H. G. (1981) 'Family construct psychology: an approach to understanding and treating families', in S. Walrond-Skinner (ed.) *Developments in Family Therapy*, 350–66, London: Routledge & Kegan Paul.

Rachman, S. (1983) 'The modification of agoraphobic avoidance behaviour: some fresh possibilities', *Behav. Res. Ther.* 21: 567–74.

—(1984) 'Agoraphobia – a safety-signal perspective', *Behav. Res. Ther.* 22: 59–70.

Ryle, A. and Breen, D. (1972) 'Some differences in the personal constructs of neurotics and normal subjects', *Brit. J. Psychiat.* 120: 483–9.

Sarason, I. G. (1978) 'Three lacunae of cognitive therapy', *Cognitive Therapy and Research* 3: 223–35.

Schwartz, R. M. and Michelson, L. (1987) 'States-of-mind model: cognitive balance in the treatment of agoraphobia', *J. Consult. Clin. Psychol.* 55: 557–65.

Semerari, A. and Mancini, F. (1987) 'Recursive self- invalidation in neurotic processes', paper presented at 7th International Congress on Personal Construct Psychology, Memphis.

Sheehan, M. J. (1981) 'Constructs and "conflict" in depression', *Brit. J. Psychol.* 72: 197–209.

Slater, P. (1972) 'Notes on INGRID 72', London: St George's Hospital.

—(1977) *The Measurement of Intrapersonal Space by Grid Technique*, volume 2 *Dimensions of Intrapersonal Space*, London: Wiley.

Snaith, R. P. (1968) 'A clinical investigation of phobias', *Brit. J. Psychiat.* 114: 673–97.

Turner, R. M., Giles, T. R., and Marafiote, R. (1983) 'Agoraphobics: a test of the repression hypothesis', *Brit. J. Soc. Clin. Psychol.* 22: 75.

Watts, F. N. and Sharrock, R. (1985) 'Relationships between spider constructs in phobics', *Brit. J. Med. Psychol.* 58: 149–54.

Winter, D. A. (1985a) 'Neurotic disorders: the curse of certainty', in E. Button (ed.) *Personal Construct Theory and Mental Health*, 103–31, London: Croom Helm.

—(1985b) 'Personal styles, constructive alternativism and the provision of a therapeutic service', *Brit. J. Med. Psychol.* 58: 129–36.

—(1988) 'Towards a constructive clinical psychology', in G. Dunnett (ed.) *Working with People: Practical Uses of Personal Construct Psychology*, London: Routledge & Kegan Paul.

Winter, D. and Gournay, K. (1987) 'Construction and constriction in agoraphobia', *Brit. J. Med. Psychol.* 60: 233–44.

Wright, K. J.T. (1969) 'An investigation of the meaning of change in phobic patients using grid methods', unpublished M.Phil. thesis, University of London.

Wright, K. J. T. (1970) 'Exploring the uniqueness of common complaints', *Brit. J. Med. Psychol.* 43: 221–32.

Chapter Six

FAILURES IN THE BEHAVIOURAL TREATMENT OF AGORAPHOBIA

KEVIN GOURNAY

This chapter reviews the relevant evidence to date and describes a study of treatment failure with agoraphobics undergoing exposure treatment.

The issue of treatment failure is perhaps the most neglected area of outcome research. Yet, as Foa and Emmelkamp (1983) point out in their landmark book, failures are a challenge, which if properly studied, can teach us much about the shortcomings of our treatment methods. The main factors which have prevented detailed systematic research are as follows.

First, there does not seem to be any universally acceptable definition of what actually constitutes failure and only Foa and Emmelkamp (1983) have attempted to tackle this thorny issue with systematic study of several treatment areas. It should be added at this point that as Barlow *et al.* (1984a) point out, Wolpe (1958) took great pains to describe failures in his legendary series. Unfortunately, very few have followed his example.

Second, definition of failure depends on clear, unambiguous target specification and the use of multiple and reliable measures of change. Therefore, it is only since the advent of behavioural practice that such methods have been used. Sadly, much of clinical psychology and psychiatric practice is characterized by the absence of objective evaluation.

Third, the 'behavioural revolution' of the past three decades has brought such enthusiastic optimism that any discussion of failure has been obscured. Outcome research has been focused on finding whether treatment A is better than treatment B, rather than looking at why treatment B was worse than treatment A. Furthermore, research reports discount failures, drop-outs, and treatment refusers in a sentence or two. Certainly, the rivalry between the various 'schools of thought' has done little to concentrate effort on examining why methods fail. It could certainly be argued that in treatment areas where behavioural methods are the most efficacious, there is a great deal of complacency.

Fourth, as Foa and Emmelkamp (1983) point out, journals discourage reports of negative results.

Finally, and of considerable importance, is that consideration of treatment failure is not very reinforcing for the clinician. While one can see intellectually that failures provide us with a valuable opportunity to learn and refine, actual confrontation with a patient who still suffers or suffers more, is another matter.

With regard to the treatment of agoraphobia, there has been little systematic evaluation of treatment failure. Rachman (1983) struck a cautionary note when he pointed out that while agoraphobic patients, in general, are improved by behavioural treatment, many are left with significant residual problems. In only two papers has there been clear definition of what constitutes clinically significant improvement or failure in the treatment of agoraphobia. Jansson and Ost (1983) in their review of twenty-four studies of outcome with agoraphobics, defined improvement in terms of the Watson and Marks (1971) combined scale of anxiety and avoidance. Treatment was considered to have accomplished a clinically significant improvement for the group of subjects if the mean rating on this 0–8 scale was three or less at post-treatment or if there was a reduction of the pre-treatment mean score of at least 50 per cent at the follow-up assessment. Thus, implicit in this definition is a definition of failure as an outcome of something less than those results.

Emmelkamp and van der Hout (1983) were more specific in defining individual failure. They defined failure as less than a three-point change on the 0–8 combined scale of anxiety and avoidance, rated over a series of five agoraphobic situations.

Foa and Emmelkamp (1983) have provided a general classification of groups of failure which seems to be a most useful system. These groups are:

1 individuals who do not accept or refuse treatment;
2 individuals who commence treatment but drop out once treatment has commenced;
3 individuals who do not respond to treatment;
4 individuals who respond to treatment but who subsequently relapse.

There are very few studies relevant to the specific area of treatment failure and agoraphobia, much of the work being found in Foa and Emmelkamp's 1983 book.

Regarding non-acceptance of treatment, Marks (1987) reported that 25 per cent of subjects referred for behavioural treatment did not pursue this when offered. This percentage seems much in accord with the rates reported in outcome studies in general. However, detail of non-acceptors and treatment drop-outs is virtually never provided in journal papers.

With regard to flooding and flooding-like treatments, Marshall and Gauthier (1983) reviewed failures and side-effects. They surveyed twenty-four practitioners and researchers of flooding therapies but could not find any evidence to suggest any major problems, major failures, or major side-effects associated with this mode of treatment. These authors went on to review factors responsible for treatment failure. It is their contention that it is the therapist, rather than the patient or the method, that is responsible for failure. They have set out a number of factors they feel are important in influencing the outcome of flooding therapy. They have divided these factors into three main categories, i.e.

1 conceptualization
2 preparation for treatment
3 implementation

Under the heading 'conceptualization', they state that a common reason for failure is an inadequate behavioural analysis, which may not take into account certain physiological variables such as autonomous panic disorder. They also discuss the possibility that the therapist may focus on a limited aspect of the client's difficulty and as Rachman (1981) suggests, not take into account patients who have 'initially a very high level of reactivity'. In these subjects, Marshall and Gauthier suggest that drugs may have a role in the facilitation of flooding. However, in the light of recent evidence concerning benzodiazepine addiction, such a course of action must be considered with an extreme degree of caution.

In discussing preparation for treatment, Marshall and Gauthier suggest that the therapist and patient may be inadequately prepared for various patient reactions to treatment. They add that one also needs to prepare the more general environment, including the reaction of the spouse to changes which may result from successful treatment. With regard to implementation, the authors suggest that there are two main areas that control effective flooding. First, the duration of exposure seems critical and second, the adaption of the procedure to the problems of specific clients is an often-overlooked but essential variable.

With regard to side-effects of flooding, Marshall and Gauthier could find no evidence that this was a major problem. This finding was in accord with the study by Shipley and Boudewyns (1980) who undertook a mail survey of therapists conducting flooding and flooding-like procedures. They had a high response rate (i.e. 83 per cent), seventy therapists covering 3,493 clients. Six of the seventy therapists reported a total of nine clients suffering serious side-effects. These side-effects involved psychotic or panic reactions. It would be tempting to speculate that this number could be a chance effect, rather than being attributable to any specific therapeutic procedure.

Until recently, only Emmelkamp (in Foa and Emmelkamp 1983) has specifically and systematically looked at the failure of exposure treatment with agoraphobics. He examined the reasons for non-acceptance of treatment by twenty-five agoraphobics referred to the psychology apartment of his hospital in the Netherlands. The treatment offered consisted of prolonged exposure *in vivo* conducted in groups, with the addition of cognitive therapy. Thus, Emmelkamp's enquiry concerned a treatment mixture, rather than exposure alone. Sixteen of the twenty-five subjects completed a questionnaire which was based on twenty-two factors related to non-acceptance of therapy. About half of the subjects reported that they were already somewhat improved and most of these subjects also gave reasons for failing to accept therapy. Some of the subjects blamed external circumstances such as problems with times of treatment for non-acceptance and said they intended to contact the department at a later date for treatment. However, two of the most important findings seemed to be that subjects were frightened of treatment and second, that overall, their expectations of therapy did fit not those of the therapist. Interestingly, thirteen of the sixteen responders agreed with the slogan 'you have to overcome your fears on your own'.

Emmelkamp then went on to examine why subjects dropped out of treatment before an adequate trial of treatment had been completed. Questionnaires were sent to fifteen agoraphobic subjects who had dropped out of group treatment over a two-year period. Eight subjects returned questionnaires which consisted of the questions used in non-acceptance study, supplemented by questions pertaining to the specific treatment received. Four subjects reported that the treatment had made them anxious and in five subjects there seemed to be discongruent treatment expectations. Two of these five subjects said that they would prefer a 'less aggressive' approach to their problem. One subject wanted to talk to a doctor and nothing further, another subject wanted pills and 'something else', and the fifth subject, although dissatisfied, did not state the kind of treatment he preferred. In addition to these findings, five of the subjects found that the therapist was either too young or did not understand their feelings. In summary, Emmelkamp felt that a pre-therapy training package might be useful in preventing drop-outs. Previously, Emmelkamp and Emmelkamp-Benner (1975) had found that showing a videotape of three ex-agoraphobics being interviewed about their treatment experiences seemed to prevent drop-outs occurring. Further, Emmelkamp suggested using former phobics as co-therapists and involving the spouse. This seems to be a relevant suggestion, particularly when demand outstrips resources. The use of the spouse has been advocated by many (e.g. Mathews *et al.* 1981, Ross 1980) and provides another saving of therapist time.

Emmelkamp (1983) examined the data of five agoraphobics who had received group exposure treatment and who were categorized as treatment failures. Failure was defined as less than a three-point change on a nine-point scale of anxiety and avoidance (Emmelkamp *et al.* 1978). There did not appear to be a relationship between pre-treatment depression or assertiveness and eventual failure. Emmelkamp also looked at the relationship of several variables (i.e. over-valued ideation concerning the phobic stimulus, age, duration of agoraphobia, previous treatment, and previous use of medication) to outcome. He could find no differences between failures and successful cases. One significant finding was that explicit complaints about marital partners seemed to correlate with poorer outcome.

Emmelkamp also examined the relationship of the therapist to the patient within the setting of group treatments. Thirteen agoraphobics completed the Dutch version of the relationship inventory (Barrett-Lennard 1973, as modified by Liataer 1976) which consists of the following sub-scales:

1 empathy
2 positive regard

3 congruity
4 negative regard
5 unconditionality
6 transparency
7 directivity

There was a significant relationship between the outcome of therapy and 'good' therapist characteristics such as empathy, positive regard, and congruity. Emmelkamp concluded the study by looking at another group of eight subjects who were regarded as therapy failures. He used a semi-structured interview centring around the following topics:

1 the current state of the agoraphobia;
2 the subject's experiences with respect to treatment;
3 the relationship with the therapist;
4 family relationships.

All subjects had had a considerable number of treatment sessions, ranging from seventeen to sixty-eight, with a range of treatment duration from six to seventeen months. Subjects had considerable difficulty dealing with the anxiety endured in treatment sessions and the subjects generally felt that therapists did not show that they understood their patients' feelings. All the married subjects (six) felt they were not understood by their husbands and the overall clinical impression was that there was often serious marital distress. As with all the other subjects studied by Emmelkamp with regard to failure, it should be emphasized that exposure was not the only treatment used. Subjects also had other treatments given within their treatment programme, e.g. assertion training and cognitive restructuring. The emphasis in Emmelkamp's treatment centre is on group treatments and as Emmelkamp points out, not all patients are suited for this method.

Fischer, Hand, and Angenendt (1987) reported on twenty agoraphobic patients who did not complete exposure treatment. These comprised fourteen refusers and six drop-outs. Their data included follow-up to at least one year. They found that treatment refusers had not changed on measures of agoraphobia and general phobia, but showed significant improvement in both social anxiety and depression. The six treatment drop-outs, on the other hand, showed dramatic improvement on several measures including agoraphobia. The authors urged caution in generalizing from such small numbers but suggested that improvement was attributable to patients carrying out the principles of exposure learned in their contact with the treatment programme.

Other variables associated with failure

As Jansson and Ost (1983) point out, there is little research directed to the question of which variables predict outcome. Although one study (Zitrin *et al.* 1978) showed that very depressed subjects did less well with exposure treatment, there is overall little evidence of a relationship between initial depression and outcome. However, the average number of subjects per study (less than twenty) in the research reviewed by Jansson and Ost may well be explanatory in not detecting some relationships between variables.

With regard to marital satisfaction (reviewed in Chapters 2 and 3 of this book), this is a complex issue and there does not appear to be any predictive quality in any of the measures of marital disharmony which have been used.

Emmelkamp (Foa and Emmelkamp 1983), in reviewing the literature and examining his own data, could find no predictive quality in measures of assertiveness, initial severity, and independent variables such as age and duration of problem. However, the few studies which examined these variables contained small numbers of subjects. Emmelkamp's failure group, for example, contained only five subjects.

In summary, there is little research on treatment failure and only the studies of Emmelkamp (Foa and Emmelkamp 1983) and Fischer *et al.* (1987) regarding agoraphobia and exposure treatment. In view of the fact that exposure treatment, while being generally effective and widely used, has its limitations, it is essential to gather more data.

THE STUDY

Subjects in the study were drawn from a cohort of 132 agoraphobic patients meeting DSM III criteria for agoraphobia. Treatment was the same for all patients and consisted of six two-hour sessions of therapist-aided exposure in real life (further details can be found in Chapter 2, Appendix I). For the sake of consistency, it was decided to base the categories and criteria for failure on the work of Emmelkamp and van der Hout (1983) and Emmelkamp (Foa and Emmelkamp 1983). Thus, the four groups of failure considered were:

1 treatment failures, i.e. those individuals who failed to respond to treatments by failing to reach predefined criteria for success (see next paragraph);
2 treatment relapsers, i.e. those individuals who met the predefined criteria for success at the post-treatment rating point but relapsed to below these criteria at subsequent rating point;
3 treatment drop-outs, i.e. those individuals who embarked on treatment but who dropped out of treatment during or at some time after the first treatment session;
4 treatment refusers, i.e. those individuals who were offered treatment but declined the offer.

The patients were assessed using the battery of measures outlined in Chapter 2 Appendix I, and including independent assessment.
Based on Emmelkamp's work, the criteria for failure were:

1 a change of less than three points on the 0–8 scale of phobic severity (after Watson and Mark 1971) between pre- and post-treatment, as rated by patient or therapist or by independent assessor;
2 an increase of less than three successfully completed items on a ten-item behavioural avoidance test.

We were interested in the following questions:

1 whether the failure groups differed from treatment responders on our measures of change;
2 how treatment drop-outs fared at follow-up;
3 how treatment failures fared at follow-up;
4 whether drop-out or failure was related to the taking of benzodiazepine medication.

Further, we were also interested in whether we could elicit factors associated with the various failure groups. To aid this enquiry, we used two questionnaires based on Emmelkamp's study (Foa and Emmelkamp 1983) (see Figures 6.1 and 6.2).

Results and discussion

Using the above criteria for failure, sixty subjects were deemed to be treatment failures. Of these:

Figure 6.1 Questionnaire given to subjects who dropped out or refused treatment

NAME: ....

Please read the statments on the left of the page and tick the response which best describes your feeling about the statement.

	Not applicable	Somewhat applicable	Is very much applicable
I am improved since my last appointment			
I am no longer troubled by my fears and phobias			
The appointments were at an inconvenient time			
The treatment was not what I wanted			
Medication would be more helpful			
I was frightened of treatment			
The therapist did not understand my problem			
I did not like the therapist			
I thought that treatment would present difficulties for my family			
I was persuaded against my better judgement to seek treatment			
'You have to overcome your fears on your own'			
I will get better in time			
Treatment will make me worse			

Nineteen subjects (thirteen women and six men) were deemed to be treatment failures.

Nine subjects (eight women and one man) were deemed to be relapsers.

128

Figure 6.2 Questionnaire given to subjects who failed or relapsed

NAME: ....

(1) How are your agoraphobic symptoms now?

(2) Are they better or worse than when you undertook treatment?

(3) Have you received further help (of any kind) with your problem?

(4) If so, can you detail this help.

(5) Were your treatment sessions involving going to various places and dealing with anxiety too much for you?

(6) During the treatment sessions was the therapist understanding?

(7) Any other comments about the therapist.

(8) Did your family help or hinder you during treatment?

Twenty-six subjects (seventeen women and nine men) were deemed to be treatment drop-outs. (Sixteen subjects dropped out after the first session. Four subjects dropped out after the second session. Six subjects dropped out after the third or fourth session.)

Six subjects (four women and two men) were deemed to be treatment refusers.

For the sake of simplicity, detail of the results is shown in table form and the text describes only the most important findings.

Follow-up

Attempts were made to follow up all subjects, including treatment drop-outs and refusers. Follow-up was usually conducted by face-to-face interviews but the questionnaires relating to failure were posted to the subject after the last follow-up point.

The total failure group consisted of sixty subjects of whom forty-eight were interviewed. Thirty-three questionnaires were returned from failures, relapsers, and drop-outs.

Of the nineteen subjects deemed to be treatment failures, eighteen were seen for follow-up interviews, one was interviewed by telephone, fourteen subjects returned questionnaires,

Of the nine subjects deemed to be treatment relapsers, eight were seen for follow-up interviews, six subjects returned questionnaires.

Of the twenty-six subjects deemed to be treatment drop-outs, fourteen were seen for follow-up interviews. Three were interviewed by telephone and thirteen subjects returned questionnaires.

Of the six subjects deemed to be treatment refusers, two were seen for follow-up interviews, two were interviewed by telephone, but none of these subjects returned questionnaires.

As Foa and Emmelkamp (1983) point out, treatment failures are indeed a challenge which need to be investigated systematically. Further, as Rachman (1983) has indicated, although results of behavioural treatment with agoraphobia are good, there is no cause for complacency. Therefore, the current study seems somewhat overdue. It is the first to describe a systematic analysis of failures in the exposure treatment of agoraphobia. The similar studies by Emmelkamp (Foa and Emmelkamp 1983) and Fischer *et al.* (1987) reported on treatment failures in agoraphobia but treatment consisted of a package of which exposure was but one part. Also in contrast, Emmelkamp investigated five subjects categorized as treatment failures (nineteen in this study), twenty-five subjects who refused treatment (six in this study), and eight treatment drop-outs (twenty-six in this study). He did not study relapsers (nine in this study).

Thus, of the 132 agoraphobics fulfilling selection criteria, sixty subjects (or 44 per cent of the sample) fulfilled the criteria for failure (thirty-two by refusing or dropping out of treatment and twenty-eight by failing or relapsing). Strictly speaking, the nine relapsers were also treatment responders, in that they reached improvement criteria at the end of treatment. Thus, for the purpose of some analyses they are included in the responder group. In fact, the pre-treatment mean scores for the relapsers were not significantly different from the other failure groups. (See Table 6.1).

Regarding the analysis of difference in pre-treatment scores between responders and the various failure groups, only the marital questionnaire score showed such a difference. Therefore, neither initial level of depression nor initial severity seem to have any predictive quality. Scrutiny of the raw scores of individual subjects shows that the sub-groups of failure contained a range of subjects from very severe to less severe problem severity. However, the significant finding regarding the marital questionnaire scores clearly establishes a positive though weak relationship between higher levels of marital satisfaction and better treatment response. This finding is in accord

Table 6.1 Comparison of some pre-treatment scores of treatment responders and failures

	Phobic problem severity (combined)	Agora-phobic sub-scale score	Wake-field inventory	Leeds inventory	Symptom check list	Marital question-naire (subject)	Mean behavioural avoidance test scores
Failure groups combined *n* = 51*	5·86 (1·41) *n* = 51	30·71 (7·20) *n* = 51	23·23 (6·14) *n* = 51	12·86 (3·59) *n* = 13	24·12 (7·58) *n* = 37	27·29 (15·71 *n* = 51	2·07 (1·19) *n* = 24 *n* = 48
Treatment responders *n* = 81*	5·80 (1.21) *n* = 81	28·43 (6·99) *n* = 81	23·59 (5·27) *n* = 81	11·71 4·19) *n* = 27	23·20 (6·71) *n* = 51	18·39 (12·98) *n* = 81	2·22 (1·31) *n* = 38 *n* = 80
t	0·512 df 130	0·940 df 130	0·193 df 38	1·358 df 86	0·648 df 130	2·422 df 60	1·011 df 126
*p***	n.s.	n.s.	n.s.	n.s.	n.s.	<	n.s.

Notes
( ) standard deviation
* Subjects categorized as relapsers are included in the responder group
** Value for two-tailed test

with the analysis reported in Chapter 2 regarding the correlation between marital satisfaction and outcome and seems logical if one considers the implications of a behaviour change programme for an individual and their immediate family. It seems obvious that positive marital relationships are necessary to provide support and encouragement during what may be a harrowing treatment experience and that in the absence of a positive marital relationship, drop-out or treatment failure become more likely.

Regarding the second area of investigation (see Table 6.2), the follow-up data of the drop-out failure groups is consistent with the data of Fischer *et al.* (1987) which shows continuing improvement after drop-out. However, the data on the drop-out group concerns only thirteen of the twenty-six subjects and therefore the findings need to be treated with some caution. Of the thirteen respondents, eight dropped out after one session and five after two or more sessions. It could be argued that the experience of exposure treatment was the important factor and that subjects used the exposure principle after

KEVIN GOURNAY

Table 6.2 Pre-treatment and follow-up scores (agoraphobic sub-scale) for treatment failures and treatment drop-outs

		Agoraphobic sub-scale score	
Drop outs n = 13 (of 26 in all)	Pre-treatment	29·62 (SD 8·00)	t = 5·329 df 24
	Follow-up rating point	18·08 (SD 10·82)	p < 0·001
Treatment failures n = 14 (of 19 in all)	Immediately post-treatment	20·17 (SD 6·20)	t = 0·616 df 34
	Follow-up rating point	19·33 (SD 9·71)	n.s.

Note
Second follow-up ratings after further professional help for three of the failure subjects were not used

dropping out. Of course, a single session of therapist-aided exposure is used in Mathews *et al.* (1977) home-based programme with further sessions being self-directed. Therefore, these results are consistent with the growing body of evidence, reviewed in Chapter 2, which suggests that the amount of therapist-aided exposure necessary to effect change may be quite small. The reduction of mean scores was certainly large (from 29.62 to 18.08 on the agoraphobic sub-scale). At first sight, this finding seems to conflict with the evidence of the questionnaire data of drop-outs, of whom only four said that they had improved since treatment. However, it should be remembered that a score of 18 or so on the agoraphobia sub-scale still indicates considerable handicap. The alternative explanation for the improvement in the status of drop-outs is that the change in scores may well be a reflection of the variability of the syndrome. While all current authorities (e.g. Mathews *et al.* 1981, Thorpe and Burns 1983, Marks 1987) agree that agoraphobia is a condition which does not remit spontaneously, there is also agreement that it fluctuates in severity.

The findings regarding the failure group are based on eighteen of the nineteen treatment failures. The mean post-treatment score of 20.17 on the agoraphobic sub-scale indicates that as a group there is a significant change for the better from pre-treatment levels (mean 29.00). However, the group comprises a spectrum of failure, from those whose scores remain unchanged on all measures, to those who only fail on one measure to achieve 'responder' criteria. Again a score of 20 on the agoraphobic sub-scale would probably mean that the

Table 6.3 Change in agoraphobic sub-scale score (pre- to post-treatment) for various drug-taking groups

	Mean change in agoraphobic sub-scale score (pre- to post-treatment)	
Subjects who completed treatment not taking psychotropic medication $n = 56$	18·09 (SD 8·15)	* $t = 2·499$ df 98 $p < 0.01$
Subjects taking benzodiazepines $n = 29$	13·14 (SD 7·08)	** Mann Whitney n.s.
Subjects taking benzodiazepines and antidepressants $n = 11$	14·40 (SD 8·42)	

Notes
* t – test between subjects taking psychotropic medication and subjects on no medication
** Mann Whitney test between subjects taking benzodiazepines alone and subjects taking a combination of benzodiazepines and tricyclic antidepressants

subject would definitely avoid each of the agoraphobic situations listed on this scale of the fear survey. Therefore, the group of subjects would remain, by any standards, severely handicapped. The lack of post-treatment improvement demonstrates a treatment 'ceiling' effect, possibly suggesting that further self-directed exposure produces no further effect on the general agoraphobic state.

Regarding the issue of concurrent benzodiazepine medication, there was no significantly greater frequency of failure in the group taking psychotropic medication. However, as Table 6.3 shows, subjects taking benzodiazepines do not do as well at post-test as subjects who are medication free. Furthermore, benzodiazepine taking was associated with a significantly greater drop-out (see Table 6.4). There is no evidence from this study that subjects taking medication differ from those not taking medication, on severity or any other readily identifiable variables. Therefore, it does seem that whether a patient is prescribed medication by his GP is a decision which is taken idiosyncratically. Certainly, in view of the range of referring doctors in the study (28 GPs and 8 psychiatrists), there must be a range of attitudes to the prescription of psychotropic medication. The present study certainly suggests that benzodiazepine medication taking does not facilitate exposure and probably detracts from treatment efficacy. (This finding merely adds to overwhelming evidence that these

Table 6.4 Drop-out rates of medication takers

	Not taking psychotropic medication	Taking psychotropic medication	Totals
Completed treatment	56 (46·5)	40 (49·5)	96
Dropped out or refused treatment	6 (15·5)	26 (16·5)	32
Totals	62	66	128

Notes
expected frequencies in parentheses
χ^2 = 15·05 1 df (corrected for continuity)
p <0·001

substances need to be treated with extreme caution.) There are probably several reasons for the negative effects of such medication. Certainly, the impairment of learning (described in Kennedy 1979) may be a major factor in preventing exposure working to a maximum effect.

Medication taking is a variable not often reported in outcome studies, although certainly the taking of benzodiazepines by agoraphobics is widespread. The present study findings suggest that future outcome studies should attempt to control for medication taking or preferably withdraw subjects from medication before inclusion in a trial. This, however, is easier said than done. The author's current clinical experience is that periods of more than a year may be needed to withdraw subjects from some benzodiazepines. MIND has recently produced a fact sheet (MIND, 22 Harley Street, W.1) compiled by eminent workers which suggests a rule of thumb of thirty days of withdrawal for each year taking benzodiazepines. Since some subjects in the current study have taken such drugs for fifteen years or more, the difficulties is this area are far from minor.

The questionnaire findings regarding drop-out (see Table 6.5) provide some indications for change in preparation for treatment. The most frequent reasons given for dropping out were that the subject thought the therapist did not understand and that treatment was frightening. The reason regarding therapist understanding indicates that more attention should be given to solving this difficulty before the point when a subject is compelled to drop out because

Table 6.5 Number of subjects responding affirmatively to questionnaire regarding drop-out from treatment

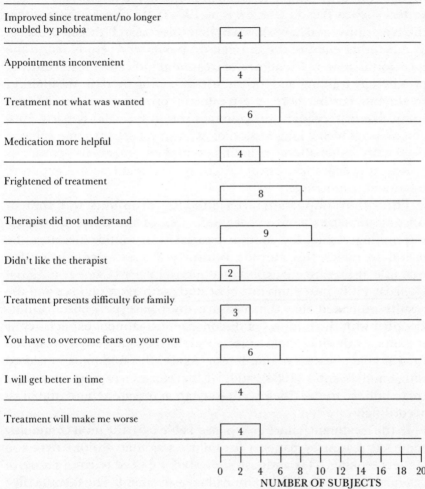

Note
Total number of subjects responding = 13 (of 26 in total)

he/she feels that he/she is not understood. Obviously, the initial interview is of paramount importance and it would therefore seem that subjects are presently given insufficient opportunity to feed back their feelings about treatment to the therapist. Emmelkamp (1983) suggests that the complex relationship between therapist and subject be further investigated but perhaps the simple mechanics of communication during assessment interviews should be the first candidate for investigation. Of course, treatment process research with behavioural treatments is still in its infancy. However, influential writers such as Barlow (Barlow *et al.* 1984a) are clearly insistent that this is a priority and have shown us how this research should proceed. The fact that eight of the thirteen drop-outs who responded to the questionnaire were frightened of treatment indicates the necessity of pre-therapy training and/or the use of coping models, via films, of treatment. Furthermore, the treatment procedure of the current study, like many clinical programmes run in specialist departments, commenced with a long session of exposure. Perhaps some subjects need more graduation, including preliminary imaginal exposure or at least a preparatory session of group discussion before exposure treatment commences.

The other important area cited by drop-outs was that of discongruent treatment expectations. Six of the thirteen subjects responding wished for another treatment. It would, therefore, be useful to check this attitude routinely at assessment, using for example, the treatment expectancy questionnaire (Caine *et al.* 1981). Gournay (1983) used this in a pilot study with agoraphobics and the results indicated that the measure does have prognostic utility. Coupled with the findings of discongruent treatment expectancy, is the apparently widely-held belief (six of thirteen subjects) that one has to overcome fears on one's own. Again, this finding is in accord with Emmelkamp's (1983) study. It therefore seems important that this belief needs to be elicited at assessment and debated accordingly.

In the treatment failure group (see Table 6.6), the most commonly reported reason by patients for failure was that sessions were too anxiety evoking. This obviously indicated the need to consider more graduation of tasks fitted to individual assessment. The fact that five of the fourteen respondees in this group reported that the therapist was not understanding is important and again, feedback opportunity for the subject during sessions may be an important factor. Also, Emmelkamp (1983) has indicated that perceived strictness (by subject of therapist) may be important in this area. Therefore, greater matching of subject and therapist seems to be indicated. However, even if such complex matching could be effected, current resource limitations would seem to be a considerable obstacle.

This study of failure gives rise to some considerable concern. 44.4 per cent of the original cohort have been defined as failures. This

Table 6.6 Number of subjects responding affirmatively to questionnaire regarding treatment failure

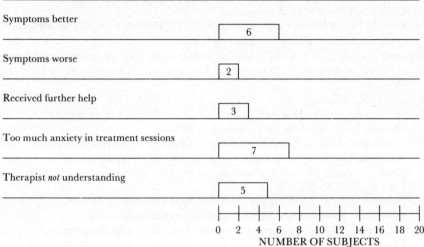

Note
Total number of subjects responding = 14 (of 19 in total)

qualification has been lacking in virtually all outcome studies to date but there is no reason to suppose that this 44.4 per cent figure is any better or worse than any of the published controlled studies with agoraphobics receiving exposure treatment. Certainly, mean scores pre, post, and follow-up of the study group as a whole are of the same order of magnitude as those of other studies. There is, however, evidence (particularly with the drop-outs in this study) that this failure figure could be much reduced by attending to pre-therapy training, more feedback during assessment and treatment, and a more conservative approach to the prescribing of psychotropic medication.

This study is a crude and preliminary attempt to look at failure with exposure treatment. Although there are indications of how treatment may be modified, perhaps the most important message is that research into failure needs to be a more routine affair.

© Kevin Gournay

REFERENCES

Barlow, D. H., Hayes, S. C., and Nelson, R. O. (1984a) *The Scientist Practitioner*, New York: Pergamon.

Barlow, D. H., O'Brien, G. T., and Last, C. G. (1984b) 'Couples treatment of agoraphobia', *Behaviour Therapy* 1: 41–58.

Barrett-Lennard, G. T. (1973) 'Relationship inventory: experimental form O SS-42', unpublished manuscript, University of Waterloo, Waterloo, Ontario.

Caine, T. M., Wijesinghe, O. B. A., and Winter, D. A. (1981) *Personal Styles in Neurosis: Implications for Small Group Psychotherapy and Behaviour Therapy*, London: Routledge & Kegan Paul.

Emmelkamp, P. M. G., and Emmelkamp-Benner, A. (1975) 'Effects of historically portrayed modelling and group treatment on self observation. A comparison with agoraphobics', *Behaviour Research and Therapy*, 13: 135–9.

Emmelkamp, P. M. G., Kuipers, A. C. M., and Eggeraat, J. B. (1978) 'Cognitive modification versus prolonged exposure *in vivo*: a comparison with agoraphobics as subjects', *Behaviour Research and Therapy* 16: 33–41.

Emmelkamp, P. M. G. and van der Hout, A. (1983) 'Failure in treating agoraphobia', in E. B. Foa and P. M. G. Emmelkamp (eds) *Failures in Behaviour Therapy*, New York: John Wiley.

Fischer, M., Hand, I., and Angenendt, J. (1987) 'Longterm developments for agoraphobics who refused or dropped out of exposure treatment', paper to 17th EABT conference, Amsterdam, Holland.

Foa, E. and Emmelkamp, P. M. G. (1983) *Failures in Behaviour Therapy*, New York: John Wiley.

Gournay, K. J. M. (1983) 'Agoraphobia: a study of some treatment variables', M.Phil. thesis, University of Leicester.

Jansson, I. and Ost, L.-G. (1983) 'Behavioural treatments for agoraphobia: an evaluative review', *Clinical Psychology Review* 2: 311–37.

Kennedy, Senator Edward M. (1979) 'Use and misuse of benzodiazapines', subcommittee report (chairman, Kennedy) on health and scientific research of the committee on labor and human resources, United States Senate.

Liataer, G. (1976) 'Nederlandstalige revisie van Barrett-Lennard's relationship inventory voor individueel therapeutische relaties', *Psychologia Belgica* 16: 73–94.

Marks, I. M. (1987) *Fears, Phobias and Rituals*, New York: Oxford University Press.

Marshall, W. L. and Gauthier, J. (1983) 'Failures in flooding', in E. B. Foa and P. M. G. Emmelkamp (eds) *Failures in Behaviour Therapy*, New York: John Wiley.

Mathews, A. M., Gelder, M. G., and Johnston, D. W. (1981) *Agoraphobia: Nature and Treatment*, London: Tavistock.

Mathews, A. M., Teasdale, J., Munby, M., Johnston, D., and Shaw, P. (1977)

'A home-based treatment program for agoraphobia', *Behaviour Therapy* 8: 915–24.

Rachman, S. (1981) 'Emotional processing', *Behaviour Research and Therapy* 18: 51–60.

—(1983) 'The modification of agoraphobic avoidance behaviour. Some fresh possibilities', *Behaviour Research and Therapy* 21, 5: 567–74.

Ross, J. (1980) 'The use of former phobics in the treatment of phobias', *American J. of Psychology* 137: 715–17.

Shipley, R. H. and Boudewyns, P. A. (1980) 'Flooding and implosive therapy: are they harmful?', *Behaviour Therapy* 11: 503–8.

Thorpe, G. L. and Burns, L. E. (1983) *The Agoraphobic Syndrome*, New York: John Wiley.

Watson, J. P. and Marks, I. M. (1971) 'Relevant and irrelevant fear in flooding. A crossover study in phobic patients', *Behaviour Therapy* 2: 275–93.

Wolpe, J. (1958) *Psychotherapy by Reciprocal Inhibition*, California: Stanford University Press.

Zitrin, C. M., Klein, D. F., and Woerner, M. G. (1978) 'Behaviour therapy, supportive psychotherapy, imipramine and phobias', *Archives of General Psychiatry* 35: 307–16.

Chapter Seven

THE TREATMENT OF AGORA-PHOBIA BY NURSE THERAPISTS: PRACTICE AND TRAINING

H. GORDON DEAKIN

In this chapter I shall briefly outline the development of nurse behaviour therapist training in the UK. This will be related to the operational training of case management skills for practitioners working with agoraphobic difficulties and demonstrate the educational and training strategies available to transfer those skills effectively. Whilst agoraphobic difficulties provide only a proportion of the clinical referrals to behavioural workers in any comprehensive community mental health service, they are a significant demand on limited resources.

NURSES AS THERAPISTS

For many outside, and some inside, the health care professions, the role of the nurse is seen as one of providing 'care', carrying out treatment procedures on behalf of medical staff, and working in teams to provide twenty-four-hour support for groups of patients. This is now, and always has been, far from the truth. It is based on a stereotyped image of nursing and a categorization of health care functions which falsely delineate roles related to decision making and responsibility.

Nurses 'treat' patients and provide 'care' for them. They have their own individual clinical responsibilities, make their own therapeutic decisions, and are accountable for their clinical actions. Whilst many hospital-based nurses work in ward, unit, or departmental teams, a very high proportion operate in more independent and more clinically autonomous roles, e.g. the midwife, the community psychiatric nurse, and a range of clinical specialists from the intensive care nurse to the AIDS counsellor.

Mental health nursing, although a less publicized branch of the nursing profession, has paralleled the other branches by encouraging expertise in group and individual psychotherapies; child, adolescent, forensic, and elderly care nursing. Recognizing this and identifying severe shortfalls in the capabilities of the psychiatric medicine and clinical psychology professions to produce sufficient numbers of specialist therapists to meet clinical demand, particularly at a time when new, effective, and experimentally validated treatment methods were becoming available in the early 1970s, a group of UK psychiatrists and clinical psychologists devised an experimental training programme to evaluate formally the effectiveness of psychiatric nurses as specialist therapists.

In a DHSS-funded experimental training project, Professor Isaac Marks of London University's Institute of Psychiatry examined the training needs, clinical and cost-effectiveness, and specialist role development of qualified psychiatric nurses (RMN) undergoing a skills-based educational programme to become autonomous clinical specialists in behavioural psychotherapy. Operated at the Bethlem Royal Hospital and the Maudsley Hospital in London between 1972 and 1975, this project successfully demonstrated the clinical effectiveness of nurse therapists with a wide range of adult neuroses (Marks *et al.* 1977). Cost-effectiveness was impressive (Ginsberg and Marks 1977); and the operation of the clinical role, not only in inpatient and outpatient settings but also in primary health care settings, was effectively demonstrated (Marks 1985).

As a result of the initial experimental training course's success, the professional accreditation body for post-basic nurse education in England and Wales, the Joint Board of Clinical Nursing Studies, approved and published an outline curriculum to facilitate national adoption of this form of clinical specialization (JBCNS, 1975). Reorganization of nurse education in 1983 led to the formation of new statutory professional nursing bodies and the absorption of the JBCNS into the national approval and accreditation organizations for England, Wales, Scotland, and Northern Ireland.

Now available as English National Board (ENB) post-basic clinical nursing studies course 650 (adult behavioural psychotherapy – short-term therapy), training for nurse behaviour therapists is established in three centres, London, Sheffield, and Plymouth. A fourth centre in Chichester closed in March 1987 when regional financing was allocated for other purposes. Since 1972, some 126 nurse behaviour therapists have been trained, of which approximately 80 per cent are either in full-time clinical practice or maintain a clinical case load alongside their other professional duties in management and education. A small number of these have subsequently undertaken clinical degrees in psychology and several practise in Australia and the USA.

With a further eighteen nurse therapists in training at present, a small but nevertheless significant number of formally trained behaviour therapists continue to be produced each year by the nursing profession. In addition, specialist ENB courses train behavioural clinical nurse specialists in mental handicap (ENB course 705) and rehabilitation (ENB course 655) whilst the Scottish National Board's course in Dundee provides a notable training programme for nurses developing behavioural skills in adult neurosis, rehabilitation, and mental handicap specialities.

The development of formal nurse therapist educational courses has significantly influenced other less specialized training courses. For example, those psychiatric nurses undergoing formal post-basic training as community psychiatric nurses (ENB course 811) receive educational modules to equip them with case management skills for therapeutic work with simple and complex phobic disorders including agoraphobia.

It is in many ways regrettable that the onset of the world economic recession should coincide with the development of nurse behaviour therapist training. This has severely affected state-funded health provision and led to marked restrictions in health authorities' investment in training courses. Mental health and psychiatric nursing developments are consequently limited by economies and efficiency savings. Fortunately, the behavioural emphasis on clinical outcome measures, effectiveness, and efficiency have preserved the small number of training centres thus far. The high demand for clinical services continues to outstrip the supply of effective behavioural therapists from any profession, so it is probable that with continuing evidence of cost-effectiveness, nurse behaviour therapist training initiatives will continue.

Nurse therapist training can be viewed as a legitimate function in the process of 'giving psychology away' (Milne 1986). As clinical psychology researchers develop new and experimentally validated treatment strategies with proven effectiveness, the range of client problems for which help is available widens. As therapeutic methods are refined and the most effective component elements are identified, skills training programmes can be devised to broaden their availability to other professionals in the mental health services. It does not appear to be either efficient or cost-effective for such clinical methods to remain the intellectual property of a single health care profession, especially when the resulting increases in clinical referrals choke departmental waiting lists and thereby prevent the research-oriented clinical practitioner from moving ahead to develop further therapeutic methods for other human difficulties.

First-level psychiatric nurse education in the UK currently takes three years (RMN), or eighteen months if the nurse is already qualified in general nursing (RGN). Entry to ENB course 650 training programmes is usually limited to those qualified RMNs who have significant post-qualification experience (eighteen months at Plymouth centre) and evidence a high standard of clinical work in either a position of recognized responsibility or clinical autonomy, e.g. team leaders, ward sisters or charge nurses, innovators, and community psychiatric nurses. Competition to gain a training post is high at selection, due in main to the limited number of training places available nationally. Consequently, course members tend to demonstrate high levels of motivation, energy, and enthusiasm. Intelligence surveys show higher than average ability (Marks *et al.* 1977), and attitudinal and personality surveys (conducted with Plymouth centre course members) suggest high levels of independence and leadership, with low levels of conformity (Gordon 1960).

ENB course 650 lasts eighteen months, operating as a small learning group within a specialized clinical unit. As the course is very skill- and role-development orientated, it is inappropriate for it to be based in a separate academic institution. Course members in most centres share a clinical base with trained nurse therapists and in some instances with psychiatrists or clinical psychologists. This leads to such departments having a clear dual function as both a clinical area and an academic teaching unit. The Plymouth centre, for example (training up to six therapists in each intake), is based in and occupies half of one floor in a three-storey community mental health centre. The course teacher and six trained therapists share offices and interview rooms with course members, supported by a secretary in a central record office. An audio-video studio and group teaching room with library area completes the unit.

This proximity facilitates modelling opportunities for course members and improves access to advice and supervision. Additional clinical space is available at a city-centre mental health clinic and in general practitioner primary health care clinics in one suburb of the city and in several of the small towns and villages outside Plymouth.

When the Plymouth course commenced in 1978, it shared facilities with the district's clinical psychology department but expansion of both services required a separation of departments in 1983. Together, trained and trainee nurse therapists are identified as the Behaviour Therapy Nursing Service, sharing a common referral and waiting list system. Each year of operation has seen a growth in referrals of a wide range of outpatient neuroses. In the accounting year ending in March 1987, the department received 513 referrals (9.9 cases per week) whilst the current rate for 1987/8 is some 10.3 cases per week. Current population of the health district is some 324,000.

Referred problems cover a wide spectrum of clinical problems. Clinical anxiety states (anxiety with depression, chronic tension, stress reactions, panic, and general anxiety disorder) make up 40 per cent of cases, agoraphobia 12 per cent, marital disharmony 7 per cent, obsessional-compulsive disorder 5 per cent, sexual dysfunctions 6 per cent, simple phobias 5 per cent, social phobias and social skills deficits 5 per cent. The remaining referrals range from unconventional sexual behaviour, anger and temper control difficulties, eating disorders, compulsive gambling, alcohol abuse, extended grief reactions to hypochondriasis, and more recently HIV/AIDS fears.

It is notable that due to therapists working in GP primary care settings, a differing clinical picture emerges than that in the outpatient clinics. In this less stigmatized setting, failed appointments are fewer and clients are often far less chronically affected. Indeed, in a significant proportion of clinical anxiety states, the presence of developing escape and avoidance strategies in recently affected people seems to indicate the early phases of agoraphobic difficulties which can be relatively easily resolved.

In 1978, over 50 per cent of referrals were from consultant psychiatrists and their registrars. Now, 60 per cent of referrals come directly from general practitioners and 25 per cent from consultant psychiatrists, with the remainder arriving from the district's crisis intervention service, staff occupational health, social workers, the sexually transmitted disease clinic, and local probation offices.

COURSE TRAINING REQUIREMENTS

The ENB course 650 outline curriculum (ENB 1983) sets out the outline objectives to be achieved in therapeutic skills development and academic learning. There is a heavy weighting given to clinical experience; and assessment strategies applied to learners require the operation of a system of continuous and intermittenta ssessment rather than formal examination. By the completion of training, course members are required to present a minimum of twelve detailed case management studies demonstrating their clinical effectiveness within adequate trials of treatment in the following categories of difficulty:

1 two specific or social phobias;
2 two agoraphobic syndromes;
3 two obsessional-compulsive disorders;
4 two sexual difficulties (dysfunction and/or unconventional sexual behaviour);
5 four miscellaneous problems, e.g. social maladjustment, personality or habit disorders, generalized anxiety disorder, eating disorders, etc.

It is necessary that marital or family contract therapy be demonstrated as part of treatment programmes; and that two cases be presented where domiciliary treatment was required.

These trainee assessment requirements for clinical practice do not, however, give a fair picture of each course member's actual clinical experience. Over the eighteen months' training, Plymouth trainees assess or 'screen' between 100 and 130 patients each and are able to provide fair trials of treatment to between 70 and 90 clients in individual, couples, and small group treatment formats. A fair trial of treatment involves a participative client receiving five or more treatment sessions with pre- and post-treatment measures completed with follow-up results available.

A detailed assessment strategy guides each course member's individual supervisor (all trained nurse behaviour therapists) in the continuous formative, and intermittent summative, assessment of skills and role development. Each course member has a case management meeting weekly with his, or her, supervisor during the first six months of training, this dropping to fortnightly and then three-weekly by the end of the course. Supervisors sit in to observe and assess 'live' interviews and treatment sessions at a high level of frequency in the first six months, fading this out to an average of four sessions per month by the end of training. Detailed skills assessment checklists and rating scales have been developed to facilitate this essentially formative, advisory and systematic feedback system. Supervisor meetings collate results from this system at quarterly meetings to provide summative results on skills acquisition. In addition, individual supervisors monitor clinical effectiveness within each case and across case load to ensure that trainees produce clinical results that are comparable with other behavioural therapists for each category of client problem. The use of standarized clinical measures within single-case outcome designs facilitates this assessment. Such monitoring of measurable clinical effectiveness is critical as the credibility of any formalized therapist training requires demonstration of both skill development and effective outcome results. Brooker and Wiggins (1983) have shown that without such monitoring it is possible for ineffective therapists to complete training without being identified.

Course design and agoraphobia

Using Plymouth ENB course 650 centre as an operational example, I intend to show how nurses with limited knowledge of behavioural psychotherapy and few behavioural treatment skills on entry to training can become effective and efficient therapists for anxiety-based disorders, including agoraphobia, in a relatively short time. That the actual duration of the course is eighteen months hides the fact that key skills in clinical intervention with clinical anxiety states and simple and complex phobic disorders, such as agoraphobia, are learnt and applied early in training. The eighteen-month duration is required to provide learning with an extensive range of clinical problems of increasing complexity, necessitating the acquisition of an extensive range of interpersonal and technical therapeutic skills. Competence, effectiveness, confidence, and efficiency are as desynchronous as emotions. Optimum therapist proficiency, we argue, necessitates a high level of clinical experience both under close supervision and in planned delegation to promote confident autonomy.

The eighteen months is separated into three six-month-long components. Each course member is allocated an individual supervisor for six months at a time, changing supervisor at the six-and twelve-month points to allow closer access to different trained therapists' case management and supervision styles.

In operational terms, the first six months form the foundation component of training. Following an orientation block of ten days, course members enter an intensive educational programme. This allocates two days each week to clinical observation of trained therapists, with graded exposure to assessment and treatment with clients selected for suitability by supervisors through the department's 'screening' system and waiting list. The remaining three days each week are assigned to academic teaching, role-play simulation workshops (with video-tape feedback for a proportion of these), case management workshops, journal and case presentations, and departmental meetings.

Teaching inputs on learning theory background are incorporated into the educational programme in two ways. The initial ten-day orientation period includes intensive teaching on the theoretical and experimental basis of behavioural and cognitive-behavioural approaches to human learning and psychological difficulty. The aim at this point is to demonstrate the breadth and variability in learning theory and derived principles. In the absence of satisfactory integrated theories, an eclectic but pragmatic approach is encouraged to provide a basis for self-directed study. Nevertheless, in an attempt to provide an over-arching model for course members in their studies and clinical practice, the cognitive social learning perspective (Mahoney 1980) is presented as a practical solution to the problem of integrating diverse theoretical approaches.

Second, research and theory inputs are presented within the continuing academic programme as component elements of problem-centred study days. Therefore, in the three agoraphobic syndrome academic teaching sessions in the course programme during weeks seven to nine (see Table 7.1), research and theory is presented to provide multiple perspectives on phenomenology, development, maintenance, and treatment specific to agoraphobia. This strategy is repeated for each clinical entity studied throughout the educational programme. Thereby, research and theory repeatedly appear as a linked theme as course members' studies progress from anxiety and fear through phobias, agoraphobia, social anxiety, social skills deficits to obsessional-compulsive disorders and beyond.

As I have mentioned earlier, the central educational focus of ENB course 650 is skills and role development. Research and theory teaching is presented as support to this central focus. Nurse behaviour therapists' learning is based on an apprenticeship model (Marks *et al.* 1977). The most effective approaches to skills learning and role development require a structured programme of practice-centred learning with access to skilled therapists as mastery models; role-play

Table 7.1 ENB course 650 first-term programme, weeks three to eleven

	Week 3	Week 4	Week 5	Week 6	Week 7	Week 8	Week 9	Week 10	Week 11
Mon.	Clinical observations and graded exposure to assessment, screening, and treatment								
Tues.	Role-play simulation workshops on interviewing and assessment skills followed by skills in the treatment of anxiety disorders and simple and complex phobias								
Wed. a.m.	Anxiety and emotion study day	Clinical anxiety states I	Clinical anxiety states II	Simple phobic disorders	Agoraphobic syndrome 1	Agoraphobic syndrome 2	Agoraphobic syndrome 3	Exposure methods workshop	Cognitive therapy for anxiety and fear
		Phenomenology Assessment	Treatment		Phenomenology	Assessment	Assessment	all day	
p.m.		Assessment methods I	Assessment methods II	Assessment methods III	Assessment methods IV	Assessment methods V	Assessment methods VI		
Thurs. a.m.	9–10 a.m. weekly CPN meeting 10–11 a.m. weekly behaviour therapy referral meeting 11–12 mid-day weekly journal seminar 12–1 p.m. weekly case management workshop								
p.m.	Clinical observations and graded exposure to assessment, screening, and treatment								
Fri. a.m.	Morning assigned to self-directed study and preparation								
p.m.	Clinical observations and graded exposure to assessment, screening, and treatment								

simulations with audio-visual and verbal feedback; graded practice of newly acquired skills with real clients supported by formative feedback from supervisors; and increasing periods of less directly supervised practice to promote confidence and autonomy (Levine and Tinkler 1974, Milne 1986).

In the early weeks of training, course members are guided by their supervisors on clinical practice days from observation to assessment interviewing and co-therapist roles. For example (see Table 7.1), a course member by week ten of training is likely to have sat in as an observer on up to thirty sessions of supervisor-led assessment and treatment and will have conducted supervised interviews with approximately ten people. They will by this point have acted as a therapist under supervisor direction on some six to ten treatment sessions involving anxiety management training methods and exposure-based treatments for individuals with clinical anxiety states, simple phobias, and agoraphobia. By this point, they will also have started to build their own individual case load as the main therapist (with sit-in supervision) for up to five clients presenting with clinical anxiety states and phobias.

By week twenty-six of training, the average course member will have amassed a considerable volume of observational experience and will have developed a high level of assessment skill. By this six-month point, most course members will have a personal case load of approximately twelve clients and will already have discharged between three and five successfully treated people. Their case load by this stage is likely to consist of up to six people with varieties of clinical anxiety states, two agoraphobics and one simple phobia, plus one or two cases of social anxiety and an obsessional-compulsive disorder. Clinically, their competence (from analysis of course members over six training intakes) will be the strongest in the delivery of *in vivo* exposure methods of treatment for phobic disorders and in the delivery of multi-method anxiety management training (progressive muscle relaxation training, cognitive-behavioural management using interventions derived from Meichenbaum's stress inoculation training, problem-solving skills training, assertiveness and fear reduction techniques such as cognitive rehearsal and paradoxical intention).

Paralleling observational learning and graded practice sessions with their supervisors, in the early weeks of training, course members undergo an exhaustive programme of extended day-long role-play simulation workshops. Using an audio-visual studio to facilitate video-tape feedback of performance, the first six workshops focus on the development of assessment skills, functional analysis, and treatment planning. Additional teaching sessions on assessment methods link academic teaching, data collection, questionnaire usage, objective setting, rating scale measurement, and report-writing skills to the more practical learning of professional interpersonal skills in role-play.

As the development of a high level of interpersonal skill in interviewing is an essential ingredient in assessment of anxiety-based difficulties such as agoraphobia, I shall at this point give examples of the skills objectives for these role-play simulation workshops. They are derived from skills analyses of practising behavioural therapists and texts on assessment skills (Priestley and Maguire 1983).

During these extended role-play simulation workshops, course members develop skills in assessment and, later, treatment with experienced therapists enacting roles as therapist (modelling) and clients. Client difficulty can be varied from uncomplicated and co-operative to complex and unco-operative.

In addition to basic skills appropriate to all client groups, specific skills in the assessment of discrete client categories are focused on. Table 7.2 provides guidance notes for trainees on specific areas to consider in the assessment of agoraphobic individuals. This is an expanded version of the 'Guide to interviewing with agoraphobia' (Marks et al. 1977). This has proved a useful learning tool with novice therapists who can include it within a set of clients' case notes for use as a prompt/check-list when assessing their first 'real' clients.

Assessment skills are more than interview skills. The therapist requires a thorough understanding of the phenomenology of the given clinical problem and how to distinguish between similar, but different, psychiatric diagnostic criteria. Although nurse therapists and behavioural therapists are not principally interested (or qualified) in medical-model diagnoses, referring agencies usually are medical practitioners with whom effective communication needs to be established using a shared language. In the mental health field misdiagnosis is remarkably easy, so it is necessary for assessing therapists to use their understanding of clinical problems to describe the client and his/her problem both behaviourally (in order to prepare functional analyses) and medically to ensure that appropriate differential diagnoses can be arrived at.

In agoraphobia, a syndrome categorization by medical

Table 7.2 ENB post-basic clinical nursing studies course 650 (adult behavioural psychotherapy) Plymouth centre: assessing people presenting with agoraphobic difficulties

Specific areas for questioning

1   What are your main fears (order of severity)? Fear of fear?

2   Duration of these fears (note starting date)?

3   Describe characteristics of environmental stimuli (are crowded buses worse than empty ones)? Distance away from home or place of safety?

4   What physical symptoms do you experience when you are in a fearful situation (e.g. palpitations, changes in breathing, churning stomach, butterflies, muscle tension, neck/head-ache, shakes, jelly legs, hairs stand up, goose flesh, go pale/flushed, urge to micturate or defæcate, aches/pains, pins and needles, feel unsteady, lose balance, staggers, feel faint, light-headed, giddy/dizzy, derealization, blurred vision, tunnel vision, objects recede, dry mouth, lump in throat, can't swallow, feel hot/cold, sweating, passing wind, etc.)?

5   What do you fear will happen? (e.g. faint, lose control, mess self, wet self, go crazy, make spectacle of self, have heart attack, die, or some other imagined consequence).

6   What happens when you anticipate entering a fearful situation?

7   What are your thoughts like during anticipation? Compare and contrast with (a) neutral situations (b) feared situations. Do you rehearse what can go wrong in imagination? (Do you notice what proportion of your thinking is positive (self-reinforcing, pleasant, confidence building, happy) and what proportion negative (awful, anxious, self-attacking, doomy, pessimistic, unpleasant, confidence weakening, desperate, escape/avoidance oriented)?

8   Have you noticed if your fears have spread? (stimulus generalization).

9   Have your responses to feared situations changed with time? If so, how? (worsened, improved, any time free of problem, variable).

10 Can you enter feared situations at all or do you avoid? If you avoid, how far can you get in approaching feared situation? If you can enter situation, how long can you stay? What makes you escape? What makes you stay when you do? What level of fear triggers escape? When you leave situations, do you run/walk, control self/scream/cry? Can you persuade yourself to stay, carry on, or enter situations by talking to yourself?

11 How are you doing things alone, with spouse, parents, your child, relatives, friends, neighbours, girl/boyfriend, strangers, or pets?

12 Do you have any particular ploys you use to feel better? (e.g. dark glasses, alcohol, pills, dog on lead, heavy bag, brolly, walking stick, shopping trolley, carry book, carry charm or bottle of fluid).

13 Have you ever had a full blown panic attack (extreme terror)? If different from general experience, describe it to me? What did you do? Frequency, intensity, duration? What happens to your breathing?

14 If you escape/avoid, what happens? Do you experience immediate relief? What happens afterwards – exhaustion, tiredness, unease, have a reaction, get the shakes?

15 What was your worst experience? Describe in detail?

Table 7.2 continued

16   What has been your most recent experience, in detail?

17   Describe how you got here today. Did you have any difficulties or take any precautions?

18   Were there any special events (new home, weddings, birth, etc.) or unpleasant circumstances (bereavement, lost job, assaults, illnesses, etc.) in your life around the time your fears began? What about the preceding six to twelve months?

19   Do you have relatives with similar fears?

20   Have you ever received any forms of treatment for your fears: what sorts and with what results?

21   Are you receiving any medication – name, dose, frequency? Do you know what they do? Who prescribes them? How long have you been taking them? With what effect? What happens if you don't take them? Do you rely on them? Do you vary the doses? (If you can't remember details, bring in the bottles.)

22   Do you ever take alcohol to reduce anxiety? (Dutch courage). Do you ever use any other drugs (pot, tobacco, smelling salts), legal or otherwise? With what effects? Any withdrawal/dependency symptoms from anxiolytics, alcohol, or drugs?

23   Describe in detail your range by foot, bus, train, car, bike, etc. What restriction do you have in your travelling? Do you *always* avoid?

24   Do you experience free floating anxiety – anxiety and panic coming out of the blue with no warning and no identifiable environmental cues? How often? With what effect? How long does it last? How long does it take to recover? In women, is there any variation related to menstrual cycle?

25   How are you in enclosed places (lifts, hair-dryers, queues, waiting rooms, public toilet cubicles, small rooms, cinema, middle of row in audiences, windowless rooms, tunnels, etc.)?

26   How do you feel when left alone at home? How do you manage/cope?

27   Do you ever take to your bed because of anxiety? Persuade spouse or children, friends, or relatives to stay home to help you cope or shop?

28   If left alone, do you (a) try to call in a friend/neighbour (how often)? (b) telephone spouse/relative/friends (how often)?

29   In crowded circumstances, do you feel people are looking at you?

30   Do you prefer open, light places (such as fields) or enclosed spaces or darkness (such as small narrow streets)?

31   Could you go into crowded city streets on a Saturday, join a crowded football stadium or sports event, shop in London's Oxford Street, go to a pop concert, or a crowded supermarket/superstore?

32   Do you find that you need to seek reassurance about your health from relatives/doctor frequently?

33   It will be helpful for me to meet and talk with your partner. When will this be most convenient?

Table 7.2 continued

Other fears and associated difficulties

a   Heights (bridges, cliffs, how many floors, steps on a ladder), thunderstorms, wind, animals, insects (spiders, wasps, beetles), illness (cancer, VD, heart disease), being alone, vomiting, surgery, injections, blood (any fainting?), hospitals, dentists, flying.

b   Social anxieties (differentiate from skills deficits). Starting conversations with friends/ strangers, parties, pubs, complaining, returning defective goods, trying on shoes/clothes in shops, eating in restaurants, carrying cups in front of others, public speaking, asking for dates, refusing requests, expressing opinions or emotions.

c   Evidence of excessive cleanliness, tidiness, or checking. Is there any obsessional-compulsive disorder? Ruminations?

d   Any marital/sexual difficulties (Men – premature ejaculation, erectile failure, ejaculatory incompetence, low libido. Women – orgasmic failure, heterophobia, vaginismus, painful intercourse, low libido)?

e   Do you ever suffer depression of mood? Regularly or periodically? Is your mood related to monthly menstruation?

f   Check for depressive symptoms (energy, appetite, libido, sleep patterns, guilt, attitude to future, suicidal ideas, health worries)?

g   Are you physically fit? Do you have any breathing or circulatory difficulties other than caused by anxiety? (Check for angina, coronary heart disease, asthma, emphysema, epilepsy, peptic ulcer, colitis – rule out flooding!).

h   What do you want to achieve in treatment? What would you be able to do, and want to do, if you were improved tomorrow? Expectations? Optimism vs. pessimism? Myths and misconceptions about behaviour therapy?

General cues

5 W H – who, why, when, where, what, how?
3 systems analysis – cognitive, physiological, and behavioural experience.
Antecedents, behaviours, consequences. Frequency and intensity.
Excesses, deficits, and assets.
Organize data collection diaries.
Questionnaire and rating scale measures.
Behavioural avoidance tests.

practitioners, the therapist requires up-to-date knowledge on classification (American Psychiatric Association 1980, Thorpe and Burns 1983), and a knowledge base in the multiple perspectives on theories of causation/development and maintenance (Chambless and Goldstein 1982). Additionally, they require skills in behavioural and cognitive assessment strategies (Hersen and Bellack 1981) both as general skills and in their application with agoraphobia (Thorpe and Burns 1983). Methods of clinical measurement, their reliability and validity, and use as change indicators is essential to demonstrate effectiveness or failure (Rachman and Wilson 1980, Foa and Emmelkamp 1983). Skills and knowledge of the process of functional analysis of clinical problems and strategies for decision making and treatment planning are fundamental requirements that differentiate the genuinely skilled behavioural practitioner from the 'cook-book' therapist (Goldstein and Foa 1980). Finally, they require an extensive range of technical treatment skills for the management of people, their fears and relationships; and up-to-date knowledge on treatment methodology, effectiveness, and intervention options (Thyer 1987, Marks 1981, Chambless and Goldstein 1982).

Just as there is no (and ought not be any) 'cook-book' approach to the management of people's individual clinical difficulties, there is no shortcut to the development of clinical skills with agoraphobia, or any other emotional disorder. Novice therapists need to be introduced to clinical practice in a prepared and structured manner that provides them with a repertoire of skills and supportive knowledge which allows them to provide both effective interventions for the client and effective learning for themselves. Clinical practice needs to be seen as a learning process for client and therapist (Clarke and Wardman 1985). Learning proceeds best when objectives are clear, active practice (and modelling) is available both in terms of quality and quantity, and when effective evaluative feedback is made available (Milne 1986).

Within ENB course 650 we have mounted a course design that, with many limitations, sets out to provide novice therapists with a repertoire of core skills and a fundamental knowledge of cognitive and behavioural interventions related to specified clinical problems as early as possible in their training. These are extended sequentially through the duration of training by additional skills learning, extensive knowledge teaching, accumulated clinical experience, and self-directed study. Supervised practice provides feedback and client-centred advice to assist in decision making and treatment applications.

It is perhaps a truism to say that all students need everything at the commencement of clinical practice, but this is not feasible. They do, however, need enough to provide a quality of intervention that effectively benefits their clients without leaving themselves feeling incompetent. It is our contention therefore that the building of core skills in the first months of a clinical practice course are critical in developing effective therapists. What are these skills and how may they best be learnt?

The sequential academic and practical introduction to each broad category of clinical problem using formal teaching sessions and role-play simulations proceeds on the basis that clinical knowledge and therapeutic skills are additive. The academic knowledge inputs and clinical skills relevant to clinical anxiety states are viewed as necessary basic precursors for developing an understanding of, and developing skills in the management of, simple phobic disorders (animals, insects, enclosed spaces, heights, etc.). Similarly, this is viewed as a necessary precursor for an introduction to agoraphobic disorders and social anxiety/social skill difficulties. The practical constraints on curriculum design prevent us from introducing other material relevant to agoraphobia, such as the inputs on marital disharmony, assertiveness, and sexual dysfunction, early in training but the availability of clinical practice supervisors enable these issues to be addressed in initial casework without noticeable detriment to the client's management.

General therapeutic orientation

Trainee therapists are in the process of role development. It is important that they are able to adopt an approach to clinical practice that enables them to relate to clients, casework, and their own learning in a consistent manner. For our purposes, this general therapeutic orientation has three components:

1 intervention strategy
2 theoretical position
3 clinical stance

Intervention strategy

The intervention strategy is the use of an intervention model/strategy which facilitates individualized therapy within a single-case design. This requires a five-stage process of clinical practice:

1 assessment
2 formulation
3 planning
4 implementation
5 evaluation

This needs to be viewed as a system where assessment is not a discrete component occurring only at the commencement of therapy but one where new information is continually added to the therapist's understanding of the client and his difficulties (Chambless and Goldstein 1980), enabling reformulations and planning changes to be made in conjunction with the feedback loop established by evaluating the effects of implementing different treatment techniques.

Table 7.3 General educational objectives matrix
Plymouth ENB course 650

	Clinical skills	Clinical knowledge	Clinical attitudes
Assessment	15	27	26
Formulation	9	13	11
Planning	13	21	14
Implementation	24	19	16
Evaluation	7	16	13

For training purposes, interpersonal and technical skills, knowledge requirements, and desirable attitudes can then be identified within each component of the intervention system. These can be expressed as educational objectives to facilitate the development of therapist competencies during course experience (Gronlund 1978). General educational objectives derived by this method at Plymouth ENB course 650 centre for the entire course can be expressed in the matrix shown in table 7.3.

The figures indicate the number of general educational objectives generated in each component area and as such are more of interest to educators than to clinicians. Such an approach greatly assists course planning although non-behavioural educationalists might consider it as evidence of obsessional-compulsive disorder.

Theoretical position

The theoretical position adopted is one within which the therapist can approach clinical data, make formulations, and generate clinical plans. The loosely integrated cognitive social learning perspective (Mahoney 1980) used in an eclectic and pragmatic way is identified as the most appropriate at this time for Plymouth centre. Additional theoretical inputs specific to presenting problems can be easily related to this integrated perspective.

Clinical stance

The clinical stance is the adoption of a therapeutic stance in which to relate to clients and to present clinical interventions. The Plymouth centre promotes the therapist as educator model as the most appropriate for our purposes. The client is viewed as a learner whose (accidental) learning experiences have generated life-style functioning difficulties which the therapist, as educator, analyses and generates new learning plans based on cognitive and behavioural research data. The client undergoes new learning experiences in clinical sessions which, reinforced by homework tasks, produce and maintain change.

CORE CLINICAL SKILLS

As mentioned previously these are identified within the five-stage process strategy.

Assessment

Interview skills with clients and their partners are developed using:

1 the three-component (three-system) model of fear and emotion (Lang 1971) to identify client experiences;
2 a detailed examination of antecedents, behaviours, and consequences (Hersen and Bellack, 1981);
3 'BASIC ID' (Lazarus 1976) examining behaviour, affect, sensation, imagery, cognition, interpersonal relations, and drugs/diet;
4 a focus on current problems in lifestyle supported by examination of factors in the development and maintenance of difficulties;
5 clinical measures that are valid and reliable; in particular, for individuals with agoraphobic difficulties, using fear survey schedules (Marks *et al.* 1977) and a reliable measure of mood such as the Beck depression inventory (Beck *et al.* 1961);
6 data collection diaries, as basic homework exercise, to identify frequency, intensity, and duration of anxiety and panic experiences in relationship to activity and whereabouts; these providing baseline information and preparing the client for the systematic recording of progress in any choice of self- controlled exposure *in vivo* (Emmelkamp 1982, Chambless and Goldstein 1980);
7 problem rating scales examining distress and impact on lifestyle (Marks *et al.* 1977);
8 behavioural avoidance tests to sample and objectively verify degree of distress and avoidance (Thorpe and Burns 1983, Mathews *et al.* 1981).

Clinical measurement and agoraphobia

Clinical measurement is an essential feature of systematic case management. Behaviour therapy has grown out of an honourable tradition of psychological and psychiatric research which has attempted to add a degree of valid and reliable objectivity to a field for too long noted for its subjectivity. The range of clinical measures available is enormous but a high proportion set out to measure areas, such as personality and trait, which have little clinical utility.

The practising behavioural therapist requires measurement devices that fulfil essentially practical purposes. In assessment, such measures need to provide valid information on the individual's current state indicating the range and severity of problems experienced. This information should indicate frequency and duration of difficulties experienced, such as anxiety and panic attacks, and demonstrate the limitations imposed on the individual's lifestyle. They add data to self-report information gained during interview.

At one level, such measures contribute to the therapist's functional analysis of the client problem by improving understanding. At a second level, they provide a pre-treatment baseline of the individual's state that can be used as a reference point to measure the impact, or otherwise, of treatment. This requires validity and test–retest reliability plus a sensitivity to actual change in the client's state. Such measures can then contribute to objective evaluation of treatment effectiveness in order to assist the therapist in modifying treatment and to demonstrate actual improvements produced.

Certain measures, such as data collection diaries, can be extremely useful in monitoring ongoing patient experiences and in providing the client with feedback on their own progress. These are nevertheless time-consuming and can become wearisome for many clients with attendant risks of misuse.

Clinical rating scales are simple and easy to use but suffer from subjective influences unless supported by a behavioural avoidance test to ensure validity.

Questionnaire measures, such as fear survey schedules (once validity and reliability are established), need to be 'user friendly' and easy to interpret and score. ENB course 650 trainees are required to use a range of clinical measures in their casework. Some of these are standard and apply to all clients seen, e.g. life history questionnaire (Lazarus 1971), fear questionnaire (Marks *et al* 1977), Beck depression inventory (Beck *et al.* 1961), and rating scales for problems, targets, and life adjustment (Marks *et al.* 1977).

Additional measures are used to examine particular clinical problems, e.g. agoraphobia or obsessional-compulsive disorder, or to assess the relevance of another life area to the main client difficulty, e.g. marital disorder, assertiveness.

In course members' management of agoraphobia, the most relevant clinical measures used, apart from rating scales and data diaries, are fear questionnaires and the Beck depression inventory. Plymouth centre use three different questionnaire measures with agoraphobic clients:

1 *Modified fear questionnaire (Marks et al.* 1977 describe a revised fear questionnaire which measures 23 fear items on a 0–8 scale of avoidance allowing scoring for agoraphobia (Ag), social phobia (Soc), and blood/injury fears (Bl)). The modified fear questionnaire examines 15 fear items on two 0–8 scales of i) fear and ii) avoidance with similar sub-scoring for Ag/Soc/Bl (Thorpe and Hecker 1987). As desynchrony between cognition/affect, physiology, and behaviour are common, we find the separate examination of fear and avoidance clinically useful (Rachman and Hodgson 1974).

2 *Agoraphobia questionnaire.* Developed by Burns (1977) in conjunction with a national survey of agoraphobics and a treatment outcome study (Thorpe and Burns 1983), this 25-item device which uses a 1–5 scale of fear and avoidance has high internal consistency, and like the modified fear questionnaire has very satisfactory concurrent validity with interview ratings and behavioural test results (Thorpe and Hecker 1987).

3 *The mobility inventory for agoraphobia* (Chambless *et al.* 1985). This 26-item questionnaire asks clients to note their degree of avoidance, on a 1–5 scale, both when alone and when accompanied by a trusted companion. It is a stable and internally consistent scale with high test–retest reliability which is sensitive to treatment changes. We find this measure useful because of its clear discrimination between accompanied and unaccompanied activity which is an important element to consider in agoraphobia assessment.

Formulation

The therapist draws together all their available sources of information on the client and the clinical problem in order to make a functional analysis of the individual's difficulties (Kanfer and Saslow 1969, Hersen and Bellack 1981, Chambless and Goldstein 1980, Beech *et al.* 1982). This analysis produces evidence and hypotheses to test, regarding the relationship between the individual and their environment, development and maintenance factors, personal and social relationships, motivation and self-control. It allows the therapist to identify intervention points and enables planning decisions and predictions to be made.

It can be particularly useful to examine the client's difficulties in terms of behavioural excesses, deficits, and assets (such as self-control and coping strategies employed) and relating these to identified antecedents, behaviours, and consequences. Then cognitive-behavioural factors can be added to this functional description to widen the therapist viewpoint and increase the therapeutic options available to be considered in planning.

Planning

Tailoring treatment to the individual—Using research-based knowledge of therapeutic methods available for the identified clinical problem and target behaviours, the therapist identifies the most appropriate strategies for change. Treatment plans need to be tailored to the individual client's identified needs and choices made about delivery method to be offered. For example, a three-component analysis (Lang 1971) will indicate the relative importance of cognitive, behavioural and physiological factors in the individual's experience. If cognitive elements such as high anticipatory anxiety related to negative cognitive rehearsals and negative internal dialogue are prominent, the therapist should consider the relevance of a cognitive treatment approach for this element. This might involve the intention to use cognitive self-guidance (Meichenbaum 1977) alongside exposure methods for agoraphobia. The presence of high levels of autonomic arousal in non-phobic situations, appearing as free-floating anxiety, might suggest the planned use of progressive muscle relaxation training (Jacobson 1938, Beech *et al.* 1982) or some variant of this (Clarke and Wardman 1985) together with cognitive strategies (Meichenbaum 1977, Beck and Emery 1985). Although cognitive behavioural treatments are less effective than exposure methods, there is suggestive evidence that they improve compliance and engagement, and have longer-term effects.

The identified occurrence of panic attacks will indicate a need to examine both cognitive strategies to facilitate exposure (Mathews *et al.* 1981) and perhaps the intention to use respiratory control training techniques where hyperventilation is an identified factor (Salkovskis *et al.* 1986, Clark 1986).

The presence of health-related fears such as anticipating a heart attack or 'stroke' whilst anxious, or when entering a fear-related environment, could suggest the intention to use paradoxical intention (Frankl 1955, Ascher 1980) within exposure sessions.

The presence of mitral valve prolapse (MVP), a non-dangerous cardiac anomaly identified in some agoraphobics and presenting with missed heart beats, extrasystoles, palpitations, syncope, fatigue, dyspnoea, and atypical chest pains, may indicate the need for a physician's educational reassurance prior to exposure (Leibowitz and Klein 1982, Emmelkamp and van der Hout 1983).

Many agoraphobic clients present with concurrent assertion difficulties. Where this is the case, the therapist needs to consider its relationship to the individual's overall social and communication skills. This may be particularly important within marital relationships where poor communication may be a factor in maintenance of agoraphobia or in marital discord. Where assertion difficulties do not appear to be a major factor in maintenance, this difficulty can be left for reassessment following exposure-based treatment; but where it occurs within a disturbed marital relationship, the therapist must consider either concurrent marital/communications therapy alongside an exposure programme or even as a preparative step before it. In such cases, exposure treatments may fail or the risk of relapse is greatly increased (Emmelkamp and van der Hout 1983).

Agoraphobia is both a distressing and depressing problem to have. Lowered mood is not an unusual feature to find at assessment. Therapists need to consider the severity of depression before commencing treatment, for although research evidence suggests that it will not generally interfere with improvement (Emmelkamp and van der Hout 1983), other workers note adverse effects (Marks 1969). In practical terms, high levels of depression produce motivational deficits with attendant problems with treatment compliance and the negative pessimistic cognitions associated with lowered mood can directly influence the therapist's attempts to promote positive expectations in treatment. On the other hand, successful exposure treatments and the high level of homework practice required within a treatment programme often lift mild to moderate degrees of depression, apparently by demonstrating positive therapeutic consequences and by increasing activity levels that allow access to a wider range of feedback and reinforcement.

Alcohol misuse is associated with a proportion of agoraphobic clients (Chambless 1982, Thorpe and Burns 1983) largely as a secondary clinical problem. Its main use appears to be for its anxiolytic properties. The therapist will find it necessary to control the patient's use of alcohol so that it does not influence exposure practice. Unless the individual is alcohol dependent, this may be a relatively simple exercise of rescheduling drinks so that they are used as reinforcers post- exposure, rather than as 'Dutch courage' pre-exposure.

Client medication can cause practical difficulties. Antidepressant medication will rarely interfere with treatment programmes but the use of anxiolytic drugs such as benzodiazepines can be problematic. By preference, we like to use exposure methods in a drug-free client, but providing doses are reduced to a minimum, they appear not to interfere seriously with exposure treatments (Marks 1981). Dependence on anxiolytic medication requires a very gradual programme of withdrawal and systematic anxiety management training (Curran and Golombok 1985).

Some clinicians prefer to combine medication with behaviour therapy for agoraphobics, but the efficacy of their results can be disputed when one considers that exposure methods have potent effects by themselves and any programme followed will require drug withdrawal at some point post-exposure (Marks 1981, Marshall and Segal 1986).

Female referrals outnumber male agoraphobic referrals by approximately two to one. Assessment often reveals the presence of variability of mood and/or anxiety symptomatology related to the menstrual cycle. Asso and Beech (1975) have shown how, in the few days prior to the onset of menstruation, the learning of aversive responses is facilitated in a proportion of women by levels of high arousability. Although little work is available to draw conclusions about the connection between premenstrual syndrome (PMS) and agoraphobia, it is our strong clinical impression that mild to moderate levels of PMS are implicated in development, maintenance, treatment progress delays, and relapse in some female agoraphobics. Should evidence of cyclical variations appear during assessment, we consider it wise to commence diary record-keeping of symptomatology and menstruation and consider this in functional analysis. Severe PMS will require medical assistance but mild to moderate levels are often relieved by self-help methods and the adaption of anxiety management training to improve the woman's coping strategies at this time. Nevertheless, predischarge counselling is usually important to ensure recurrent effects do not provide the foci for relapse.

Sexual dysfunctions, in both male and female agoraphobic clients, are not unusual. They appear most frequently as secondary to the high anxiety levels that disrupt the individual's lifestyle in agoraphobia. Although not a major focus in treatment, it may be necessary to provide psychosexual therapies for couples after exposure treatment is completed.

There are few contraindications for exposure methods in agoraphobia but the behaviour therapist will need to assess physical fitness for prolonged exposure *in vivo* where high levels of anxiety and panic may occur. In particular, the presence of angina, coronary heart disease, asthma, emphysema, peptic ulcer, or colitis should direct the therapist to slower graded exposure and self-controlled exposure methods rather than rapid (flooding) strategies.

Central treatment strategy

In agoraphobia, research evidence shows that the most effective strategies involve prolonged exposure *in vivo* (Chambless and Goldstein 1982, Foa and Emmelkamp 1983). Such a programme ought to be the central strand in a therapist's plans, but in what manner exposure is utilized requires therapeutic judgement based on assessment data, clinical experience (or with novice therapists the advice of the supervisor), and most vitally, client choice.

Agoraphobia is essentially 'fear of fear', associated with public places, transport, and with being away from home or a place of perceived safety (Chambless and Goldstein 1982). Whether treatment success functions through a process of habituation, increased self-efficacy (Bandura 1977), some multi-modal or non- specific factors, e.g. expectancy, is unclear (Thorpe and Burns 1983, Marks 1981). Whatever the process, all successful interventions utilize exposure in some form or other (Marks 1981).

Evidence suggests that therapist choice should focus on either:

Table 7.4 Central treatment strategy options

Option I	Option II	Option III	Option IV
Prolonged exposure *in vivo*.	Self-controlled exposure *in vivo*.	Prolonged exposure *in vivo* in a group.	Programmed practice.
Graded therapist accompaniment.	Therapist appointments to monitor unaccompanied exposure practice.	Between four and eight clients sharing similar fear environments.	Home-based appointments involving client, partner, and therapist.
Session duration: two hours plus.			
Session frequency: once, twice, or three times per week.	Session duration: one-and-a-half hours minimum.	One or two therapists directing sessions and managing graded accompaniment.	Five appointments in one-month period to advise and monitor programme management.
Daily self-directed homework for two hours duration.	Session frequency: daily as homework and once or twice each week from therapist's clinical base.	Session duration: two hours minimum to whole day exposures (perhaps six hours).	Daily homework practice.
(Thorpe and Burns 1983, Thyer 1987)		Session frequency: once, twice, or three times per week.	Therapist follow-up visits after two weeks, one month, three and six months.
	(Emmelkamp 1982)	Daily self-directed homework for two hours duration.	Requires programmed practice client's manual and partner's manual.
		(Hand *et al.* 1974, Emmelkamp 1982, Thorpe and Burns 1983, Jasin 1983)	(Mathews *et al.* 1981).

Individualized adjuncts

Adjunct 1 Progressive muscle relaxation training (Jacobson 1938, Bernstein and Borkovec 1973) where chronic anxiety accompanies agoraphobia.

Adjunct 2 Cognitive behaviour therapy methods.
      a Cognitive rehearsal and cognitive self-guidance
        (Meichenbaum and Genest 1980)
      b Cognitive therapy (Beck and Emery 1985)
      c Systematic rational restructuring and problem solving
        (Goldfried and Goldfried 1980)

Adjunct 3 Paradoxical intention (Frankl 1970, Ascher 1980, Gertz 1970) for specific fears of physical catastrophes in fear environments.

Adjunct 4 Respiratory control training (Salkovskis *et al.* 1986, Clark 1986) where cognitive catastrophizing is associated with panic and hyperventilation.

1. prolonged sessions of *in vivo* exposure involving the client entering and remaining in phobic situations for one-and-a-half hours or more; initially accompanied by the therapist who acts as advisor and withdraws from escorting the client in a planned manner. Frequently spaced sessions, perhaps two

or three in each week, are better than one each week. Homework exposure accompanied by partner or family and then alone facilitates the quantity and quality of exposure (using situations more personally relevant to the client). (See Table 7.4, Option I).

2. self-controlled exposure *in vivo* (Emmelkamp 1982) where the client manages his/her own prolonged exposure programmed after therapist instruction, but without therapist accompaniment, and which should include specific advice about duration of sessions and spacing of homework. In this approach, controlled avoidance of extreme anxiety is allowed providing that escape behaviour does not occur and ensuring that avoiding is followed by re-exposure. (See Table 7.4, Option II.)

3. prolonged exposure *in vivo* in groups. Taking advantage of group support and cohesion, individuals undergo exposure with fellow agoraphobics, initially accompanying each other but with the passage of time increasing the quantity of time unaccompanied. This has the advantage of greater cost-effectiveness but the disadvantage that individual goals can be given secondary priority to shared goals (Hand *et al.* 1974, Emmelkamp 1982, Thorpe and Burns 1983). (See Table 7.4, Option III).

As research evidence suggests equal effectiveness for all of the exposure procedures described, therapist choice may not be as material as client preference when the therapeutic plans are discussed.

A further consideration is the choice of a home-based treatment method such as the programmed practice treatment system devised by Mathews *et al.* (1981). This self-directed exposure programme operates through practice manuals for client and homework partner with a very low time cost to the monitoring therapist and has proven itself effective for a large number of agoraphobic clients. It is unclear, however, exactly how wide its applicability may be. (See Table 7.4, Option IV).

Agoraphobic individuals are nowadays bombarded with self-help manuals of limited effectiveness and inadequate validation. Some are excellent learning materials for trainee therapists, to learn instructional ideas from; but most do not effectively deal with accurate self-diagnosis and issues of compliance and interpersonal factors

(Rosen 1982). Agoraphobics in particular find self-help materials difficult to utilize without therapist support. Their role in conjunction with therapist-directed treatment is worth further investigation. Personally, the only self-help text my own clients have valued is Weekes (1977) but these were nevertheless people seeking therapist-directed treatment programmes.

Targeting outcome goals

An important element in planning is to negotiate agreed definitions of treatment goals with each client. Agoraphobia is recognized as a difficult clinical problem to treat (Emmelkamp and van der Hout 1983). The therapist and client need to agree exactly what the client wants to gain by the culmination of treatment if maximal co-operation and compliance are to be achieved. This appears to be most easily determined by asking the client to describe what they would be able, and want to do frequently if they were already improved. Such descriptions of intended outcome need to be operationalized into more concrete and specific wordings that are then open to objective testing and measurement (through behavioural avoidance tests and diary analysis).

For example, one client might state that they want to be able to travel from home into the city centre and be able to shop without an escort and free from fear as one aim. The therapist needs to break this global statement down into its component elements before it can be used as a valid outcome objective. This might finally appear as four outcome statements that together represent the original goal. 'At the end of my treatment programme I will be able to:

1 travel by crowded bus for twenty minutes from my home to the city centre unaccompanied;
2 walk through the pedestrianized city centre on a busy Saturday for up to two hours alone;
3 shop in a busy city-centre department store for up to one hour unaccompanied; and
4 shop in a crowded supermarket for forty-five minutes and be able to wait in the checkout queue until served, while unaccompanied.'

Together these outcome statements can be seen to sample and describe the client's original statement, but in a manner that allows the therapist to objectively measure partial success or partial failure in achieving the goals. Pre-treatment measurement can then be made

Table 7.5 Patient ratings

Subjective rating scale of distress

0   No anxiety or distress. I feel calm.
1   Very slightly anxious.
2   Slightly anxious or fearful, but easy to cope with.
3   More than slightly anxious, but fear manageable.
4   Moderately anxious or fearful, not very easy to cope with.
5   Fear is distressing, but not close to panic though it's hard to cope.
6   Very anxious and fearful, requires great effort to manage. I could easily lose control and panic.
7   I feel extremely afraid and panicky but I know I could feel worse.
8   Panic or terror. I feel unable to cope with my feelings of distress. I cannot imagine feeling any worse than I do now.

Subjective rating scale of personal satisfaction

8   I'm extremely pleased with what I've achieved today. Overjoyed.
7
6   I'm very pleased with my progress today. I feel very good.
5
4   I'm moderately happy with today's achievements. Fifty per cent satisfied with my efforts/ progress.
3
2   Only slightly pleased with today's modest progress/achievement.
1
0   No feeling of achievement or satisfaction.

Note
In all such subjective scales, odd numbers reflect intervening levels between fixed statements on even number rating points (0 = 0 per cent, 2 = 25 per cent, 4 = 50 per cent, 6 = 75 per cent, 8 = 100 per cent). Adaptability to a range of client experiences can make them widely valuable in treatment, e.g. disgust, anger, dirtiness, confidence.

using a standardized rating form (Marks *et al.* 1977). We prefer one which allows two parameters to be rated on 0–8 subjective rating scales of i) distress experienced and ii) avoidance/success in achieving the objective (see Table 7.5).

Clients are encouraged to use these 0–8 rating scales throughout treatment as a means of giving themselves and the therapist feedback on the level of distress experienced and even satisfaction with each session of treatment or homework. Such feedback of subjective units of distress (SUDs) is speedily learnt and avoids less quantifiable verbal responses like 'I feel terrible now, but not as awful as when I was in that queue.' In crowded public places, 'How do you rate now?' gives the client a socially discreet means of communicating distress, e.g. 'four now, but six ten minutes ago'. Whilst other workers prefer to use 0–100 scales for SUDs (Wolpe 1969), it is our experience, and that of other workers (Marks *et al.* 1977), that client feedback can sometimes deteriorate to meticulous discriminations between ratings of, say, 75 and 70.

General behavioural clinical practice versus research practice

Therapists working in a general behavioural clinical practice environment have a freedom that research workers do not possess. The research therapist is obliged to work within the constraints of an experimental design which will usually require the use of a rigidly defined treatment method for a specified number of hours or sessions. Where a number of techniques can be used, it is usually necessary for them to be delivered in a particular order so that their individual effects can be separately determined. This freedom for the general service therapist widens their range of choice in selecting treatment methods, mix of methods, and frequency/duration of clinical sessions. It also allows the therapist the opportunity to adapt, modify, or radically change their intervention in response to client feedback or changes in client need.

Clinical freedom places a responsibility on the therapist, and in a training course upon their supervisors and teachers, to ensure that they do have sufficient background knowledge and technical skills across a range of effective methods to actually apply that freedom of choice appropriately. Clinical decision-making skills need to be refined to a high level of expertise. The trainee behavioural therapist is probably best viewed as an individual who is building a portfolio, or repertoire, of clinical methods from which to choose. These will not only include the cognitive and behavioural skills that they are acquiring through the process of training and clinical practice, but also those they have brought with them from previous training and experience in non-behavioural methods of work. Teachers and supervisors need to familiarize themselves with these pre-existing repertoires in order to ensure that inappropriate methods are not used. Trainee therapists may need to unlearn certain response styles and techniques, as well as to learn their new repertoires.

In many respects, it is easier for the novice therapist learning their skills within a research project for the number of methods they will be required to develop are necessarily constrained, or confined, to those demanded by the immediate project. As ENB course 650 is essentially a programme to produce a general cognitive and behavioural therapist, the course design requires a high level of teaching inputs in its first six months in order to facilitate this development of a wide clinical repertoire to allow effective choices to be made. We therefore emphasize modelling and role-play simulation methods of learning in the first six months to meet that objective for anxiety-based clinical difficulties (clinical anxiety states, simple and complex phobias, agoraphobia, social anxieties/skills deficits, and obsessional-compulsive disorders). Thereafter, the course members' clinical skills repertoires are widened by moving the teaching emphasis on to sexual dysfunctions, marital discord, unconventional sexual behaviour, anger/temper control, eating disorders, and a range of lower frequency referrals such as compulsive gambling, in a similar manner.

Implementation

The final stage of planning is essentially the first stage of implementation. Having comprehensively assessed the individual's difficulty and made a functional analysis which directs the therapist to feasible options in therapeutic management, these need to be presented to the client in an understandable form so that both therapist and client can together discuss the option choice.

Part of this process involves sharing information about the problem. How common is the individual's difficulty? Despite increased publicity about clinical problems such as agoraphobia, a high proportion of clients feel peculiarly alone and isolated. 'Surely no one else is going through what I'm experiencing?' Even well-read clients often view themselves as essentially different from the other agoraphobics they have read about – as they are, due to their uniqueness as individuals – but not in the sense that many express this difference. This is frequently a belief that what has worked for others will not in fact work for them because they cannot, with their experience of 'fear of fear', imagine themselves capable of engaging in exposure activities in the way others have; or if they can, their anticipatory fears predict their own response will be catastrophically different.

The value of the 'therapist as educator' role can excel at this point. The giving of information, the explanation of development and maintenance, and the vital listening and empathic reflection skills establish communication in the therapeutic partnership which values the client's participation, even if only in the honest examination of the client's doubts. The clinical dialogue needs to assure the client that they are not silly, stupid, or going crazy. The difference between explanation as assurance and the unhelpful giving of reassurance needs to be recognized at this point. Most agoraphobics have received exhortations ('pull yourself together') and reassurances ('Of course you'll be alright!', 'There is no chance that you will collapse and die of a heart attack!') from partners, family, friends and physicians with little or no effect. Indeed, where reassurances have produced temporary anxiety relief, some individuals have found themselves driven to repeatedly ask for it until their families and GPs have been driven to distraction. A therapist can listen, answer by explanation, and discuss what is likely to happen (as probability) but not effectively provide certainty for, in this life we all lead, no guarantees do exist. Therapists are aiming to provide the client with learning that involves reality-testing. Reality is risky because certainties do not exist and none of us can be reassured that we will not experience a coronary thrombosis or cerebrovascular accident in the next hour. The therapist aim should be to suggest likelihoods, and by expressing confidence with calm self-assurance (verbally and non-verbally), propose that by approaching fears of personal disasters as hypotheses to be tested, the individual client will discover the only effective reassurance possible. That is, exposure without disaster, engagement in feared activity without catastrophe, experiencing fear and watching it recede (rather than explode) without escape or avoidance.

An important component in preparation for treatment is creating a positive expectation in the client (Emmelkamp 1982, Mathews *et al* 1981). It is also true that trainee, or novice therapists, require a similar expectation, for with their first clients they will have no direct personal experience that this treatment will work, and if it does, will it work with this client, or will it work effectively when they use it? How can a novice therapist develop and communicate positive expectations? As with the client, information is necessary, as is an open discussion of doubts, before reality-testing by taking an individual agoraphobic through the process. In addition, of course, the trainee therapist will have the benefit of modelling, from real-life and videotaped recordings of experienced therapists in action, and the opportunity of practising the component skills in role-play simulations of varying difficulty (including uncooperative, disbelieving, and clinically unresponsive clients).

Agoraphobic clients can also be introduced, as a process of pre-therapy training (Emmelkamp and van der Hout 1983), to videotaped recordings of previously successful clients describing their treatment experiences and outcomes (as can their doubting relatives). Although more time consuming, an introduction to a willing ex-client can be as useful, with the additional advantage that, unlike passive video viewing, dialogue enables exploration of doubts and fears in a more personal manner. Information handouts and a selected reading list can complement this, e.g. Clarke and Wardman's (1985) account of treatment from both the client's and therapist's perspective in a severe case. I do not suggest that all agoraphobic clients require such pre-therapy training as studies show (Emmelkamp 1982) that introducing ex-patients to present clients, or watching historical videotape recordings, do not improve treatment effectiveness. They may, however, hold particular benefits for the more doubting client and for those whose compliance or motivation to proceed is questionable. In such cases, they may improve engagement and reduce the risk of drop-out before a fair trial of treatment is experienced.

What option choice is there to present? As discussed earlier in our 'Planning' section, the central treatment strategy gives therapist and client three main choices, i) prolonged exposure *in vivo*; ii) some form of self-controlled exposure *in vivo*; or iii) prolonged exposure *in vivo* in a group. As we can see by examining other planning factors in the 'Tailoring treatment to the individual' section, the therapist can offer a wider range of choice.

In some respects the therapist is a salesman displaying their wares. Clearly the therapist is likely to favour one approach over another, particularly so the experienced practitioner. It is more honest to state this preference with supportive explanatory reasons than attempt to shape choice by subtle verbal/non-verbal strategies. Where the client rejects an important component, e.g. involving their partner as co-therapist or rejecting marital therapy, the therapist should examine the client's reasons and recommend the importance of the component but not reject the client from treatment. The therapist can be wrong (and the client might gain from proving them wrong) and in any case, if positive results are delayed by the absence of this component, the therapist can still negotiate acceptance later.

Some option rejections are more critical. The client who rejects exposure under any conditions acceptable to the therapist or whose misuse of alcohol or medication continues, are probably best rejected from a behavioural programme at this point. Therapists are unwise to proceed when the most effective techniques at their disposal are banned or when unhelpful chemical interference with the client's learning experience occurs. If pre-therapy training, discussed earlier, still does not change the client's view, an alternative therapist and intervention method may be recommended (e.g. individual or group psychotherapy) or the client's case referred back to their GP for long-term support. Proceeding is likely to be ineffective and is certainly unlikely to be cost-effective or efficient. Our experience suggests that those clients rejected as unsuitable, for method refusal, often do return at a later date with increased willingness to comply and just as much chance of success.

An alternative that might prove fruitful with some clients is to purposely choose a largely cognitive treatment method as an intentional preparation for exposure. Cognitive restructuring through rational-emotive therapy (Ellis and Harper 1975, Wessler and Wessler 1980) can often produce attitudinal and belief change sufficient to facilitate later exposure, but the level of therapist skill required might require (as in Plymouth) the supervisor taking on this element of treatment from a novice therapist.

Once therapist and client have agreed on the treatment programme to be followed, an immediate start on therapy is to be recommended. Delays in commencing the programme can facilitate the return of doubt and lead to missed appointments or 'drop-out' from treatment. The agreed treatment plan should be viewed as a verbal contract to which both partners in treatment (therapist and client) assent. The therapist agrees to provide an initial series of treatment appointments over perhaps six weeks, making themselves available for telephone consultations between appointments to monitor home- work practice and to troubleshoot difficulties. The client agrees to follow the treatment programme and makes practical arrangements to allocate time for exposure *in vivo* at specified appointments and as homework. This may involve them in taking time off from work and/or arranging for a partner, relative, or friend to sit with their children.

Table 7.4 illustrates the main recommended option choices for the central treatment strategy and the principal adjuncts that may be chosen to accompany them. I shall illustrate how therapists may utilize an initial session of Option I, prolonged exposure *in vivo*, with adjuncts 2 and 3 in this section. For other option choices and the practical use of other adjunctive methods, readers are directed to reference sources.

Session 1: prolonged exposure in vivo to walking in pedestrianized city centre and entering crowded stores—Starting point is an outpatient clinic ten minutes' walk from city centre. Planned duration of session is two hours plus. The first twenty minutes of the appointment involves discussing the main elements the client is to focus on in exposure:

1 Anxiety and fear will rise as exposure to the threatening environment takes place. This will be anticipatory at the start, in the clinic, but will reflect environmental cues as the session commences. For example, the client may be reminded that more crowded areas are likely to produce increments in fear and that difficult-to-leave situations will exacerbate this.

2 Exposure means following the therapist into the streets and stores with their attention focused on the here-and-now. This requires them to pay attention to the people around them, the streets, and stores they will enter.

3 They should not fight the rising fear but attempt to 'float' through it without resistance. Do not hurry – haste increases arousal – slow down!

4 They should recognize negative catastrophizing thinking and challenge it; give themselves instructions to carry on when escape thoughts arise and discuss these with the therapist accompanying them.

5 When approaching a difficult area such as a denser grouping of other pedestrians, they should not move around or away from them but boldly move towards them.

6 Anxiety and fear will rise and fall throughout the exposure session; but the longer they remain engaged in the environment, the less fear they will experience, as arousal reduces, and the more capable they will feel.

7 If fear rises after falling, it will fall away again if they continue to engage with and attend to their environment.

8 The therapist will ask them to increase the physical distance separating them progressively but will always return to their side if they stop walking and will rejoin them periodically, as they walk, to monitor their SUDs and coping thoughts.

9 The therapist will set them tasks to do alone (like walk around a block and walk through a store) but will always wait at a pre-set rendezvous for them to return.

10 The therapist will not trick them. They will always be at a specified rendezvous or a pre-set distance ahead or behind them on the street (and they can check this themselves).

11 If fear rises to panic, they should concentrate on slowing their

breathing and replacing catastrophe thoughts with instructions on what to do, and praise for being where they are. In panic, they should stand (or sit) waiting for the fear to abate. They should look around themselves and not run for cover or attempt to shut out of their thoughts where they really are.

12 Time in the environment matters. Awareness of the environment and the people around them matters. 'Keep going one step at a time.'

13 They are not silly, stupid, sick, or crazy. They are not weak or cowardly to experience fear. Courage is the ability to continue when afraid, so they are courageous by being where they are and continuing to follow their route.

14 As fear and arousal reduce, they may feel weak and shaky; they may feel exhausted. This is normal and a good indicator of their passage through fear and out the other side.

15 Boredom is a triumph. If they feel so familiar with any part of the environment that it bores them, they have achieved an enormous personal victory.

16 The session will last as long as necessary. It will not end at any specified time so they should not try to keep going just because it's almost x o'clock. The therapist will monitor their progress and discuss ending the session when satisfied that they have 'worked-over' the place enough.

Entering the exposure environment –Therapist and client walk side by side directly into the city centre heading for the main streets and stores. Conversation will focus on attending to the people in the streets, the window displays, and busy junctions. Every few minutes the therapist will ask about SUDs ratings and the physical/cognitive experiences they are aware of. The therapist will praise, encourage, and coach on thinking and attention strategies. If the therapist feels conversation is being used as a means of partial avoidance, they will ask for periods of silent walking.

The therapist should be superfamiliar with the city environment, knowing the busiest days, streets, and stores. They should know the whereabouts of sitting areas, cafés and public toilets. They should know the busiest departments in stores, the shops with the longest queues, and where any required elevators and escalators are situated. In particular, they should know the locality of entrapment cues that might exacerbate fear unnecessarily or provide especially useful practice venues, e.g. limited exits from stores, densely crowded covered market areas.

Within twenty minutes of entering the city streets, the therapist should start their graded distancing from the client (unless panic management has been required) by reviewing SUDs and praising the progress over the route. It is usually immaterial whether, or not, any fear reduction has taken place. The client is engaged in, and attending to, the exposure environment without escape or avoidance. The fear will reduce so continue to expose. Personally, I find that it is usually best to make the first stage of graded distancing one where the client leads the therapist by 100 metres or so. This way the client can cope with sudden fear increments by standing still until the therapist catches up with them; and the therapist can easily catch up by walking more briskly to monitor SUDs and cognitions periodically.

The following scenario may illustrate the therapist's graded distancing over this session.

1 20 minutes side-by-side.
2 10 minutes client leading by 100 metres.
3 10 minutes client and therapist parallel on opposite sides of thoroughfare.
4 10 minutes therapist leading client by 100 metres.
5 10 minutes client leading therapist by 200 metres.
6 10 minutes client walking ahead to landmark then returning by direct route to therapist waiting at start point rendezvous.
7 10 minutes client walking alone round one city block to rendezvous with therapist at start point rendezvous.
8 15 minutes client walking alone round two city blocks to rendezvous with therapist at start point rendezvous.
9 10 minutes client walking alone round two city blocks to landmark rendezvous (differently situated from start point).
10 20 minutes client walking alone back to clinic base. Therapist to meet at clinic base having returned by alternative route.

Practice item 10 will always depend on sufficient decrement in fear ratings on SUDs. If the client has experienced a four-point drop in SUDs (0–8 rating scale) between items 2 and 9, this will be appropriate. If not, the session should continue for up to a further hour with variations on the distancing-from-accompaniment theme, with rendezvous for monitoring. Some clients' SUDs will remain low throughout exposure but these still require prolonged exposure time.

It is not unusual for clients' ratings to make such a four-point drop more rapidly – say within 60 minutes of starting item 2 (or less). Where this occurs, I personally prefer to increase practice demands more rapidly by incorporating in-store graded exposure within this first session. This is not to induce increments in fear but to facilitate more rapid achievement of exposure goals. Example: after 30 minutes of 100 metre separation, client ratings of SUDs have dropped to 3. A further 20 minutes have covered activity items 7 and 8, with SUDs at 4 and client satisfaction high. This might be an appropriate point to follow the following scenario.

1 20 minutes side-by-side exposure to two or three floors of a department store or indoor shopping mall.
2 10 minutes of 100 metres separation within the same department store/mall.
3 10 minutes separation on either different floors of a different store, or client in-store whilst therapist waits at specified exit rendezvous.
4 20 minutes client exposure to a different store whilst therapist waits with tea and buns in specified café rendezvous.

Planned variations on this theme utilizing elevators, supermarkets, and queues are of course endless. The principal requirement is prolonged client exposure with graded therapist withdrawal to maximize patient achievement, measured by decrements in fear and increments in time unaccompanied.

Should panic occur, the therapist is available near at hand. A calm but warm support through panic is essential, with the therapist advising on cognitive self-guidance, respiratory control, and attention to the environment. Escape is the undoing of achievement and whilst it cannot be prevented, the warm praise of achievement, calm advice with physical contact ('Hold my hand'), and reminders of management strategies will usually prevent its occurrence. It can be very useful to remark how glad you are, as the therapist, to be able to guide them through such a marvellous practice opportunity. On the rare occasions where panic, or its impending appearance, leads the client to escape, or avoid, the therapist needs to follow and uncritically provide remedial counselling. The client is likely to feel terrible about giving in to fear by such escape/avoidance and may feel guilt or depression at 'failing'. They might further catastrophize by writing themselves off as hopeless cases.

Such thinking is unhelpful and needs reversal by the therapist, directing their conversation to achievement up to the point of escape, praise of gains made, and perhaps self-criticism for misjudging the situational demands they asked the client to face too early in the session. The therapist objective is 'repair and salvage': bringing the client back into active exposure again so that they do continue the full exposure session up to, and preferably beyond, the point where panic ensued. The therapist will find it useful to remind themselves that this, like any incident, is an opportunity for the client (and themselves) to learn from.

The use of cognitive strategies (adjunct 2) within an exposure session make practical sense, if only weakly supported by research evidence at present. The recognition of negative self-statements ('I'm useless', 'I can't cope'), catastrophizing ('I'm going to die now if I can't get out!'), and negative rehearsals ('She's going to take me into that awful market and I'm going to faint/collapse/wet myself') is an important element in making effective use of exposure. By identifying the presence of such cognitions, the therapist can give *in vivo* coaching on alternative thinking strategies and self-instructions for the client to focus on. It may be useful to emphasize the need to balance the cognitive ledger by generating opposing positive, helpful cognitions each time a negative thought enters awareness. Using the client's own coping thoughts (used in other experiences of stress and anxiety), self-disclosure of the therapist's own cognitive strategies, and those utilized by other clients, can give this client a menu of more positive options to practise on during exposure. These can be written down *in vivo* on cue cards for the client to carry in a pocket, or handbag, so that they can pause to refer to them when entering an unaccompanied area within the session. They may also be generated to give self-praise on achieving sub-goals within the exposure session (Meichenbaum 1977, Meichenbaum and Genest 1980).

The utility of viewing therapy impact through a three-systems model (Lang 1971) of emotion is rewarding. Change will often be desynchronous and, for both client and novice therapist, confusing. Monitoring client responses in these three systems helps focus the therapist's advice and feedback, providing situationally relevant means of attending to the client's experience.

During exposure, the client is learning something about themselves, and their environment, through 'reality-testing'. Decrements in fear during prolonged exposure disprove the negative hypotheses they hold about themselves and allows the generation of more positive coping hypotheses which enable future exposures to be aided by positive cognitive rehearsals. Whether cognitive strategies are purposely used by the therapist, or not, the client's experience of successful exposure produces them (Marks 1981). I prefer to encourage their appearance rather than to wait hopefully for their generation.

Where agoraphobic clients actively fear particular consequences occurring in the presence of fear, or in their feared environments (e.g. fainting, collapse, heart attacks, strokes, or madness), the therapist may find paradoxical intention (adjunct 3) a useful strategy. Anticipation of these consequences helps to maintain fear. Prolonged exposure should effectively remove these fears but anticipatory anxiety tends to linger longer than situational fear. Such a client may successfully relinquish escape and avoidance behaviour during treatment but retain an apprehensive fear that just because a coronary did not occur during exposure does not mean that it will not occur the next time they enter the crowded city. This might provide a cognitive focus for the return of fearful behaviour.

Some clients may not fully participate in prolonged exposure lest the environmental demands, perhaps producing rapid heart rate, are perceived to put them at risk of the anticipated consequence. In such an instance, the client may refuse further exposure, escape or avoid, or drop out of the therapy programme.

Paradoxical intention (Frankl 1960, 1970, Gertz 1970) is a technique developed within the psychotherapeutic method of existential logotherapy (Frankl 1955). Clients are asked to purposefully and consciously bring on the state or condition they fear. As the anticipated consequences are not accessible to voluntary intention, it will not be possible for the individual to induce them, even in the anxiety-loaded exposure environment. The therapist can ask the client to try as hard as possible to faint, or have a heart attack. I find it useful to do this with a dead-pan facial expression whilst holding a stopwatch. Very often the client will try hard when the method is explained but the harder they try, with the therapist exhortations to try harder ('you've got sixty seconds to have a coronary'), the more they realize the ridiculousness of the situation and accept that such an intention is impossible. If they cannot faint or have a heart attack even when they try, and in a fear-evoking environment at that, the probability of such an event occurring in future will be perceived as low. It is very common for such clients to burst out laughing at the incongruousness of their situation.

Paradoxical intention can be set as a homework task between formal exposure sessions to reinforce the experience and facilitate homework exposure.

Ending the prolonged exposure in vivo session and planning homework—At whatever point of achievement reached by the client, the therapist needs to close the session in a planned manner. Therapist and client together need to debrief from the session, reviewing progress and achievements. Particular events that hold significance for homework exposure require close discussion in order to ensure the client knows how to respond when unaccompanied, e.g. impending panic. This debriefing should emphasize the active participation in the client's own learning that has occurred, with warm objective feedback and effusive praise.

Homework exposure (Griest *et al.* 1980), with and without the assistance of a partner, should be planned for daily practice between sessions. These homework sessions should be based on the same prolonged exposure model. It can be useful to write out the homework objectives explicitly and require the client to provide written diary data on results for return to the next therapist-directed session. It will be useful to arrange periodic telephone monitoring of the client's homework practice (and for discussion of the partner's contributions), particularly in those individuals where motivation is considered weak or non-compliance is predicted.

As many agoraphobic clients notice a daily variability in their fear experiences and may describe themselves as having 'good days' and 'bad days', it will be important to ensure that homework practice does not only take place on 'good days' (O'Brien and Barlow 1984). Personally, in these cases, I emphasize that if daily practice exposure is not feasible, the practice they should do must be on 'bad days' rather than 'good ones' for it is then that they most need the relearning experiences.

Further therapist-accompanied sessions of prolonged exposure *in vivo* should be planned to rapidly extend the individual client's range of travel and activity. The therapist aims should be to target personally relevant areas for the client, reversing avoidance behaviour by expanding access to activities that will become high frequency aspects for them when recovered, e.g. bus and train travel, shopping, queuing, and entering social environments such as cafés, cinemas, and theatres. Frequent sessions supported by homework practice are important.

The therapist will usually be able to fade out their escort support rapidly so that within two or three sessions they may only be involved at their beginning and closure.

It is worth noting that therapists frequently have difficulty learning to help with often simple activities. The therapist who travels everywhere by car will need to relearn how to travel by bus, underground, or train. When did they last have to find their way across the city by bus? Do they know the route numbers, timetable frequencies, and fares system? Are they familiar with one-man-operated buses and the necessity of paying with the exact cash? Are they aware of the flexibility of daily and weekly 'Saver/Rover' tickets and the financial savings they make within exposure sessions? The therapist who is lost and unfamiliar with such issues does not inspire client confidence.

Assessing course members' skill development in agoraphobia treatment.

Plymouth ENB course 650 centre have now adopted a new skills assessment tool for use in formative trainee assessment and feedback (see Table 7.6). The course members' supervisor will accompany them on their first prolonged exposure session and use this form to assess technique application. Subsequently, the supervisor can arrange to sample exposure sessions with other clients, or rendezvous with them to assess, say, a one-hour section of such a session.

Evaluation

Agoraphobia is a complex problem which is difficult to treat. Partial success rather than complete success is more common (Emmelkamp and van der Hout 1983). Major improvements in the majority of clients reported in the research press should not disguise the evidence that some clients do not improve at all and that most have some residual difficulty remaining after treatment. Even where treatment is successful, client progress is not linear. It is more usual for progress to follow a pattern of ups and down, gains and set-backs, often with plateau periods (O'Brien and Barlow 1984).

The majority of clients will be discharged from active treatment substantially improved, but until recent years with the expectation that they would make further gains in post-treatment follow-up phases. Some individuals do continue to reduce residual difficulties post-treatment but most appear not to do so (Emmelkamp and van der Hout 1983). There is suggestive evidence that cognitive

Table 7.6 ENB post-basic clinical nursing studies course 650 (adult behavioural psychotherapy) Plymouth centre: supervisor's assessment of exposure-based treatment session for a person presenting with agoraphobic syndrome

Course member:　　　　　Supervisor:　　　　　Date:

Client's identification:

Duration of session:　　　Duration of exposure:　　　Duration of supervision:

Assessment factor	Supervisor's comments and notes	Supervisor's skill ratings

Session orientation

Has therapist planned session adequately?

Therapist's ability to define objectives of session?

Has therapist chosen appropriate environment, stimuli, and/or route?

Is sufficient time allocated?

Homework review

Verbal report?

Diary sheets or log book?

Quality of therapist feedback?

Appropriate reinforcement?

Did therapist emphasize positive client activity?

Problem-solving advice?

Did therapist avoid criticism of client errors?

Exposure treatment

Exposure method adopted?

Is therapist's description of method, instructions, or advice to client clear and appropriate?

Did therapist seek feedback to check understanding?

Does therapist invite and answer client's questions effectively?

Does therapist avoid giving unhelpful reassurance?

Appropriate cognitive/behavioural modelling given?

Does therapist seek regular subjective ratings of distress during exposure?

Table 7.6 Continued

Assessment factor	Supervisor's comments and notes	Supervisor's skill ratings
Is effective use made of client's statements to promote appropriate cognitive self-guidance?		
Therapist's use of feedback, encouragement, and reinforcement?		
Does therapist appropriately balance time accompanying client with unaccompanied exposure in session?		
Do rendezvous meetings between client's unaccompanied exposures provide adequate feedback, reinforcement, and preparation for continuing practice?		
Has therapist made the most appropriate use of features of the exposure environment (e.g. stores, queues, crowds, lifts, busy streets, distance walking, and public transport)?		
Is escape behaviour prevented?		
Is avoidance allowed for appropriate reasons to prevent panic-induced escape?		
Is avoidance prevented to promote flooding experience?		
Is client appropriately reintroduced to exposure after avoidant withdrawal?		
Are exposure times sufficient to allow decrements in distress?		
Is pacing of exposure appropriate?		
Appropriate advice on anxiety or distress management?		
Does panic reaction occur?		
Therapist's skill in managing client's handling of panic?		
Does therapist maintain calm, confident demeanour and promote positive expectations during client distress?		
Does therapist use appropriate explanation, teaching, coaching, and/or prompting to improve compliance during exposure?		
Does therapist prevent haste/hurry and unhelpful micro-avoidance?		
Does client show appropriate compliance with therapist advice and instructions?		

Table 7.6 Continued

Assessment factor	Supervisor's comments and notes	Supervisor's skill ratings

Closure

Did therapist end exposure session at an appropriate point?

Did client show sufficient progress (decrements in distress and behaviour change) in session?

Has therapist made the most effective use of the total time available for exposure?

How could therapist have improved this exposure session?

Did therapist provide client with effective and appropriate debriefing feedback at end of session?

How did therapist arrange for client's return to home or work at end of session (does this complement exposure achievements)?

Homework setting

Was appropriate exposure homework set?

Was frequency, duration, and locality of exposure homework made clear?

Did therapist seek feedback to ensure client understands homework requirements?

Was appropriate explanation and advice given to support homework practice?

Did therapist invite and answer client's questions about homework effectively?

What non-exposure homework is required?

Is an effective data collection system available (diaries/log book) for client to record homework practice?

Has therapist made a new appointment for the next session?

Is telephone monitoring and feedback arranged? (if appropriate)

What arrangements have been made to appropriately involve spouse, family, or significant others in homework programme?

Difficulty of this session: uncomplicated/difficult:

State reasons:

Overall rating of therapeutic skills demonstrated:

Table 7.6 Continued

Supervisor's debriefing notes:

Skills rating scale:

0	1	2	3	4	5	6	7	8

No skill apparent	Shows some skill	Fairly skilled	Generally good level of skill	A very high level of skill

Therapeutic skills are a mixture of complex interpersonal social skills (verbal and non-verbal) and technical skills and competencies in utilizing specific techniques with a client. The client may be distressed, uncertain, and have difficulty in complying with the therapist's advice and instructions. Ratings of skill and competence need to take into account the therapist, the client, and the environment.

As supervisor, you need to make your skill ratings based on the therapist's demonstrated competence as compared with what you would expect to see with the same client from other trained and experienced behaviour therapists (Norm Reference Group).

restructuring, although less effective than prolonged exposure *in vivo*, may have delayed effects which enable clients to continue making further improvement post-treatment (Emmelkamp and Mersch 1982). The majority of clients making successful gains in treatment maintain those gains but relapse does occur in a proportion of individuals (Emmelkamp and van der Hout 1983, O'Brien and Barlow 1984).

Therapists need to evaluate their clinical interventions in at least three ways. First, during the process of active treatment, they need to monitor the effectiveness of each therapist-directed exposure session and each homework practice period. When using self-controlled exposure *in vivo* (Emmelkamp 1982) or programmed practice (Mathews *et al.* 1981), they and the client need to monitor effectiveness and progress. In this sense, evaluation is a continuous process completing the therapist's feedback loop in the operation of a systematic treatment programme. It will facilitate fine tuning of the programme to maximize effectiveness and allow rapid decisions to be made to drop redundant treatment components or introduce alternative strategies when progress is delayed or arrested.

Second, each case is best viewed as a single-case experimental design (of varying complexity) where pre-treatment measures of problem state and intended outcomes are remeasured and rated for post-treatment successes. It is highly advisable for behaviour therapists to adhere to measurement strategies that demonstrate both objectively and subjectively the actual impact of therapeutic interventions. Although the general clinical service therapist may not be involved in clinical research, they have a responsibility to demonstrate their actual clinical effectiveness, cost-effectiveness, and efficiency. Increasing managerial stringency in state-funded care requires therapists to produce valid and reliable data on these issues to ensure continuing finance and development monies to expand service provisions, or at least to defend services from economies by contraction.

Third, evaluation of clinical effectiveness requires client follow-up. Treatment interventions that lead only to short-term maintenance of clinical gains are neither cost-effective nor appropriate for clients who invest considerable effort in achieving those gains. Follow-up ought not to be seen as a means of gathering clinical data to attest to the benefits derived from treatment. Follow-up appointments provide the therapist with a means of encouraging generalization of improvement and continuing client practice in reducing residual difficulties. A proportion of clients view discharge from active treatment as the point where they no longer need to apply the clinical methods that have produced improvement. Therapists need to use their educational skills in preparing clients for discharge so that they can develop skills in maintaining their gains and creatively dealing with set-backs in future. For example, those female clients who have a history of premenstrual symptoms may be viewed as vulnerable to relapse should these difficulties continue to produce attrition effects on confidence, mood, and autonomic arousal. Physical ill health can produce re-emergence of symptoms that mimic previous agoraphobic experiences. Influenza that leads to some days ill at home may produce anxiety-like symptoms, depress mood, and unintentionally re-establish avoidance behaviours. We find it important to warn clients that such illness experiences will affect their confidence and that recovery must be followed by planned self-directed re-exposure.

It is an important subsidiary aim in treatment to increase the client's sense of personal effectiveness, independence from others, and development of a stronger internal locus of control. Improvements produce a social role change for many clients that may require additional advice and counselling.

How frequent follow-up appointments should be, and how long it should continue for, is probably best viewed as a departmental issue. Follow-up requires significant therapist time (unless telephone and postal means are used) that might more appropriately be used for active treatments so its cost-effectiveness ought to be examined. At Plymouth centre, improved clients are called for follow-up at one month, three, six, and twelve months from the date of discharge. Not all clients respond to follow-up appointments, however. Nevertheless, all clients are advised to contact the department directly should they experience re-emergence of symptoms that they feel unable to manage themselves.

A proportion of clients whose clinical gains have been minimal may require longer-term support while extended self-management programmes are followed. The use of a long-term support group for partially improved agoraphobics can enable therapists to provide economical means of maintaining gains and promoting further improvements. These may be operated by the clinical service or as consumer-led resources.

Where clients have not benefited from the main choices in treatment method, therapists are well advised to reassess and replan their interventions using perhaps slower exposure methods, alternative cognitive strategies, or interventions directed to marital and assertiveness difficulties. Similarly, the use of pharmacological interventions (Zitrin *et al.* 1983) together with behavioural methods should be considered.

Evaluation is not only an assessment of client progress and improvement but should also be seen as assessment of therapist skill and effectiveness. This is particularly important in a training course where course teachers have a responsibility to ensure that course members are skilled, knowledgeable, safe, and effective practitioners. Course supervisors' assessments of skill (see Table 7.6) in treatment method are important as is the assessment of more general case management abilities (assessment interviewing, decision making, programme design). Course members benefit from being taught self-assessment skills so that they may apply critical and reinforcing feedback on their own performance.

The client's view of therapy and therapist skill is an under-investigated area. Questionnaire surveys (anonymous or otherwise) of consumer views should be considered in any self-evaluating department. An analysis of clients' views of their treatment and therapist, e.g. Emmelkamp and van der Hout (1983) and in Gournay's chapter on failures in this book, reveals interesting information on where they perceive clinical weaknesses. These include patients who do not experience decrements in anxiety during exposure, exposure demands paced too high for the individual, therapists who are viewed as lacking understanding of the client's feelings, are too young, and excessively technique oriented.

CONCLUSION

In this chapter I have attempted to illustrate how psychiatric nurses can be trained as effective therapists for a wide range of anxiety difficulties, with particular attention to the management of agoraphobia. The advanced clinical training available in the United Kingdom on ENB post-basic clinical nursing studies course 650 is a significant departure from conventional treatment practice, using psychiatrists and clinical psychologists (Marks *et al.* 1977), which has proven both effective and economical (Marks 1985). It is not the only means of making psychiatric nurses more effective as therapists but it does provide a means of creating widely skilled and largely autonomous cognitive-behavioural practitioners to meet the present shortfall of therapists. It is disheartening, however, that investment in such training is so limited.

Agoraphobia is a severely limiting and distressing disorder which is complex to treat. Although behavioural methods are the treatments of choice, further development of clinical technique is required to increase effectiveness for those clients who are only partially helped, left with residual difficulties, or fail to improve (Emmelkamp and van der Hout 1983, O'Brien and Barlow 1984). A high level of clinical skill is essential to produce maximal effectiveness from the methods currently available. Too little attention has been paid to such skills development because of the adoption of an uncritical attitude to technique-centred treatment.

© H. Gordon Deakin

REFERENCES

American Psychiatric Association (1980) *Diagnostic and Statistical Manual of Mental Disorders* (3rd edn), Washington DC: APA

Ascher, L. M. (1980) 'Employing paradoxical intention in the treatment of agoraphobia', *Behaviour Research and Therapy* 18: 229–42.

Asso, D. and Beech, H. R. (1975) 'Susceptibility to the acquisition of a conditioned response in relation to the menstrual cycle', *J. Psychosomatic Research* 19: 337–42.

Bandura, A. (1977) 'Self-efficacy: toward a unifying theory of behaviour change', *Psychological Review* 84: 191–215.

Beck, A. T. and Emery, G. (1985) *Anxiety Disorders and Phobias: a Cognitive Perspective*, New York: Basic Books.

Beck, A. T., Ward, C. H., Mendelson, M., Mock, J. E., and Erbaugh, J. K. (1961) 'An inventory for measuring depression', *Arch. Gen. Psychiat.* 4: 561–71.

Beech, H. R., Burns, L. E., and Sheffield, B. F. (1982) *A Behavioural Approach to the Management of Stress: a Practical Guide to Techniques*, Chichester: J. Wiley & Sons.

Bernstein, D. A. and Borkovec, T. (1973) *Progressive Relaxation Training*, Champaign, Illinois: Research Press.

Brooker, C. and Wiggins, R. D. (1983) 'Nurse therapist trainee variability: the implications for selection and training', *J. Advanced Nursing* 8: 321–8.

Burns, L. E. (1977) 'An investigation into the additive effects of behavioural techniques in the treatment of agoraphobia', unpublished doctoral dissertation, University of Leeds.

Chambless, D. L. (1982) 'Characteristics of agoraphobia', in D. L. Chambless and A. J. Goldstein (eds) *Agoraphobia: Multiple Perspectives on Theory and Treatment*, 1–18, New York: J. Wiley & Sons.

Chambless, D. L., Caputo, G. C., Jasin, S. E., Gracely, E. J., and Williams, C. (1985) 'The mobility inventory for agoraphobia', *Behaviour Research and Therapy* 23: 35–44.

Chambless, D. L. and Goldstein, A. J. (1980) 'The treatment of agoraphobia', in A. J. Goldstein and E. B. Foa (eds) *Handbook of Behavioural Interventions*, New York: J. Wiley & Sons.

—(1982) *Agoraphobia: Multiple Perspectives on Theory and Treatment*, New York: J. Wiley & Sons.

Clark, D. M. (1986) 'A cognitive approach to panic', *Behaviour Research and Therapy* 24: 461–70.

Clarke, J. C. and Wardman, W. (1985) *Agoraphobia: a Clinical and Personal Account*, Sydney: Pergamon Press.

Curran, H. V. and Golombok, S. (1985) *Bottling it up*, London: Faber & Faber.

Ellis, A. and Harper, R. A. (1975) *A New Guide to Rational Living*, Englewood Cliffs, New Jersey: Prentice-Hall.

Emmelkamp, P. M. G. (1982) '*In vivo* treatment of agoraphobia', in D. L. Chambless and A. J. Goldstein (eds) *Agoraphobia: Multiple Perspectives on Theory and Treatment*, 43–76, New York: J. Wiley & Sons.

Emmelkamp, P. M. G. and Mersch, P. P. (1982) 'Cognition and exposure *in vivo* in the treatment of agoraphobia: short-term and delayed effects', *Cognitive Therapy and Research* 6: 77–90.

Emmelkamp, P. M. G. and van der Hout, A. (1983) 'Failure in treating agoraphobia', in E. B. Foa and P. M. G. Emmelkamp (eds) *Failures in Behaviour Therapy*, 58–81, New York: J. Wiley & Sons.

English and Welsh National Boards for Nursing, Midwifery, and Health Visiting (1983) *Outline Curriculum in Adult Behavioural Psychotherapy for*

RMNs: Short Term Therapy, Course 650, London: ENB.

Foa, E. B. and Emmelkamp, P. M. G. (1983) *Failures in Behaviour Therapy*, New York: J. Wiley & Sons.

Frankl, V. E. (1955) *Man's Search for Meaning: an Introduction to Logotherapy*, New York: Knopf.

——(1960) 'Paradoxical intention: a logotherapeutic technique, *American J. of Psychotherapy* 14: 520–35.

——(1970) *Psychotherapy and Existentialism: Selected Papers on Logotherapy*, New York: Souvenir Press.

Gertz, H. C. (1970) 'The treatment of the phobic and obsessional patient using paradoxical intention', in V. E. Frankl (ed.) *Psychotherapy and Existentialism: Selected Papers on Logotherapy*, New York: Souvenir Press.

Ginsberg, G. and Marks, I. M. (1977) 'Cost effectiveness of behavioural psychotherapy by nurse therapists', *Psychological Medicine* 7: 685–9.

Goldfried, M. R. and Goldfried, A. P. (1980) 'Cognitive change methods', in F. H. Kanfer and A. P. Goldstein (eds) *Helping People Change: a Textbook of Methods* (2nd edn), 97–130, New York: Pergamon Press.

Goldstein, A. J. and Foa, E. B. (1980) *Handbook of Behavioural Interventions: a Clinical Guide*, New York: J. Wiley & Sons.

Gordon, L. V. (1960) *Survey of Interpersonal Values*, Chicago: Science Research Associates.

Griest, J., Marks, I. M., Berlin, F., Gournay, K., and Noshirvani, H. (1980) 'Avoidance versus confrontation of fear', *Behaviour Therapy* 11: 1–14.

Gronlund, N. E. (1978) *Stating Objectives for Classroom Instruction* (2nd edn), New York: Macmillan Publishing.

Hand, I., Lamontagne, Y., and Marks, I. M. (1974) 'Group exposure (flooding) *in vivo* for agoraphobics', *British J. of Psychiatry* 124: 588–602.

Hersen, M. and Bellack, A. S. (1981) *Behavioural Assessment: a Practical Handbook* (2nd edn), New York: Pergamon Press.

Jacobson, E. (1938) *Progressive Relaxation*, Chicago: University of Chicago Press.

Jasin, S. (1983) 'Cognitive-behavioural treatment of agoraphobia', in A. Freeman (ed.) *Cognitive Therapy with Couples and Groups*, 199–220, New York: Plenum Press.

Joint Board of Clinical Nursing Studies (1975) *Outline Curriculum in Adult Behavioural Psychotherapy for RMNs: Short Term Therapy, course 650*, London: JBCNS.

Kanfer, F. H. and Saslow, G. (1969) in C. M. Franks (ed.) *Behavioural Diagnosis in Behaviour Therapy: Appraisal and Status*, 417–44, New York: McGraw-Hill.

Lang, P. (1971) 'The application of psychophysiological methods to the study of psychotherapy and behaviour modification', in A. E. Bergin and S. L. Garfield (eds) *Handbook of Psychotherapy and Behaviour Change: an Empirical Analysis*, New York: J. Wiley & Sons.

Lazarus, A. A. (1971) *Behaviour Therapy and Beyond*, New York: McGraw-Hill.

——(1976) *Multimodal Behaviour Therapy*, New York: Springer.

Leibowitz, M. R. and Klein, D. F. (1982) 'Agoraphobia: clinical features, pathophysiology, and treatment, in D. L. Chambless and A. J. Goldstein (eds) *Agoraphobia: Multiple Perspectives on Theory and Treatment*, 153–82, New York: J. Wiley & Sons.

Levine, F. M. and Tinkler, H. A. (1974) 'A behaviour modification approach to supervision of psychotherapy', *Psychotherapy: Theory, Research and Practice* 2: 182–8.

Mahoney, M. J. (1980) *Abnormal Psychology: Perspectives on Human Variance*, San Francisco: Harper & Row.

Marks, I. M. (1969) *Fears and Phobias*, London: Heinemann Medical and Academic Press.

—(1981) *Cure and Care of Neuroses: Theory and Practice of Behavioural Psychotherapy*, New York: J. Wiley & Sons.

—(1985) *Psychiatric Nurse Therapists in Primary Care: the Expansion of Advanced Clinical Roles in Nursing*, London: Royal College of Nursing.

Marks, I. M., Hallam, R. S., Connolly, J., and Philpott, R. (1977) *Nursing in Behavioural Psychotherapy: an Advanced Clinical Role for Nurses*, London: Royal College of Nursing.

Marshall, W. L. and Segal, Z. (1986) 'Phobia and anxiety', in M. Hersen (ed.) *Pharmacological and Behavioural Treatment: an Integrative Approach*, 260–88, New York: J. Wiley & Sons.

Mathews, A. M., Gelder, M., and Johnston, D. W. (1981) *Agoraphobia: Nature and Treatment*, New York: the Guilford Press.

Meichenbaum, D. (1977) *Cognitive-Behaviour Modification: an Integrative Approach*, New York: Plenum Press.

Meichenbaum, D. and Genest, M. (1980) 'Cognitive behaviour modification: an integration of cognitive and behavioural methods', in F. H. Kanfer and A. P. Goldstein (eds) *Helping People Change: a Textbook of Methods* (2nd edn), 390–422, New York: Pergamon Press.

Milne, D. (1986) *Training Behaviour Therapists: Methods, Evaluation and Implementation with Parents, Nurses and Teachers*, Beckenham, Kent: Croom Helm.

O'Brien, G. T. and Barlow, D. H. (1984) 'Agoraphobia', in S. M. Turner (ed.) *Behavioural Theories and Treatment of Anxiety*, 143–86, New York: Plenum Press.

Priestley, P. and Maguire, J. (1983) *Learning to Help: Basic Skill Exercises*, New York: Tavistock Publications.

Rachman, S. J. and Hodgson, R. (1974) 'Synchrony and desynchrony in fear and avoidance', *Behaviour Research and Therapy* 12: 311–8.

Rachman, S. J. and Wilson, G. T. (1980) *The Effects of Psychological Therapy*, (2nd edn), Oxford: Pergamon Press.

Rosen, G. M. (1982) 'Self-help approaches to self-management', in K. R. Blankstein and J. Polivy (eds) *Self-Control and Self-Modification of Emotional Behaviour*, 183–99, New York: Plenum Press.

Salkovskis, P. M., Jones, D. R. O., and Clark, D. M. (1986) 'Respiratory control in the treatment of panic attacks: replication and extension with concurrent measurement of behaviour and pCO', *Br. J. Psychiatry*.

Thorpe, G. L. and Burns, L. E. (1983) *The Agoraphobic Syndrome: Behavioural Approaches to Evaluation and Treatment*, Chichester: J. Wiley & Sons.

Thorpe, G. L. and Hecker, J. E. (1987) 'Clinical validation of the Fear Questionnaire and the Agoraphobic Questionnaire', paper presented to the 15th annual conference of the British Association for Behavioural Psychotherapy, Exeter, 25 July.

Thyer, B. A. (1987) *Treating Anxiety Disorders: a Guide for Human Service Professionals*, Newbury Park, California, Sage Publications.

Weekes, C. (1977) *Simple, Effective Treatment of Agoraphobia*, New York: Hawthorne Books.

Wessler, R. A. and Wessler, R. L. (1980) *The Principles and Practice of Rational-Emotive Therapy* (2nd edn), San Francisco: Josey-Bass.

Wolpe, J. (1969) *The Practice of Behaviour Therapy*, New York: Pergamon Press.

Zitrin, C. M., Klein, D. F., Woerner, M. G., and Ross, D. C. (1983) 'Treatment of phobias I: comparison of imipramine hydrochloride and placebo', *Arch. Gen. Psychiat.* 40: 125–38.

Chapter Eight

COGNITIVE CHANGES DURING THE BEHAVIOURAL TREATMENT OF AGORAPHOBIA

KEVIN GOURNAY

The clinical picture in agoraphobia is dominated by a range of distressing thoughts and fears. These fears generally concern some sort of loss of control or physical incapacity and are heightened during panic attacks. Such fears and thoughts are linked with physiological arousal and for a long time it has been accepted that the anxious thoughts and increased physiological arousal found in agoraphobia feed each other in a vicious circle. Eventually, as Chambless (1978) points out, the anticipation or 'Fear of Fear' becomes the central element in a great majority of cases.

However, despite the central nature of abnormal cognitive styles in agoraphobia, the question of whether agoraphobia cognitions are cause or effect remains to be answered. Furthermore, there is little evidence to show that cognitive therapies for agoraphobia produce cognitive change over and above that produced by behaviour therapy and indeed little is known about what cognitions change in response to behaviour therapy.

The purpose of this chapter is to look at some of these issues and to describe some pilot attempts to define some of the cognitive consequences of behaviour therapy.

It is only recently that the issue of detailed cognitive assessment in relation to the behavioural treatment of patients has been addressed. Kendall and Hollon (1983) argue convincingly that an analysis of the contribution of cognitive change to behavioural change is long over-due. They go on to indicate that there are considerable problems in effecting this. This same area of concern has been addressed by Merluzzi, Glass, and Genest (1981) and Meichenbaum (1976). Kendall, in Kendall and Hollon (1981) sets out four primary purposes for cognitive assessment and these are worth repeating in full. They are:

1 to study the relationships among covert phenomena and their relationship to patterns of behaviour and expressions of emotion;
2 to study the role of covert processes in the development of distinct psychopathologies and the behavioural patterns associated with coping;
3 to confirm the effects of treatment;
4 to check studies where cognitive factors have either been manipulated or implicated in the effects of the manipulation.

Very little attention has been paid to the specific cognitive processes of agoraphobics. However, some of the research carried out with anxious subjects may provide some indications of what these processes are. Beck *et al.* (1974) gave an account of the cognitive components of subjects with general anxiety disorder and proposed that certain kinds of stress activate schemata relative to 'personal danger'. This leads to a pattern of cognitive activity with the following characteristics:

1 systematic misconstruing of experiences along lines very similar to those observed in depression (arbitrary inferences, over-generalization, misinterpretation, etc.);
2 specific thoughts or images which are often clearly related to past experience;
3 cognitions generally preceding the onset or exacerbation of experienced anxiety;
4 the amount of anxiety being proportional to the degree of plausibility (to the patient) of the hypothetical danger, the patient's own notion of the severity of harm, and his estimate of the likelihood of the dreaded event occurring.

Hibbert (1984) was prompted by Beck *et al.*'s (1974) paper to study some aspects of cognitive function in general anxiety disorders (he excluded phobics from his sample). Hibbert found that patients with panic attacks demonstrated cognitions centring on personal danger such as death and heart attacks. However, patients without panic attacks had less dramatic fears. Hibbert also reported that with severer levels of anxiety, thoughts tended to be more intrusive, more credible and harder to exclude. Hibbert also concluded that his data supported the findings of Teasdale *et al.* (1980) and Clark and Teasdale (1982) who demonstrated that there tends to be increasing accessibility of negative thoughts with increasing dysphoric mood.

In an attempt to examine how subjects estimated personal risk, Butler and Mathews (1983) studied three groups of twelve subjects, i.e. generalized anxiety, major depressive disorder, and normal controls. The method used questionnaires containing brief, ambiguous scenarios (e.g. hearing a noise in the middle of the night). Subjects were then asked to rank the likelihood of their thinking each of the three alternatives in response to the scenario. In turn, subjects then rated subjective cost (value) and subjective probability of alternative outcomes. The study demonstrated that anxious subjects were more likely to interpret ambiguous material as threatening and that anxious subjects also rated subjective cost (value) of threatening events higher than the control group. The depressive group showed a similarity to the anxious group. In other respects, the study showed some differences between the anxious and depressed subjects and the authors commented that at present there was a need to more clearly distinguish anxious from depressed cognitions. In summary, the study seemed to support an interaction between anxiety and the availability of danger schemata.

Recently, in reviewing this and subsequent studies of cognitive processing in anxiety, Mathews and MacLeod (1987) have suggested that anxiety and depression are associated with cognitive biases at different stages of processing, such that the acquisition of threat-related information is facilitated in anxiety, while the recall of negative memories is more characteristic of depression.

With regard to agoraphobia, there have only been isolated accounts of what cognitive processes may be important in treatment outcome. For example, Barlow *et al.* (1984) reported the case of an agoraphobic who responded to exposure treatment and improved on behavioural, physiological, and self-report measures but who continued to think of avoidance. This patient later relapsed. This type of finding, which is commonly reported by experienced clinicians, is in accord with the argument of Hollon and Kriss (1984) who stated that permanent changes in schemata would have to be made in therapy to prevent relapse. It could also be argued that isolated exposures can do little in themselves to alter entrenched self-schemata and that exposure should be complemented by procedures designed to change cognitive 'styles'.

Before reviewing the evidence regarding the use of cognitive strategies in agoraphobia, there are two papers worthy of mention. First, as long ago as 1976, Beck observed that clients' subjective estimates of harm would shift as a function of exposure to the feared situation. Second, in 1983, Rachman reviewed the possibility of using some fresh approaches to modify agoraphobic avoidance. Pursuing Beck's argument, he reviewed the work of Seligman and Johnston (1973), pointing out that an essential part of their cognitive theory of avoidance was that behaviour is most effectively weakened by repeated disconfirmations. Technically speaking, a disconfirmation is the discrepancy between the expected outcome and the actual outcome. Rachman suggested that probability estimates be systematically used prior to exposures. Rachman felt that such a therapeutic procedure could be extended to disorders other than agoraphobia. One obvious disorder which would lend itself to such an approach would be obsessional neurosis, particularly where there were specific cues such as contamination.

STUDIES OF COGNITIVE TREATMENT WITH AGORAPHOBICS

In the area of treatment, there has been a recent trend to treating agoraphobia with strategies involving manipulation of cognitions while carrying out exposure treatment. However, evaluative research in the clinical area is confined to just a few published studies with agoraphobic subjects.

Emmelkamp *et al.* (1978) studied the comparative effectiveness of cognitive restructuring *in vivo* in a group of agoraphobics and demonstrated that exposure *in vivo* was clearly superior. However, the cognitive therapy lasted only 5 days (two hours per day) and one could argue that this was insufficient time to assimilate and practise new strategies. In a later study, Emmelkamp (1979) used a between-group design to compare exposure *in vivo* with cognitive restructuring and a combined treatment of exposure *in vivo* and cognitive restructuring. Emmelkamp concluded that exposure *in vivo* was a superior treatment with respect to anxiety and avoidance and that cognitive restructuring did not add to outcome. Again, this study used only a brief time period (two-and-a-half weeks) for the cognitive treatment. Emmelkamp has stated elsewhere (Emmelkamp 1982) that cognitive modification should be reserved for subjects whose cognitions did not change with exposure treatment.

In the third study, Williams and Rappoport (1983) used a combination of exposure *in vivo* and cognitive therapy on the driving fears of agoraphobics. Again, the cognitive addition did not seem to produce any additional effect.

In the best designed and controlled experiment of this group of studies, Mavissakalian *et al.* (1983) compared self-statement training and paradoxical intention in a group of agoraphobics who all had concurrent self-directed exposure *in vivo*. Treatment lasted three months and the duration, in author's view, allowed adequate time for the strategies to be 'learned, integrated and practised'. The study demonstrated no difference between treatments and the order of change on the outcome measures seemed much the same as studies using exposure alone. Cognitive changes were marked by a decrease in self-defeating statements but there was no parallel increase in coping statements. Perhaps the greatest flaw in this and the other studies reviewed was that there was no attempt to control for the nature and variability of 'faulty' cognitions and consequently treatment was given in blanket fashion to (cognitively) heterogeneous samples.

TWO STUDIES OF COGNITIVE CHANGE DURING THE BEHAVIOURAL TREATMENT OF AGORAPHOBIA

These studies were designed to look at whether behavioural treatment produced cognitive changes and to generate hypotheses which could be tested by larger controlled enquiry.

The first study (Gournay 1986) was at a pilot level and therefore only general predictions were made. It was hoped that this sort of enquiry would help to differentiate between subjects for whom the simple behavioural treatment of exposure would produce extensive cognitive change (for the better) and subjects who still retained, after treatment, cognitive abnormalities.

Hypotheses

1 Subjects will, before treatment, rate highly the probability of negative outcomes occurring.
2 Subjects will, before treatment, rate highly the value (subjective cost) of negative outcomes.
3 The ratings of subjective probabilities of negative outcomes will decrease during successful treatment.
4 Subjects' ratings of value of negative outcomes will decrease during successful treatment.

5 Unsuccessful outcomes and relapses will be generally characterized by unchanged ratings of subjective probability and value.

Method

Subjects The subjects were twelve agoraphobics fulfilling the inclusion criteria of a larger treatment outcome study (i.e. DSM III criteria for agoraphobia). The twelve subjects comprised ten women and two men, mean age 38.08 years (SD 9.86). The mean problem duration was 10.17 years (SD 5.22).

Allocation Subjects were allocated randomly to several therapists of varying experience.

Treatment This consisted of six sessions of two hours of therapist-aided exposure in real life. A range of situations were used, including travelling by bus and tube, shopping centres, and other situations commonly a problem for the agoraphobic. The six sessions took place over a period of approximately twenty-one days. There were no additions to treatment, such as spouse involvement, instruction manuals, or any anxiety management training. Subjects were simply instructed in staying in the situation until they felt better and told that repeated exposure to their feared situations would lead to a decrease in fear.

Measures

Outcome measures In the main outcome study, a battery of outcome measures were used. However, for the purposes of this study, two main outcome measures were selected.

Phobic problem severity This was 0–8 rating of severity based on that of Watson and Marks (1971). Ratings were made by subject, therapist, and independent assessor.

Behavioural avoidance test This was a ten-item test with situations ranging from a 100-yards walk to a long city-centre excursion, using bus and underground train. The test was scored by simply counting the number of items successfully completed.

Rating points—The above were completed at pre-treatment, post-treatment, and at one-year follow-up.

Cognitive change measures
1 subjective probability of negative outcome (see Fig. 8.1)
2 value (subjective cost) of negative outcomes (see Fig. 8.2)

Figure 8.1 Subjective probability of negative outcomes

Target ....

Outcome ....

The probability of this outcome occurring is:

0	10	20	30	40	50	60	70	80	90	100%
certain not to happen	almost certain not to happen	very unlikely to happen	quite unlikely to happen	slightly unlikely to happen	could go either way	slightly likely to happen	quite likely to happen	very likely to happen	almost certain to happen	certain to happen

Rating

Date

Figure 8.2 Value (subjective cost) of negative outcomes

Target ....

Outcome ....

If this outcome occurs it will be:

−5	−4	−3	−2	−1	0	+1	+2	+3	+4	+5
the worst thing ever in my life	extremely bad	very bad	moderately bad	slightly bad	neutral	slightly good	moderately good	very good	extremely good	the best thing ever in my life

Rating

Date

Rating method

Six target behaviours were elicited from each subject by asking 'What would you like to be able to do at the end of treatment?'. The response was then operationally defined. For example, a subject may respond that 'she wished to go shopping'. This would then be defined, after mutual negotiation, in unambiguous terms, also defining the role of safety signals or modifying factors. Therefore, the shopping example may be to shop alone in a large supermarket for a twenty minute period in the afternoon (without using a walking stick as a support in case of feeling faint). Also, a feature of the exercise should be queuing and browsing for items, rather than buying the first available item.

These targets were then entered on to the target rating form. Six targets were elicited for each subject. Each subject would, therefore, have a range of target behaviours from, in their terms, the easiest to the most difficult items. Subjects were asked to state the negative outcomes for each target. For example, 'if you were in a large supermarket tomorrow for a twenty minute period without a walking stick, etc., what would be the worst thing to happen?'. This would yield the negative outcome. In this way, a list of targets with negative outcomes was compiled. The subject was then asked to rate the outcomes of subjective probability and value on the rating scales shown in Figures 8.1 and 8.2.

Rating points Subjects rated subjective probability and value at pre-treatment, before and after each session of exposure, at post-treatment, and at one-year follow- up.

Criteria for failure

These criteria were predetermined and were:

1 a change of less than three points on the phobic problem severity rating from pre- to post-treatment (on either therapist, assessor, or patient rating);
2 an increase of less than three successfully completed items on behavioural avoidance test from pre- to post-treatment.

Results

Table 8.1 shows the mean ratings of subjective probability and value of negative outcomes for six targets for each subject.

Of the twelve subjects, three met the criteria for failure, i.e. subjects nos. two, three, and six. Two of these subjects (nos. two and six) however, made significant improvements during the follow-up period and no longer met failure criteria of any kind. One subject (no. twelve) dropped out of treatment at the end of the second session of treatment. Two subjects (nos. five and eight) met the criteria for relapse. The remaining six subjects (nos. one, four, seven, nine, ten, and eleven) had successful treatment outcome which was maintained to follow-up. Table 8.1 shows the mean ratings of subjective probability and value of negative outcomes for the various groups according to treatment response. As the numbers involved were so small, statistical testing seemed pointless.

Discussion of results

The subjects in this study would seem typical of populations of agoraphobics in general. Their level of handicap pre-treatment was severe and long standing. They had a range of central agoraphobic fears; indeed, eleven of the twelve subjects had more than one central fear. The subjects, overall, selected targets which were common to agoraphobics coming for treatment. However, the precise definition of target behaviour made at assessment showed considerable individual difference. Thus, for example, many subjects chose shopping in a supermarket as a target but subjects differed considerably in what factors modified the situation, to make it more or less frightening. This would seem to be a reflection of the variations of fear in agoraphobic populations. This factor thus prevented using standard targets for the population of subjects under study.

Regarding the first hypothesis concerning subjective probability ratings, ten of the twelve subjects had a mean subjective probability rating (at pre-treatment) of a negative outcome occurring if they performed a target as specified, of over 80 per cent. During exposure treatment, there was a reduction in these ratings for all subjects (see Tables 8.1 and 8.2). This confirms Beck *et al.*'s (1974) hypothesis that subjective probability estimates change as a function of exposure to the fear stimulus.

Taking into account that the number of subjects was small, there were clear differences in subjective probability ratings at post-treatment between the responder group and the group of treatment failures. However, at pre-treatment, these ratings were similar for all subjects and groups, thus indicating that subjective probability estimates may have little prognostic value.

Scrutiny of individual data demonstrates that subjective probability

Table 8.1 Mean ratings of subjective probability and value of negative outcomes

		Mean rating* of value for six targets			Mean rating* of subjective probability for six targets		
	Subject no.	Pre-treatment	Post-treatment	Final follow-up	Pre-treatment	Post-treatment	Final follow-up
Treatment responders	1	-5.0	-4.8	-5.0	95.0	36.6	45.0
	4	-4.0	-3.8	-4.0	93.3	30.0	13.3
	7	-4.3	-2.5	-2.5	45.0	10.0	13.3
	9	-4.7	-5.0	-5.0	81.6	6.6	10.0
	10	-5.0	-4.0	-4.0	85.0	20.0	20.0
	11	-5.0	-3.3	-3.3	80.0	23.3	25.0
Treatment failures	2	-4.1	-4.1	-4.16	81.6	40.0	46.6
	3	-4.1	-4.1	-4.1	91.6	45.0	48.3
	6	-5.0	-5.0	-5.0	63.3	48.3	40.0
Drop-out	12	-4.8	-2.8	-2.3	98.3	91.6	73.3
Relapsers	5	-4.3	-2.0	-4.0	95.0	15.0	70.0
	8	-5.0	-4.0	-4.0	85.0	40.0	46.6

Note
* The mean of six ratings per subject (these ratings refer to those made using the scales shown in Figures 8.1 and 8.2)

Table 8.2 Cognitive ratings for subjects according to treatment response

	Mean ratings of subjective probability			Mean ratings of value		
Responders n = 6	79.9 (18.2)	21.0 (11.3)	21.1 (12.9)	4.7 (0.4)	3.9 (0.9)	4.0 (1.0)
Failures n = 3	78.8 (14.4)	44.4 (4.2)	45.0 (4.4)	4.4 (0.5)	4.4 (0.5)	4.4 (0.5)
Relapsers n = 2	90.0 (7.1)	27.5 (17.7)	58.3 (16.6)	4.7 (0.5)	3.0 (1.4)	4.0 (0.0)
Drop-outs n = 1	98.3	91.6	73.3	4.8	2.8	2.3

Note
( ) standard deviation

ratings change not only between assessment and treatment but within and between exposure sessions. However, because most agoraphobics continue to go out between exposure sessions, it becomes impossible to quantify the 'carry over' effect of treatment. We did ask subjects in the study to keep a diary of homework and all exposure. There was, however, no obvious relationship between homework and change in ratings. There was also the additional problem that subjects' records were generally very incomplete and therefore this data, we felt, was unreliable.

One very interesting observation from the individual data is the way in which individual sessions of exposure seem to influence subjective probability estimates of all targets simultaneously. There were, however, exceptions to this. For example, for subject number nine, target number one was travelling by car on a motorway. While the other targets showed a parallel change in subjective probability ratings, the ratings for this target were unaffected until session five, when the exposure trip consisted of a motorway drive. After this session, there was a dramatic drop in ratings for this target.

Scrutiny of individual treatment responders shows no net change between the end of treatment and follow-up in subjective probability ratings. It is interesting to note that this is despite very significant change on the dependent measures of agoraphobia for the responder group. The main follow-up subjective probability ratings were ranged from 10–45. Thus, at post-treatment, these subjects apparently still had a significant estimation of something aversive occurring if they attempted a target behaviour. This personal estimation of an aversive outcome would seem to be a factor in maintaining avoidance behaviour or at least, performance of certain behaviours only under specified conditions. For example, subjects would go shopping but only in the company of a trusted companion.

Regarding Rachman's (1983) point that repeated disconfirmations will lead to reduction of fear and avoidance in agoraphobics, the experimental data support this assertion (i.e. the strong relationship between pre- to post-change in agoraphobic avoidance and change in subjective probability estimates). However, it does seem that other variables are responsible for maintaining a conviction on the part of the agoraphobic that her/his fears will come to fruition. One hypothesis would be that the evidence for maintaining a conviction comes from continuing physiological disturbance. Thus, if the agoraphobic continued to be highly aroused, with tachycardia, hyperventilation, etc., she/he will continue her/his high estimation of an aversive outcome occurring. This hypothesis would be in accord with the view that agoraphobia is caused and maintained by a mixture of organic and psychological processes. Specifically, an anomaly of physiological arousal, such as beta-adrenergic over-activity would continue to provide the physiological cues for anxiety. Another way of viewing the continuing over-estimation of risk would be to say that the agoraphobic subject continued to scan the environment for danger signals at a greater rate than would a normal subject. Alternatively, it could be argued that incoming information was incorrectly processed or both these factors contributed to this over-estimation. These hypotheses would be in accord with the view of Butler and Mathews (1983) in the discussion of their experiment with generally anxious subjects and consistent with the hypotheses of Mathews and MacLeod (1987).

The measurement of the variable of value attached to outcome in this study gives an additional perspective on the cognitive processes involved in agoraphobia and its treatment. Scrutiny of individual and grouped data demonstrate that prior to treatment, all of the study subjects attached an extremely negative value to their feared outcomes. Interestingly, three of the six treatment responders (subjects one, four, and nine) maintained virtually the same value to the feared outcome at post-treatment follow-up as at pre-treatment, despite apparently significant change in subjective probability and the other dependent measures. Furthermore, all three failures showed no change in mean ratings of value between the three rating points. Certainly, the value rating would seem to have no predictive quality regarding outcome and the indication is that any change in value is independent of the behavioural change reflected in the dependent measures. Indeed, the value attached to outcome is theoretically independent of the probability estimate (Azjen and Fishbein 1980).

It would be tempting to argue that in order to reduce or cease avoidance behaviour, a subject would need not only to see an aversive outcome as less likely but to attach a lesser value to such an outcome. This relationship is, of course, well known in social psychology and some authors would argue (e.g. Azjen and Fishbein 1980) that both variables, if properly measured and considered together, would predict very accurately the likelihood of performing (or not performing) a behaviour.

It would thus seem to be important to change the extreme view of the agoraphobic towards these feared outcomes. The two routes to this would seem to be either exposure to outcome or some form of rational persuasion. Exposure could be effected by imaginal rehearsal of the various aversive outcomes. Exposure to these outcomes would thus continue until the subject habituates. Persuasion that such an outcome may not be as bad as is thought could be systematically effected by rational emotive approaches (Ellis 1961, 1970). Indeed, workers such as Ellis would argue (e.g. Ellis 1979) that exposure is an integral part of such cognitive restructuring.

The results of this study indicated that, in the subjects, there was a modification of faulty cognitive function occurring over treatment. There was, however, no evidence to suggest that there was a radical change in such function which would amount to a 'cure' of the agoraphobia. This result could be explained by arguing that the exposure given to subjects was primarily to situations which were avoided rather than to feared outcomes. This issue seems of central importance.

If one examines the method of imaginal exposure used in the various outcome studies, there is little indication of what specifically the subjects were exposed to. The evidence concerning imaginal exposure which was reviewed by James (1985) is overall rather ambiguous. The varying findings can be explained thus: in some of the studies there may have been emphasis on exposure to aversive outcomes, rather than to situations. This exposure would then possibly lead to a significant reduction in the aversive values attached to such outcomes. Conversely, imaginal exposure to the situation would lead only to minimal, if any, change in the value attached to the outcome. Thus James's (1985) reviewed studies may contain both methods of exposure described above or varying mixtures of the methods.

It would be tempting, therefore, to suggest that exposure should be carried out by preparing the subject through imaginal exposure to outcome. This would affect the value attached to this outcome. Then the subjects would be exposed to the situation in real life and undergo the experience of repeated disconfirmation and a lessening of the perceived risk. Therefore, a trial of comparing exposure in imagination to the aversive outcomes, with exposure in imagination to the situation avoided, in an additive design, would seem to be a research priority.

The study attempted to measure only two attitude variables and it could be that additional variables not measured are responsible for some of the rather ambiguous results. Certainly, as Azjen and Fishbein

(1980) argue, behaviour is crucially influenced by social belief factors. Therefore, if, as Hallam (1985) argues, agoraphobia is part of a general staying-at-home behaviour, the social influences of important others may be central to the behaviour change, or otherwise, of agoraphobics in treatment. Specifically, if one's family believes that avoidance of anxiety is the best method of coping, then the social pressure from a family may prove stronger than the advice of the therapist to confront fear.

This study attempted to investigate some cognitive variables during exposure treatment but does not pretend to provide other than preliminary data. The call for more experimental analyses of agoraphobia (Rachman 1983) seems particularly relevant in the area of agoraphobic cognitions.

In the second study (Winter and Gournay 1987), we used repertory grids to look at agoraphobia from a personal construct perspective. (David Winter's chapter of this book reviews this area in detail, therefore only a summary of our study is presented.)

The experimental group consisted of thirty females and five males, fulfilling DSM III criteria for agoraphobia. These subjects were treated by giving six two-hour sessions of graduated exposure *in vivo*, during a twenty-one-day period. Subjects were simply instructed to stay in the phobic situation rather than escape and treatment sessions were assisted by a therapist. Subjects were allocated randomly to therapists (six therapists were used for the thirty-five subjects). The treatment procedure did not include any additions to the exposure method and therefore no formal cognitive strategies were used.

Subjects were assessed with a range of measures, including a behavioural avoidance test and independent assessment. Rating points were pre- and post-treatment and follow-up. In addition to the standard measures, we used a supplied repertory grid. This had sixteen elements and sixteen constructs. The constructs were chosen from two sources. The first source was previous pilot work with agoraphobic subjects. The second source was from previous research which indicated that agoraphobics had poor awareness of interpersonal conflict (e.g. Fisher and Wilson 1985). Thus, the chosen constructs reflected such awareness. Additionally, we asked the spouses of the subjects to complete similar grid measures. We also used two control groups (one non-phobic neurotic and one normal) and their spouses. The three groups did not differ significantly in age, social class, or sex ratio.

Results

In accord with Fisher and Wilson's (1985) findings, we found that agoraphobics had little awareness compared with the control groups of interpersonal conflict. Generally speaking, the agoraphobics/ subjects had poor self-image.

The simple behavioural treatment produced changes in the grid measures which were wide ranging and these changes were mirrored by positive changes in the grids of spouses. In particular, agoraphobics showed an increase in self-esteem and their spouses saw the agoraphobic (after successful treatment) as closer to their ideal partner. The obvious explanation is that many interpersonal problems are the effect of the agoraphobic state and that as in the Cobb *et al.* (1980) study, exposure treatment generates generalizing changes.

In summary, the two studies described above clearly produce positive cognitive change which is not solely specific to the agoraphobic state. These changes seem to be durable and would counter arguments to the effect that behavioural treatment produces only superficial changes.

However, the literature on cognitive change during behaviour therapy is sparse and much wider investigation is urgently needed, in order to understand the process of change and to refine treatment methods. These future directions will be considered in Chapter 10.

© Kevin Gournay

REFERENCES

Azjen, I., and Fishbein, M. (1980) *Understanding Attitudes and Predicting Social Behaviour,* Englewood Cliffs, NJ: Prentice Hall Inc.

Barlow, D. H., O'Brien, G. T., and Last, C. G. (1984) 'Couples treatment of agoraphobia', *Behaviour Therapy* 1: 41–58.

Beck, A. T. (1976) *Cognitive Therapy and the Emotional Disorders,* New York: International University Press.

Beck, A. T., Laude, R., and Bohnert, M. (1974) 'Ideational components of anxiety neurosis', *Archives of General Psychiatry,* 31: 319–25.

Butler, G. and Mathews, A. M. (1983) 'Cognitive processes in anxiety', *Advances in Behaviour Research and Therapy* 5: 51–62.

Chambless, D. L. (1978) 'The role of anxiety in flooding with agoraphobic clients', unpublished doctoral dissertation, Temple University, PA, USA.

Clark, D. M. and Teasdale, J. D. (1982) 'Diurnal variation in clinical depression and accessibility of memories of positive and negative experiences', *Journal of Abnormal Psychology* 91: 87–95.

Cobb, J. P., McDonald, R., Marks, I. M., and Stern, R. S. (1980) 'Psychological treatments of coexisting marital and phobic obsessive problems', *Behavioural Analysis and Modification* 4, 3–16.

Ellis, A. (1961) *A Guide to Rational Living*, London: Prentice Hall.

—(1970) *The Essence of Rational Psychotherapy: a Comprehensive Approach to Treatment*, New York: Institute for Rational Living.

—(1979) 'A note on the treatment of agoraphobics with cognitive modification versus prolonged exposure *in vivo*', *Behaviour Research and Therapy* 17: 162–4.

Emmelkamp, P. M. G. (1979) 'The behavioural study of clinical phobias', in M. Hersen, R. Eisler, and P. M. Miller (eds) *Progress in Behaviour Modification*, vol. 8, New York: Academic Press.

—(1982) Chapter '*in vivo* treatment of agoraphobia', in D. L. Chambless and A. J. Goldstein (eds) *Agoraphobia: Multiple Perspectives on Theory and Treatment*, New York: John Wiley.

Emmelkamp, P. M. G., Kuipers, A. C. M., and Eggeraat, J. B. (1978) 'Cognitive modification versus prolonged exposure *in vivo* : a comparison with agoraphobics as subjects', *Behaviour Research and Therapy* 16: 33–41.

Fisher, L. M. and Wilson, G. T. (1985) 'A study of the psychology of agoraphobia', *Behaviour Research and Therapy* 23, 2: 97–108.

Gournay, K. J. M. (1986) 'Cognitive change during the behavioural (exposure) treatment of agoraphobia', paper to EABT Congress, Lausanne, Switzerland.

Hallam, R. S. (1985) *Psychological Perspectives on Panic and Agoraphobia*, London: Academic Press.

Hibbert, G. A. (1984) 'Ideational components of anxiety. Their origin and content', *British Journal of Psychiatry* 144: 618–24.

Hollon, S. D. and Kriss, M. R. (1984) 'Cognitive factors in clinical research and practice', *Clinical Psychology Review* 4: 35–76.

James, J. C. (1985) 'Desensitization treatment of agoraphobia', *British Journal of Clinical Psychology* 24: 133–4.

Kendall, P. C. and Hollon, S. D. (1981) *Assessment Strategies of Cognitive-Behavioural Interventions*, New York: Academic Press.

—(1983) 'Methodology and cognitive behavioural assessment', *Behavioural Psychotherapy* 11, 4: 285–301.

Mathews, A. and MacLeod, C. (1987) 'An information-processing approach to anxiety', *Journal of Cognitive Psychotherapy* 1, 2: 105–16.

Mavissakalian, M., Michelson, L., Greenwald, D., Kornblith, S., and Greenwald, M. (1983) 'Cognitive behavioural treatment of agoraphobia. Paradoxical intention versus self statement training', *Behaviour Research and Therapy* 21, 1: 75–86.

Meichenbaum, D. (1976) 'A cognitive behaviour modification approach to assessment', in M. Hersen and A. S. Bellack (eds) *Behavioural Assessment: a Practical Handbook*, New York: Pergamon Press.

Merluzzi, T., Glass, C., and Genest, M. (1981) *Cognitive Assessment*, New

York: Guilford.

Rachman, S. (1983) 'The modification of agoraphobic avoidance behaviour. Some fresh possibilities', *Behaviour Research and Therapy* 21, 5: 567–4.

Seligman, M. E. P. and Johnston, J. C. (1973) 'A cognitive theory of avoidance', in F. McGuigan and O. Lumsden (eds) *Contemporary Approaches to Conditioning and Learning*, New York: Wiley.

Teasdale, J. D., Taylor, R., and Fogarty, S. J. (1980) 'Effects of induced elation-depression on the accessibility of memories of positive and negative experiences', *Behaviour Research and Therapy* 18: 339–46.

Watson, J. P. and Marks, I. M. (1971) 'Relevant and irrelevant fear in flooding. A crossover study in phobic patients', *Behaviour Therapy* 2: 275–93.

Williams, S. and Rappaport, J. (1983) 'Cognitive treatment in the natural environment for agoraphobics', *Behaviour Therapy* 14: 299–313.

Winter, D. A. and Gournay, K. J. M. (1987) 'Construction and constriction in agoraphobia', *British Journal of Medical Psychology*, 60: 233–44.

Chapter Nine

AGORAPHOBIA: A WOMAN'S PROBLEM? THE SEX-ROLE PERSPECTIVE

KEVIN GOURNAY

As Barbara Hudson has pointed out in Chapter 3, the public perception of agoraphobia is that of a 'woman's problem'. Feminist writers compound this error by stating that 95 per cent of agoraphobics are women (Eichenbaum and Orbach 1983) and by their construction of the problem in sole terms of male oppression (Fodor 1974). The purpose of the chapter is to critically examine agoraphobia from a sex-role perspective and to look at the differential response of men and women to behavioural treatment.

BACKGROUND

Dwyer (1984) comprehensively reviewed the historical aspects of psychological disorder. She argued convincingly that the theories of mental illness developed in the nineteenth century continue to dominate current thinking. In particular, these theories saw 'female instability' as a significant aetiological factor. Indeed, today, common lore dictates that women are more prone to succumb to life stresses. This belief was notably reflected in the classic study of Broverman *et al.* (1970) who investigated a group of mental health professionals and found that these workers associated masculine, rather than feminine, attributes with mental health.

It goes without saying that women are relegated to inferior roles, both socially and occupationally, and that this process begins very early in development.

Weinraub and Brown (1983) reviewed the development of sex-role stereotypes in children and gave a very gloomy picture of how females' expectations are limited at a very early age. They reviewed research regarding children's awareness of sex differences in possessions and toys and in adult occupations and household tasks. They concluded that there is evidence that the acquisition of sex-typed behaviour begins before the age of two and that even among pre-school children, girls choose nurturing roles more often than boys.

There are many studies demonstrating how children acquire stereotyped roles. For example, Kagen and Moss (1962) showed that adults tend to reinforce dependent and helpless behaviour in female children, while encouraging male children to be more independent. Bandura (1977) demonstrated quite clearly that behavioural contingencies differentially reinforce stereotyped behaviour in boys and girls and that cross-typed behaviour is generally punished. Hoffman (1972) summed up the developmental literature by stating that girls get less encouragement for independence than boys. Moreover, they are more protected than boys and less independent in exploring their environment. Consequently, they develop fewer skills and less confidence and continue to be more dependent on others.

Sex differences in the incidence of fear

In the general developmental literature, there is no evidence that male and female children up to the age of eight differ in incidence of fears (Maccoby and Jacklin 1974). However, in a recent study of older children in Japan (Abe and Masui 1981) girls had a greater incidence of fears. These authors looked at a group of school children and students, aged eleven to twenty-three, to obtain prevalences of various fears in normal adolescents. Overall, the data from this study, which suggested that sex differences seemingly become more apparent with increasing age, were reinforced by a more recent study.

Kirkpatrick (1984) carried out an investigation of common intense fears in an adult population of 345 women and 200 men and showed that males and females had different patterns of fear as the ages increased. The data suggested that in common intense fears, males and females were potentially equally vulnerable at earlier ages, but that the higher numbers of females with intensive fears in older populations were due to cultural and experiential influences.

There have been several major community studies of adult populations carried out in the United States, Switzerland, Germany, and the United Kingdom. Marks (1987) has reviewed these studies and demonstrates that women are roughly twice as likely to develop anxiety states and panic disorder as men. However, in social phobia, prevalence rates are much more similar and in obsessive compulsive disorders some varieties are commoner in men. Marks also points to the considerable evidence that anxiety states are not the prerogative of western cultures and that the general prevalence rates of Europe and the USA are similar to those found in Asia, Africa and South America. However, the results of these findings should be treated with some caution as it does seem that women will more readily admit their fears (Rachman 1978).

Differences in incidence of agoraphobia between males and females

The earliest descriptions of agoraphobia were based, as Mathews *et al.* (1981) point out, on descriptions of male sufferers. Westphal (1871), in his description, reported the cases of three male agoraphobics and Legrand du Saule (1885) concluded that agoraphobia was uncommon in females. The contemporary scene, however, seems quite different. Thorpe and Burns (1983) suggested that the percentage of female sufferers presenting for treatment in this country averages about 80 per cent. Agras and his colleagues (1969) in the USA reported an equal incidence of agoraphobia between the sexes. However, it should be pointed out that their sample was relatively small (325 subjects).

Since that time, large community studies have been carried out which show a higher incidence in women. In two major community studies in the USA (Uhlenhuth *et al.* 1983, Myers *et al.* 1984), females accounted for roughly 75 per cent of agoraphobic populations. This rate has also been approximated in other studies in other parts of the world, e.g. Angst and Dobler-Mikola (1983). Thus, the general impression is that agoraphobia is largely a woman's problem, but no means as much as was suggested by Eichenbaum and Orbach (1983). Having said that, one must take into account two other factors before making any assumptions about sex difference. First, as previously stated, men tend to deny or hide their fearfulness (Rachman 1978). Second, as reviewed in Chapter 1, two careful studies (Mullaney and Trippett 1979 and Bibb and Chambless 1986) show a close association between alcohol abuse and agoraphobia. The data from these studies suggest that many men may attempt to deal with agoraphobia by using alcohol, eventually only coming to the notice of treatment agencies because of alcohol abuse. Therefore, the sex incidence of 3:1 reported in clinical and epidemiological samples needs to be treated with some considerable caution.

Factors relating to apparent sex differences

Biological factors

Several writers have suggested that the male/female difference in phobias may be partly caused by endocrine factors. Zitrin *et al.* (1976) suggested that oestrogen fluctuation may be partly responsible for the acquisition of phobic avoidance. Marks (1970) has pointed to the fact that because testosterone is linked to dominance behaviour, men will more likely face situations rather than avoid them. Further, Asso and Beech (1975) found evidence to suggest that women are more likely to be conditioned to anxiety responses when their levels of oestrogen and progesterone drop in the pre-menstrual week. However, as Chambless and Goldstein (1982) point out, the issue of expectancy was not controlled for. This factor is important and, as in menstrual cycle research, needs to be considered as a confounding variable which may considerably influence the individual's response(s) to events occurring at different points of her cycle (Sommer 1973).

Emmelkamp (1979) has argued that hormonal fluctuations may account for the excess of females in agoraphobic populations, but he does not give any specific data to back his assertions. However, Buglass *et al.* (1977) specifically asked their sample whether their agoraphobia increased in severity during the pre-menstrual phase of their cycles. Only six of the eighteen subjects who were having menstrual cycles reported such an increase. Overall, the data tends to disconfirm any simple relationship between hormonal factors and the genesis and maintenance of the syndrome.

Sex roles

Within the psychiatric field there has, for a long time, been a view of agoraphobia as a classic female response. Indeed, in a most derogatory statement, Terhune, who was a leading authority in his day, in considering factors relating to the evolution of the agoraphobic syndrome, stated that women were predisposed because 'they had been brought up soft' (Terhune 1949). The stereotyping of the agoraphobic as a dependent female was reinforced by Andrews's review (1966), which at that time was a most influential piece of writing. He said he 'had never heard of a phobic who had been described as self-assertive, independent or fearless' and went on to say that 'the phobic individual is characterised by dependency relationships and avoids activities involving self-assertion and independence in coping with stressful situations'.

Fodor (1974) has argued that women who become stereotyped as helpless and dependent are susceptible to developing phobias. Fodor saw agoraphobic women as exhibiting an extreme stereotype of female behaviour. She argued that such conditioning processes begin in childhood, and continue unremittingly. She further argued that agoraphobic women choose complementary spouses. Fodor went on to conclude her 1974 paper by saying that agoraphobia appeared to be 'a natural outcome of sex role socialisation, rather than an illness'.

Wolfe (1984) has recently reviewed the issue of gender ideology and phobias in women. He cites wide-ranging evidence to suggest that much of the time we are hardly recognizant of the extent to which our behaviour is controlled by gender imperatives, but that such influences account for the development of phobias. Wolfe points to the literature on sex-role socialization to provide convincing evidence that the rearing of male and female children, and the differences of such rearing, correlate with the differences between males and females in personality characteristics and behavioural styles. While Wolfe's stance is to view the issue of sex roles behaviourally, he looks not only at social learning and behavioural prospectives, but also cognitive developmental theory and psychoanalysis. He argues that with regard to developing an anti-phobic style, females are particularly disadvantaged. Wolfe goes on to review the extension of gender imperatives and the connection between agoraphobia and women's marital imperative. He cites the work of writers such as Chambless and Goldstein (1982), and Fodor (1974), to argue that many agoraphobic women develop their problems at a time when they feel trapped in a marital situation, especially when there are young children demanding care and attention. From there, Wolfe goes on to describe the work of writers who suggest an extension of this basic entrapment into a number of conflicts which in turn produce the agoraphobic syndrome. This line of thinking is interesting, but one is again drawn to the rather conflicting evidence of both descriptive studies, e.g. Buglass et al. (1977), and outcome studies, e.g. Cobb et al. (1984) and Hafner (1977a, 1977b), which seem to deny a simple cause-and-effect explanation of agoraphobia and the marital state. Again, many of the arguments reviewed by Wolfe seem to rest on unsubstantiated psychodynamic explanations of the phobia, which use a conflict/symptom production model. Wolfe describes the various limitations to the gender imperative model and particularly draws attention to the fact that women are more vulnerable to depression and therefore more prone to phobias. Lastly, he states what is probably the greatest limitation of the gender imperative model; this is that as we are all exposed to the ideology of gender, there should in fact be more phobics than one actually sees. Of the minority of males who are agoraphobic, Wolfe points out that we know very little about their backgrounds as these have not been systematically studied.

Measurement of femininity and masculinity

The measurement of the constructs of masculinity and femininity has long formed an important part of personality testing. Nonconformity with an appropriate gender role was, and to an extent still is, viewed as constituting an abnormality. A turning point in the way that sex roles were construed came with the critique of Constantinople (1973), who reviewed the various psychological scales purporting to measure masculinity and femininity as bipolar opposites which were, in effect, mutually exclusive. Further, a subject who scored responses on both of these scales would, using most criteria, be far from the ideal for males and females. Further to this, Bem and co-workers (Bem 1974, 1975, Bem and Lenney 1976, Bem *et al.* 1976) argued convincingly that ideal adjustment was characterized by the possession of behaviours of both sex types, i.e. androgynous behaviour. Bem (1974) subsequently developed her now widely accepted sex-role inventory. The various authors pointed out that while people with a high level of one sex typing will be highly competent in situations requiring responses consistent with such typing they will be deficient in responses in situations calling for oppositely typed responses. Therefore, subjects with high levels of male and female typing, i.e. androgynous individuals, will be effective in a range of situations and will demonstrate behavioural flexibility. Bem (1977) was among several workers who have shown a high correlation between high self-esteem and subjects who possess androgynous and masculine-typed sex responses. Conversely, subjects with low self-esteem tend to have feminine typing, or be low on both masculine and feminine typing (i.e. undifferentiated sex typing).

The Bem Sex Role Inventory (BSRI)

The BSRI (Bem 1974) was one of several measures published after Constantinople's (1973) critique. It is a widely used measure of sex-role stereotyping and is similar in general principle to the Personal Attributes Questionnaire (Spence and Helmreich 1975). It consists of 60 items, 20 masculine, 20 feminine and 20 neutral, scored by the subject on a seven point scale. The inventory gives masculinity and femininity scores which are simple sums of item responses. Androgyny has been scored in two ways. Originally, Bem (1974) devised the following method. The androgyny score is defined as student's t ratio for the difference between a person's masculinity and femininity scores. Thus, the closer to zero, the closer was the person to androgyny. However, this did not differentiate between subjects with very high or very low scores on masculinity and femininity. Spence et al. (1975) therefore suggested that this differentiation could be effected by using a median split in a group for each scale. Subjects scoring high on both scales (androgynous subjects) are therefore differentiated from subjects scoring low on both scales (undifferentiated). Bem (1977) subsequently accepted this revised method. This method of scoring is used in the current study.

Research using the BSRI and shortcomings of the scale

There are two main criticisms of the BSRI. First, and this is not confined to the BSRI, there is the well-known problem of whether self-description correlates with behaviour in real life. Second, the feminine items of the scale have a rather negative tone when compared with the masculine items. Despite these two criticisms, the BSRI has been widely used in research. However, there is only one study of direct relevance to agoraphobia. Brehony (1983) used a new Agoraphobia Research Questionnaire (ARQ) and a fear survey (among other measures) with a group of college students. These students also completed a BSRI. The data showed that females scored more highly on the ARQ, and that subjects typed as masculine (using the BSRI) scored lower on the ARQ. This finding, suggesting a relationship between adherence to a sex-role stereotype and self-report of agora- phobic symptoms, must be tempered with some caution, as the ARQ had not been validated at the time of the research being carried out.

One other isolated finding should also be mentioned. Jasin (1981) used the Minnesota Multi-phasic Personality Inventory (MMPI) to look at the relative masculinity and femininity of agoraphobics. She found that agoraphobic women were not excessively feminine, but that male agoraphobics tended to score high on femininity according to clinical norms.

Male agoraphobics and treatment outcome

The literature on male agoraphobics is somewhat sparse and to compound this, as Chambless and Mason (1986) point out, male agoraphobics are commonly excluded from treatment outcome studies to ensure greater sample homogeneity. Liotti and Guidano (1976) carried out a retrospective review of the records of twenty-one agoraphobic males and concluded that they did poorly compared with females. They cited resistance to treatment as the major problem. Furthermore, they stated that a poor treatment response was more likely if the subject had a fear of being left alone or was hypochondriacal. However, the *post hoc* nature of their review casts some doubt on their findings.

Prior to the study, which will be described presently, there have only been three properly controlled studies which have looked at the differential treatment response of male and female agoraphobic subjects.

In the first study, Hafner (1983) looked at a sample of 18 male and 49 female agoraphobics conforming to DSM III criteria for agoraphobia. From this sample, 10 males completed treatment, which consisted of twelve hours of graduated exposure *in vivo*. Hafner then matched these with 10 females, using age as the basis of matching, and looked at outcome. On the various measures used, the post-treatment and twelve-month follow-up state of the male agoraphobic subjects was broadly comparable to that of the female agoraphobic subjects. However, there were two major differences between the two groups. Women experienced significantly more panic attacks during treatment than men, but males had significantly more fears of losing control of aggressive impulses. The rate of drop-out from treatment was 44 per cent for males and 12 per cent for females and this led Hafner to conclude that while exposure *in vivo* may be an effective treatment for males, it may not be as acceptable to them as for females.

In a second study, Mavissakalian (1985) also considered 10 males and 10 matched female agoraphobic subjects. In this study, subjects received not only exposure treatment with a therapist or exposure instructions, but were also treated by imipramine or by an imipramine placebo. The study was limited by the fact that post-treatment follow-up was only to one month. Treatment outcome was significantly better for females than males and no drop-outs were reported.

In the third study, Chambless and Mason (1986) looked at the outcome of 14 male and 67 female agoraphobics, who received a comprehensive programme of treatment, totalling ten complete days, and including twenty-seven hours of graduated exposure *in vivo* and other treatment strategies. There were no differences between males and females on either pre-treatment measures or on outcome. The study reported no follow-up period and there were only two female drop-outs and no male drop-outs from the total sample. The study also considered the responses of all subjects on the Personal Attributes Questionnaire (Spence and Helmreich 1978). This measure yields scores of masculinity and femininity. The results of Chambless and Mason's study will be considered with the results of the current study to be described below.

AREA OF THE CURRENT STUDY

1 The outcome of male and female agoraphobics with exposure treatment.
2 The differential drop-out rate from treatment.
3 Whether male and female agoraphobic subjects demonstrate extremes of feminine sex-typed behaviour as measured by a sex- role inventory.

METHOD

Subjects were 100 females and 32 males conforming to DSM III criteria for agoraphobia who took part in the large outcome study (reported in other chapters of this book). Unlike American studies, there was no delineation on the basis of panic disorder. To recap, subjects were accepted for standardized behavioural treatment. This comprised six two-hour sessions of exposure in real life with no other additions. Treatment was given over a twenty-one-day period by a range of therapists, who were randomly allocated to patients.

Measures
Subjects were assessed with a range of outcome measures, including

ratings of general phobic state by patient, therapist, and independent assessor; a Leeds depression inventory; a fear survey schedule (Marks and Mathews 1978); a behavioural avoidance test; and a rating of dysfunction of work, home management, social leisure, and private leisure (Marks et al. 1977).

In addition, 20 male and 54 female subjects from the same sample also completed the Bem sex role inventory (Bem 1974). This measure was reviewed in detail above.

The Bem measure was given at pre- and post-treatment rating points. In order to compare the agoraphobic subjects with normal controls, a control population of equal numbers and in the same proportions of the sexes was recruited from the non-psychiatric departments of two district general hospitals. Subjects consisted of staff and patient attenders at out-patient orthopaedic clinics.

RESULTS AND DISCUSSION

For the sake of simplicity, the main results are tabulated.

Pre-treatment scores

As Table 9.1 shows, the only significant difference in scores was on the marital questionnaire scores of the subjects, with males having significantly higher levels of marital satisfaction. Surprisingly, the level of depression and general symptoms was not greater among the female group. This result is at variance with more general research on sex differences in depression and with the results of both the Mavissakalian (1985) and Chambless and Mason (1986) studies.

Drop-out rates for males and females

As Table 9.2 shows, the drop-out rate for male subjects in the study was higher than that for female subjects, but this did not reach significance (χ^2=3.263 $p<0.10$). This finding is similar to that of Hafner's 1983 study where males had a higher drop-out rate. However, in Mavissakalian's 1985 study there were no drop-outs at all and in Chambless and Mason's (1986) study (which was a highly selected group) there were only two female drop-outs and no male drop-outs in a sample of eighty-one.

The current study used a population which is probably more typical of routine clinical services and probably the drop-out/refusal rates of about one in four are more realistic and in keeping with general

Table 9.1 Comparison of pre-treatment scores of all male and all female subjects

						Pre-treatment scores							
	Fear survey total	Agoraphobic sub-scale score	Symptom check list	Wakefield inventory	Leeds scales	Problem rating, assessor	Problem rating, therapist	Problem rating, subject	Work, home, social, private	Marital quest. subject	Marital quest. spouse	Behavioural avoidance test	Change in ag. sub-scale (pre–post)
Male subjects n = 32	69·81 (20·24)	30.22 (6·49)	25·50 (7·28)	23·43 (4·86)	12·24 (4·52)	5.80 (0.84)	6.84 (1.00)	7.19 (1.20)	21.17 (6.31)	17.93 (12.11)	16.92 (12.68)	2.52 (1.44)	15.93 (7.10)
Female subjects n = 100	67.15 (19·27)	28.92 (6·80)	22·92 (6·80)	23·51 (5·72)	12·18 (3·77)	6.00 (1.27)	6.85 (0.98)	7.01 (1.11)	18.73 (5.62)	22.63 (15.17)	18.44 (13.09)	2.02 (1.15)	15.81 (8.42)

Note
* all subjects completing follow-up (including drop-outs)

Table 9.2 Chi square analysis of male and female subjects completing treatment or dropping out/refusing

	Females	Males	n
Completed treatment	81 (77·3)	19 (22·7)	100
Dropped out/refused	21 (24·7)	11 (7·3)	32
Total	102	30	132

Notes
Expected frequencies in parentheses
$\chi^2 = 3.263$ 1/df (corrected for continuity) n.s.

drop-out rates for outpatient treatment. The likelihood therefore remains that males will tend to drop out of treatment more often. Hafner suggested that this is more so in the case of males who either feared being alone or who were hypochondriacal and suggested that effective techniques may be evolved for them. The current study did not look at this hypothesis and the small numbers of males involved in these studies will tend to make this a difficult task.

Reasons for drop-out

As part of a wider study which also looked at various aspects of treatment failure (see Chapter 6), we also looked at why subjects dropped out. We used a questionnaire based on that used by Emmelkamp (1983) in his study of treatment failures. Probably because the numbers involved were small, we could see no differences between the responses of the male and female subjects. To recap, the main factors which were reported as important in drop-out accounts were that the therapist did not understand, that the patient was frightened of treatment, the treatment was not what the patient wanted, or there was a belief on the part of the patient that one had to overcome fears on one's own. These results do indicate that there should be more comprehensive preparation for treatment, and therapist's behaviour may need some modification.

Comparison of male and female subjects' scores in matched groups

Because of the very uneven numbers it was decided to match subjects on initial agoraphobic sub-scale scores (subjects were also of similar ages). This was the procedure adopted in both the Mavissakalian (1985) and the Hafner (1983) studies. In the current study, we looked at 20 males and 20 females, the Mavissakalian study looked at 10 males and 10 females, and Chambless and Mason's study looked at 14 males and 14 females. As Table 9.3 shows, there were no major significant differences between the groups. However, the change on the agoraphobic sub-scale for male subjects was a mean of over three points greater than that of the female group. This result approaches significance. This more positive change in our male subjects is at variance with the Mavissakalian study where the males' outcome on scores was poorer.

In the matched groups, as in the total overall groups, males seemed to have significantly higher levels of marital happiness, but contrary to

Chambless and Mason's study and as previously pointed out in other more general research, there was no difference in levels of depression. Comparison of the pre- and post-treatment scores of the matched female group with the other females by non-parametric analysis showed no significant differences, indicating that it would be reasonable to generalize from the results of the matched comparison.

Table 9.3 Comparison of matched male and female subjects who completed treatment

	Initial agoraphobia sub-scale score	Initial symptom check-list score	Age	Change in agoraphobia sub-scale (pre–post)	Change in agoraphobia sub-scale score (post – 1 yr. f.u.)
Male n = 19	31·00 (5·87)	23·21 (6·67)	36·47 (7·07)	17·68	0·16
Female n = 19	30·95 (5·84)	22·01 (6·40)	39·42 (8·71)	14·47 (7·72)	0·06
t	0·027 df 36 n.s.	0·970 df 36 n.s.	0·82 df 36 n.s.	1·33 df 36 n.s.	0·061 df 32 n.s.

Note
( ) = standard deviation

Comparison of female agoraphobic subjects and normal female controls

Scores on the F scale (feminine typing) of the Bem were remarkably similar between the two groups, but the agoraphobic subjects had significantly lower M (masculine typing) scores than the control group. The Bem scale did not appear sensitive to treatment change; there was no significant difference between pre- and post-scores.

Comparison of male subjects and normal male controls

For male subjects, again there was no sensitivity of the Bem scale to treatment change and scores on the F scale were similar. However, although the agoraphobic males had lower scores on the M scale, this was only significant at the 10 per cent level.

Implications of study for theories of sex typing in agoraphobia

The data for both males and females would suggest that rather than agoraphobia being an extreme of feminine typed behaviour, the disorder was one characterized by low masculinity. This finding is in accord with the Chambless and Mason study. However, as these authors point out, this profile may be accounted for by the detrimental effects of the agoraphobia. The male items on the scale, which are self-descriptions, are instrumental items which are the antithesis of agoraphobic behaviour.

The lack of post-treatment change on the Bem scale may well be a reflection of the very brief treatment programme, in that self-perception changes may be far from complete at post-test. One could speculate that the pre-morbid profile of the subjects on the Bem scale may well be indistinguishable from 'normal'. This would fit with the theory that agoraphobics are no different in psychological profile than the population at large. This theory, of course, has considerable evidence behind it (see, for example, Fisher and Wilson 1985).

The Bem Sex Role Inventory as a predictor of outcome

Various analyses showed that there were no differences in outcome between the various Bem groups. In particular, subjects classified as androgynous did no better on the outcome measures than the other groups. However, androgynous and male-classified subjects had a significantly lower drop-out rate than subjects classified as female or undifferentiated. It therefore seems that there is little evidence that the Bem scale has any prognostic utility.

SUMMARY

This study showed that male and female agoraphobics referred for treatment were, overall, not significantly different on pre-treatment measures. Of those who completed simple exposure *in vivo* treatment, outcome was equivalent, with results maintained to one-year follow-up. However, there was a trend, as in Hafner's study, for males to drop out or refuse treatment at a greater rate. With regard to the issue of sex-role stereotyping, the data suggest that agoraphobia should not be considered as an extreme of feminine sex typed behaviour. Rather, it suggests that agoraphobics, both male and female, lack certain instrumental responses. This, of course, could well be a consequence of the problem. Therefore, it would seem that the various aetiological theories based on the notion of agoraphobia being an expression of extreme feminine behaviour are in need of radical revision.

© Kevin Gournay

REFERENCES

Abe, K. and Masui, T. (1981) 'Age–sex trends of phobic and anxiety symptoms in adolescents', *British Journal of Psychiatry* 138, 4: 297–302.

Agras, S., Sylvester, D., and Oliveau, D. (1969) 'The epidemiology of common fears and phobias', *Comprehensive Psychiatry* 10: 151–6.

Andrews, J. (1966) 'The psychotherapy of phobias', *Psychological Bulletin* 66: 455–80.

Angst, J. and Dobler-Mikola (1983) 'Anxiety states, panic and phobia in a young general population', in *World Congress of Psychiatry, Vienna*, New York: Plenum.

Asso, D. and Beech, H. R. (1975) 'Susceptibility to the acquisition of conditioned response in relation to the menstrual cycle, *Journal of Psychosomatic Research* 19: 337–44.

Bandura, A. (1977) *Social Learning Theory*, Englewood NJ: Prentice-Hall.

Bem, S. L. (1974) 'The measurement of psychological androgyny', *Journal of Consulting and Clinical Psychology* 42: 155–62.

—(1975) 'Sex role adaptability: one consequence of psychological androgyny', *Journal of Personality and Social Psychology* 31: 634–43.

—(1977) 'On the utility of alternative procedures for assessing psychological androgyny', *Journal of Consulting and Clinical Psychology* 45: 196–205.

Bem S. L. and Lenney, E. (1976) 'Sex typing and the avoidance of cross sex behaviour', *Journal of Personality and Social Psychology* 33: 48–54.

Bem, S. L., Martyna, W., and Watson, C. (1976) 'Sex typing and androgyny: further explorations of the expressive domain', *Journal of Personality and Social Psychology* 34: 1016–23.

Bibb, J. and Chambless, D. L. (1986) 'Alcohol use and abuse among diagnosed agoraphobics', *Behaviour Research and Therapy* 24: 49–58.

Brehony, K. A. (1983) 'Women and agoraphobia', in V. Franks and V. Rothblum (eds) *The Stereotyping of Women*, New York: Springer.

Broverman, I. K., Broverman, D. M., Clarkson, F. W., Rosenkranz, P., and Vogel, S. R. (1970) 'Sex role stereotypes and clinical judgements in mental health', *Journal Consulting Psychology* 34: 1–7.

Buglass, D., Clarke, J., Henderson, A., and Kreitman, N. (1977) 'A study of agoraphobic housewives', *Psychological Medicine* 7: 73–86.

Chambless, D. L. and Goldstein, A. J. (1982) *Agoraphobia: Multiple Perspectives*, New York: John Wiley.

Chambless, D. L. and Mason, J. (1986) 'Sex, sex-role stereotyping and agoraphobia', *Behaviour Research and Therapy* 24, 2: 231–5.

Cobb, J. P., Mathews, A. M., Childs-Clarke, A., and Blowers, C. (1984) 'The spouse a cotherapist in the treatment of agoraphobia', *British Journal of Psychiatry* 144: 282–7.

Constantinople (1973) 'Masculinity–femininity: an exception to the famous dictum', *Psychological Bulletin* 80: 389–407.

Dwyer, H. (1984) chapter in C. Spatz Widom (ed.) *Sex Roles and Psychopathology*, New York: Plenum.

Eichenbaum, L. and Orbach, S. (1983) *Understanding Women,*
Harmondsworth: Penguin.

Emmelkamp, P. M. G. (1979) chapter in M. Hersen, R. Eisler, and P. Miller
(eds) *Progress in Behaviour Modification,* New York: Academic Press.

Emmelkamp, P. M. G. (1983) chapter in E. N. Foa and P. M. G.
Emmelkamp (eds) *Failures in Behaviour Therapy,* New York: John Wiley.

Fisher, L. M. and Wilson, G. T. (1985) 'A study of psychology of
agoraphobia', *Behaviour Research and Therapy* 23, 2: 97–108.

Fodor, I. D. (1974) 'The phobic syndrome in women', in V. Franks and V.
Burke (eds) *Women in Therapy,* New York: Brunner/Mazel.

Hafner, R. J. (1977a) 'The husbands of agoraphobic women: assortative
mating or pathogenic interaction', *British Journal of Psychiatry* 130: 233–9.

—(1977b) 'The husbands of agoraphobic women and their influence on
treatment outcome', *British Journal of Psychiatry* 130: 280–94.

—(1983) 'Behaviour therapy for agoraphobic men', *Behaviour Research and
Therapy* 21, 1: 51–6.

Hoffman, L. W. (1972) 'Early childhood experience and women's
achievement motives', *Journal of Social Issues* 28: 129–55.

Jasin, S. E. (1981) 'A comparison of agoraphobics, anxiety neurotics and
depressive neurotics', unpublished doctoral dissertation, Temple
University, USA.

Kagen, J. and Moss, H. A. (1962) *Birth to Maturity,* New York: John Wiley.

Legrand du Saule, H. (1885) *De l'agoraphobie practicien,* vol. 8, 208–10.

Liotti, G. and Guidano, V. (1976) 'Behavioural analysis of marital
interaction in agoraphobic male patients', *Behaviour Research and
Therapy* 14: 161–2.

Maccoby, E. and Jacklin, C. (1974) *The Psychology of Sex Differences,*
California: Stanford University Press.

Marks, I. M. (1970) 'Agoraphobic syndrome', *Archives of General Psychiatry*
23: 538–53.

—(1987) *Fears, Phobias and Rituals,* New York: Oxford University Press.

Marks, I. M., Connolly, J., Hallam, R. S., and Phillpot, R. (1977) *Nursing in
Behavioural Psychotherapy,* London: RCN.

Marks, M. and Mathews, A. M. (1978) 'A brief standard self-rating for
phobic patients', *Behaviour Research and Therapy* 17, 3: 263–7.

Mathews, A. M., Gelder, M. G., and Johnston, D. W. (1981) *Agoraphobia:
Nature and Treatment,* London: Tavistock.

Mavissakalian, M. (1985) 'Male and female agoraphobia: are they
different', *Behaviour Research and Therapy* 23, 4: 469–71.

Mullaney, J. and Trippett, C. (1979) 'Alcohol dependence and phobias',
British Journal of Psychiatry, 135: 565–73.

Myers, J., Weissman, M., and Tischler, G. (1984) 'Six month prevalence of
psychiatric disorders in three communities', *Archives of General Psychiatry*
41: 959–67.

Rachman, S. (1978) *Fear and Courage,* San Francisco: Freeman.

Sommer, B. (1973) 'The effect of menstruation on cognitive and motor
behaviour', *Psychological Medicine* 35: 515–34.

Spence, J. T. and Helmreich, R. L. (1975) *Masculinity and Femininity: Their Psychological Dimensions, Correlates and Antecedents*, Austin, Texas: University of Texas Press.

Terhune, W. B. (1949) 'The phobic syndrome', *Archives Neurology Psychiatry* 62: 162–72.

Thorpe, G. L. and Burns, L. E. (1983) *The Agoraphobic Syndrome*, London: John Wiley.

Uhlenhuth, E., Balter, M., Mellinger, G., Cisin, I., and Clinthorpe, P. (1983) 'Symptom checklist syndromes in the general population', *Archives of General Psychiatry* : 40: 1167–73.

Weinraub, B. and Brown, R. (1983) chapter in V. Franks and V. Rothblum (eds) *The Stereotyping of Women*, New York: Springer.

Westphal, C. (1871) *Die Agoraphobie: eine Neuropathische Aich, für Psychie. Und Nervenkrank-heiten*, vol. 3, 138–61.

Wolfe, B. (1984) Chapter in C. Spatz Widom (ed.) *Sex Roles and Psychopathology*, New York: Plenum.

Zitrin, C. M., Klein, D. F., Lindeman, D., Tobak, P., Rock, M., Kaplan, J., and Ganz, V. H. (1976) 'Comparison of short-term treatment regimens in phobic patients', in R. L. Spitzer and D. F. Klein (eds) *Evaluation of Psychological Therapies*, Baltimore: Johns Hopkins University Press.

Chapter Ten

CONCLUSIONS AND FUTURE DIRECTIONS

KEVIN GOURNAY

There is no adequate conclusion to this book as there are so many questions which have yet to be answered. However, there are several areas worthy of comment and issues which demand more research.

Aetiology

The nature of agoraphobia remains unclear. We are certainly beginning to understand some of the cognitive factors, but this returns us to the fundamental question of whether the cognitive state of agoraphobics is causal or consequential. As Marks (1987) points out, the biological data is equivocal and at present we do not know of any biological anomalies found in agoraphobia which are not found in panic and general anxiety. This leads us back to Mathews *et al.'s* (1981) suggestion that what is needed is a prospective study of at risk populations. Although this would necessitate the use of a complex battery of cognitive and physiological measures and the monitoring of the subject group over a number of years, it may be in the long term cost-effective. For example, we need to set against the costs of such a study facts such as the 26 million prescriptions for benzodiazepines in 1986.

Therapist issues

Gordon Deakin's chapter clearly shows that nurse therapists in the UK are trained to standards that should be the envy of many clinical psychology and psychiatrist training courses. Indeed, the training he describes has arguably more adequately supervised and properly evaluated training experience than any other offered in this country and probably elsewhere (other than a couple of notable Psy D programmes in the USA). However, at the risk of being unpopular, it should be asked whether such training is necessary for such therapists to treat the vast majority of agoraphobics. Given the very encouraging results of self-exposure and the use of manuals and computer programs, the real question would seem to be where such sources of therapeutic excellence as nurse therapists be placed. Should they, and clinical psychologists for that matter, be attached to primary care settings, where given current resources, only small segments of the population can be treated? Or should they act as trainers and advisors to more numerous groups such as community psychiatric nurses or locally organized self-help groups and reserve individual treatment expertise for difficult cases? The answer to deployment should ideally lie with health care planners who work fairly centrally. This, of course, contrasts with the current position where there are some local services run by forward-thinking managers who manage resources very effectively and yet others where ill-informed managers waste therapeutic talent on very limited areas.

Exposure treatment

The evidence presented in Chapter 2 indicates that the dismantling of exposure as a research endeavour is virtually complete. The picture is now emerging of a simple, powerful principle which can probably be self-administered by a majority of patients. However, as the Preface points out, there are a sizeable proportion of patients who either fail to respond to exposure or refuse it before or during treatment. Research effort therefore could profitably be directed to such ill-defined areas as 'motivation' and 'commitment'. Further, as the chapter on failure indicates, communication with the client at assessment seems to be worth investigating in more detail. With regard to self-exposure, we probably need to widen the range of instruction manuals and extend our educative efforts to the many commendable self-help groups.

Treatment preparation

One area of the behaviour therapy field which has been largely unresearched is that of client's expectations of treatment. The data from the failure study in Chapter 6 suggest that not all patients desire the exposure method or at least, not in the form that it is usually offered. With the very strong evidence regarding patient's expectation being a crucial variable, perhaps it is time that we attempted to assess more objectively the patient's perception of the treatment offered. This would hopefully pick up discongruent expectations and each case could then be dealt with accordingly. Measures to assess treatment expectancy already exist (eg.Caine *et al.'s* 1981) and therefore these need to be used both in research enquiry and treatment practice. This issue naturally leads to the question asked by both Emmelkamp's (1983) study and the data presented in Chapter 6. Do we give enough pre-therapy information and training? The answer seems to be a resounding no. It is inexcusable that most treatment services do not routinely inform and prepare patients for treatment. Perhaps many professionals suffer the authoritarian legacy of the psychoanalytic movement where the patient, by definition, is incapable at the beginning of therapy of understanding both problem and treatment. Obviously, Mathews *et al.*'s (1981) programmed practice manuals and Mark's (1980) *Living with Fear* are excellent introductions for the agoraphobic contemplating treatment, but perhaps we can do better with more comprehensive packages. At the agoraphobia treatment programme at Barnet General Hospital we prepare patients by breaking individual assessment into two parts, allowing time for the assimilation of information. Furthermore, we use two long introductory group sessions which include didactic input, the use of two videos of fears, phobias, and exposure treatment, group discussion, a spouse/co-therapist session, written handouts, and an introductory exposure session designed to elicit problems. We also use measures of treatment expectancy to screen for potential problems. This set of strategies seems to have reduced drop-out and refusal rates, but obviously the use of this sort of method needs further controlled investigation.

Cognitive factors

With regard to cognitive change, the data in Chapter 8 does demonstrate that the cognitive changes that result from exposure treatment are wide ranging and positive, though incomplete. These findings underline the earlier call of Mathews and his colleagues (1981) to undertake more research to understand, more adequately, the cognitive variables involved in both the agoraphobic syndrome and its treatment. This call has largely gone unheeded, although some workers (e.g. Foa and Kozak 1986, Hecker and Thorpe 1987, and Mathews and MacLeod 1987) have produced some very interesting research and writing in the areas of anxiety and simple phobias. Such research is badly needed as current cognitive therapies do not seem to add to treatment effectiveness. It could be argued that these therapies incorrectly match the very processes that they set out to modify and that adequate cognitive treatment strategies can only evolve from a sound theoretical base. Having said that, there does not seem to be any argument for maintaining that the cognitive therapies currently used for treating agoraphobia should be anything but adjunctive. David Winter's chapter indicates that we need to look at a range of wider possibilities and go through a process of systematic hypotheses testing. However, it should be said that there is a danger that in adopting a cognitive approach to the problem performance-based (exposure) methods will be minimized during treatment and therapists may well neglect doing the obvious. In fact, as Marks (1987) points out, exposure treatment may in itself be a cognitive therapy because of the possibility of the generalizing effects of exposure in producing more efficient coping strategies.

Social factors and social worker roles

Barbara Hudson has demonstrated that the sociological aspects of agoraphobia are under-researched. In particular, there seem to be many popular and professional misconceptions of agoraphobia as a woman's problem, caused solely by sexual inequality, etc., etc. What we really need is data on how families and social structures may reinforce the problem and how such influences may be modified during treatment. Of specific interest is the issue of the background belief systems referred to in the chapter on cognitive change. In this area, it is possible that lack of commitment to treatment may relate to the belief of patient and family in the utility of avoidance as a coping mechanism. Another area ripe for research is the issue of how spouse-training programmes can be most effectively delivered and maintained in the long term.

Barbara Hudson clearly shows that social workers may make ideal therapists for many clients, although the reality is that social workers are rarely put into the role of autonomous behaviour therapist. The answer to this problem clearly lies with basic social work training, which is still dominated by the anachronism of psychoanalysis.

Fortunately, there are trends which indicate a changing climate, but it may be a decade or more before the large work-force of social workers starts to deliver any sizeable amount of behavioural treatment.

The role of drugs

As Cherrie Coghlan's chapter demonstrates, the role of drugs as a treatment for agoraphobia is far from clear. There is, as yet, no evidence that any drug provides anything more than a partial treatment. Perhaps one could tentatively suggest that agoraphobics who have autonomous depressive illnesses should have a trial of tricyclic anti-depressants. However, against this positive recommendation one needs to look at the negative side of the balance sheet. At best there are a number of drugs which confer absolutely no benefit, but at worst there is now overwhelming evidence that many drugs create iatrogenic problems which are far worse than the agoraphobia they were meant to cure. In the area of drug treatment, there is no need to call for future research as our society manages to provide all the incentive the drug companies need.

Conclusion

The concluding lines of this book are left to a plea which has much more applicability than to agoraphobia alone. This plea is for research findings to be acted on and used as a base for clinical practice. It is a fact that the treatment of agoraphobia in this country is woefully inadequate across the whole spectrum of clinical practice. For example, general practitioners are largely uninformed about the condition and its management and continue to prescribe addictive tranquillizers. Furthermore, they tend not to refer highly suitable patients to appropriate services. Many psychiatrists continue to prescribe drugs without giving any other vital exposure advice. Many psychologists continue to deliver treatment in fifty-minute sessions, once a week and carefully omit exposure, restricting behavioural interventions to relaxation training. Unfortunately, these examples are the rule rather than the exception. One wonders whether these poor levels of practice are also found in other areas of psychological treatment. Perhaps the one final direction for future research should be, how do we transfer the benefits of research to the patient?

© Kevin Gournay

REFERENCES

Caine, T. M., Wijesinghe, O. B. A., and Winter, D. A. (1981) *Personal Styles in Neurosis: Implications for Small Group Psychotherapy and Behaviour Therapy*, London: Routledge & Kegan Paul.

Emmelkamp, P. M. G. (1983) chapter in E. B. Foa and P. M. G. Emmelkamp (eds) *Failures in Behaviour Therapy*, New York: John Wiley.

Foa, E. and Kozak, M. J. (1986) 'Emotional processing of fear: exposure to corrective information', *Psychological Bulletin* 99: 20–35.

Hecker, J. E. and Thorpe, G. L. (1987) 'Fear reduction processes in imaginal and *in vivo* flooding: a comment on James' review', *Behavioural Psychotherapy* 15: 215–23.

Marks, I. M. (1980) *Living with Fear*, London: McGraw-Hill.

——(1987) *Fears, Phobias and Rituals*, New York: Oxford University Press.

Mathews, A., Gelder, M. G., and Johnston, D. W. (1981) *Agoraphobia: Nature and Treatment*, London: Tavistock.

Mathews, A. and MacLeod, C. (1987) 'An information processing approach to anxiety', *Journal of Cognitive Psychotherapy* 1, 2: 105–16.

NAME INDEX

SUBJECT INDEX

SUBJECT INDEX